AF521981

MEXICO
EXPECTED / UNEXPECTED

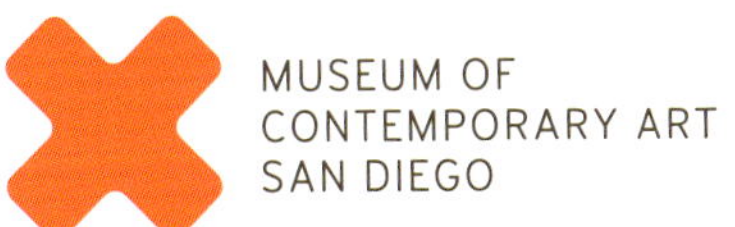

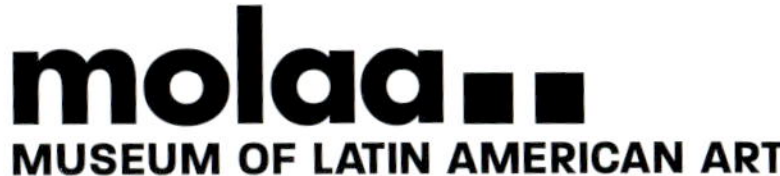

This book was published on the occasion of the exhibition *Mexico: Expected / Unexpected* at the Museum of Contemporary Art San Diego, February 5 to May 15, 2011, and the Museum of Latin American Art, Long Beach California, February 20 to May 15, 2011.

Mexico: Expected / Unexpected was originally curated by Mónica Amor with project advisor Carlos Basualdo for the Maison Rouge, Paris (2008). The MCASD and MOLAA installations are the result of a curatorial dialogue between Mireya Escalante and Ana Belén Lezana (CIAC), Lucía Sanromán (MCASD) and Cecilia Fajardo-Hill and Idurre Alonso (MOLAA).

Mexico: Expected / Unexpected is organized by CIAC with support from La Secretaría de Relaciones Exteriores, México, and the Consulado General de México in San Diego and Los Angeles.

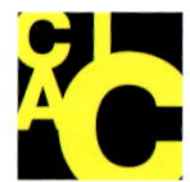

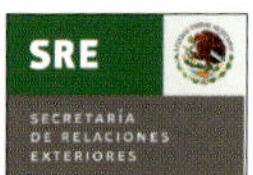

At MCASD, programs related to the exhibiton are supported by grants from The James Irvine Foundation Arts Innovation Fund, the County of San Diego Community Enhancement Fund, and the Institute of Museum and Library Services. Institutional support for MCASD is provided, in part, by the City of San Diego Commission for Arts and Culture.

the James Irvine foundation

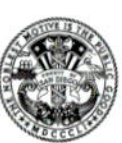
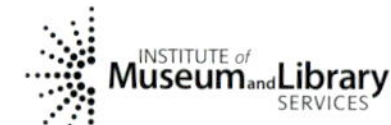

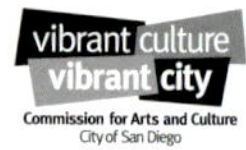

At MOLAA, the exhibition is presented by Wells Fargo and Thank Goodness It's Sofia, with additional funding from the Robert Gumbiner Foundation, Arts Council for Long Beach, City of Long Beach and the MOLAA Annual Exhibition Fund.

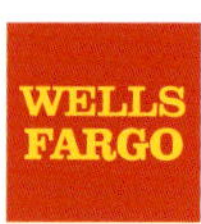

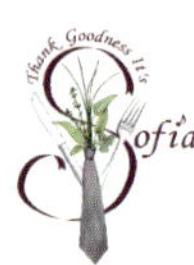

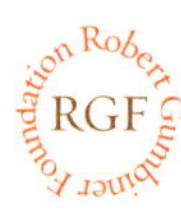

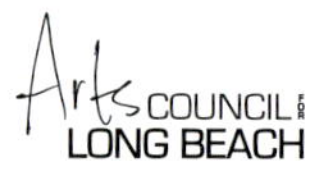

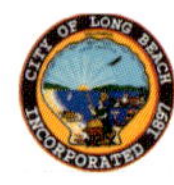

ISBN: 978-0-9801080-3-3
Catalogue Design: Steve Vladimiroff
Editors: Idurre Alonso, Susan Golden and Martha Guzmán
Translators: Idurre Alonso, Selene Preciado
Printed in Brea, CA, by Dual Graphics, Inc.

TABLE OF CONTENTS

FOREWORD

The Museum of Contemporary Art San Diego and the Museum of Latin American Art are delighted to jointly show presentations, that combined, comprise the exhibition *Mexico: Expected / Unexpected*, drawn from the collection of Isabel and Agustín Coppel. This collaboration between MCASD, MOLAA, CIAC (Colección Isabel y Agustín Coppel) and Mexico's Secretaría de Relaciones Exteriores (Ministry of Foreign Affairs) is a happy one, by bringing this renowned collection to the United States for the first time—after an extensive European tour—and also sharing it between these two Southern California institutions in order to bring it to a wider audience.

It is altogether appropriate that this exhibition include not only impressive examples by today's leading Mexican artists—Gabriel Orozco, Francis Alÿs and Damián Ortega spring to mind—but other prominent Latin American artists as well, ranging from such past masters as Lygia Clark and Hélio Oiticica to current international practitioners like Rivane Neuenschwander and Tatiana Trouvé. More to the point, these artists are joined by their peers from Europe and the United States such as Ed Ruscha and Maurizio Cattelan, Doug Aitken and Terence Koh. The resulting contextualization is a significant achievement of the exhibition, as it seeks to question and expand upon what is "Mexican" about Mexican contemporary art, and how others, within and without, perceive it. While MCASD has long demonstrated its commitment to this type of approach, MOLAA is now pleased to join in such an effort.

First and foremost, we thank Isabel and Agustín Coppel, who have proven to be both astute collectors and generous patrons. We deeply appreciate the efforts of Mireya Escalante, CIAC Director and Ana Belén Lezana, CIAC Curatorial Manager, who through their tireless efforts have made this exhibition possible. The original curator of *Mexico: Expected / Unexpected*, Mónica Amor and project advisor Carlos Basualdo, are to be congratulated on their brilliant concept. Additional curatorial work has occurred since: the thoughtful division of the exhibition between the two venues and the addition of works new to the show. To that end, we, the Directors of both institutions, want to thank Lucía Sanromán, Associate Curator at MCASD, and at MOLAA, Cecilia Fajardo-Hill, Chief Curator, and Idurre Alonso, Curator. We are grateful for the fundraising efforts of Edwina Brandon, Vice President of External Affairs, and Wendy Celaya, Associate Vice President of Development, both from MOLAA. MCASD also wishes to acknowledge the tireless fundraising work of Jeanna Yoo, Chief Advancement Officer, and her team. The catalogue has been skillfully designed by MOLAA's Art Director, Steven Vladimiroff.

Finally, we thank our sponsors, without whom we would not have been able to bring this provocative and stimulating exhibition to the public. At MOLAA we thank our presenting sponsors Wells Fargo and Thank Goodness It's Sofia and additional funders, the Robert Gumbiner Foundation, Arts Council for Long Beach, City of Long Beach and the MOLAA Annual Exhibition Fund. MCASD is grateful to the Consulado General de México in San Diego for its support of this exhibition, and to The James Irvine Foundation Arts Innovation Fund, the County of San Diego Community Enhancement Fund, and the Institute of Museum and Library Services. Institutional support for MCASD is provided, in part, by the City of San Diego Commission for Arts and Culture and we are deeply grateful for their continued support towards this exhibition.

Our hope is that the public will travel the short distance between San Diego and Long Beach to visit both museums and view both halves of the exhibition. We are certain that they will enjoy this singular opportunity to see "one" exhibition in two contemporary art venues which simultaneously examines the dualities of the local and the international, the established and the emerging, the expected and the unexpected.

Hugh M. Davies
The David C. Copley Director and CEO
Museum of Contemporary Art San Diego

Richard P. Townsend
President and CEO
Museum of Latin American Art

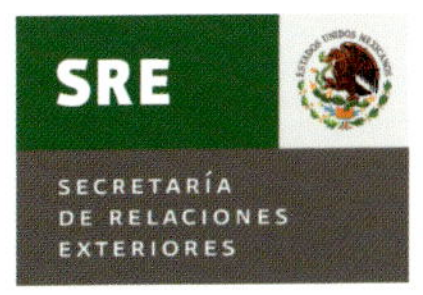

PRESENTATION

The United States and Mexico are two nations that are dynamic, ever-changing and that grow and develop at a steady rate. They are also two countries that are proud of their rich cultural roots and their diverse societies.

The significance of the new artistic identity common to the many communities that coexist and meet each other at the border is without a doubt something worthy of a profound analysis. The same is true of the influence of such an identity being used to create a better and closer relationship of friendship and brotherhood between both countries.

The exhibition *Mexico: Expected / Unexpected*, from the collection of Isabel and Agustín Coppel, is comprised by works of art that were mostly created by Mexican artists. They not only highlight the meeting points and disagreements between tradition and innovation in contemporary art in Mexico, but also how these agreements and disagreements can go beyond our borders. Furthermore, these works of art show that Mexican artists are making visions a reality.

I am certain that the exhibition *Mexico: Expected / Unexpected*, presented simultaneously at the Museum of Contemporary Art in San Diego and at the Museum of Latin American Art in Long Beach, California, will contribute to a better understanding of Mexican contemporary art.

I thank the Museum of Contemporary Art San Diego and the Museum of Latin American Art for displaying these works which illustrate the cultural diversity in Mexico and which make us so proud. A special thanks, of course, to the Isabel and Agustín Coppel Collection and to the vision and effort of all of those who have made this possible.

Patricia Espinosa C.
Secretary of Foreign Affairs, Mexico

Mexico: Expected / Unexpected

Original catalog essay by Mónica Amor (Exhibition Curator) and Carlos Basualdo (Project Advisor) for the inaugural exhibition of Mexico: Expected / Unexpected *at La Maison Rouge, Paris, 2008*

The intent of this exhibition is to highlight the role of the collection as a sort of epistemological tool, one related to the cultural locus occupied by the agents responsible for its formation. This mainly refers to collectors in general who advise curators, specialists and galleries. This complex network of institutions and operators doesn't lend itself to a clear-cut analysis, and the same can be said about the objects accumulated in the Isabel and Agustín Coppel Collection. The latter is the result of shifting and uneven trajectories that bespeak the productive uncertainties and ambivalences that inform any cultural operation in our current global economy. As a result, the "Mexicanness," to use a geographical neologism which Roland Barthes[1] associated with the expectations brought forth by the signifier of identity, of this collection and this exhibition will be dealt with by suggesting venues of investigation. At its foundation lie exchange, dialogue, influence, impurity, dissonance and multiplicity.

Another goal of this ever-changing Coppel Collection is to try and explore contemporary [Mexican] art while emphasizing relations and connections with its canonical predecessors and its contemporary producers. Furthermore, there are two frames of reference which ground the curatorial effort in this exhibition. On the one hand, this presentation attempts to address a collection which is open to the global dynamics that fuel the contemporary art of our period. However, it also tries to convey that the Coppel Collection is equally committed to a growing group of Mexican contemporary artists and a constantly increasing local audience. That both projects are complementary is one of the premises that inform this exhibition and the logic proposed to the viewer in the physical spaces of La Maison Rouge. It is strategically done this way in hopes of increasing an appreciation for how the Isabel and Agustín Coppel Collection champions contemporary national and international art. In doing so, it also interrogates the fundamental differences between those two categories. These are of course old preoccupations, fraught with perils and difficulties. But through this exhibition it is our intention to show, that now more than ever the local and the global, the authentic and the foreign, the original and the copy, are concepts that permeate each other and have little to say about cultural production when thought separate.

---

[1] Roland Barthes, "Rhetoric of the Image," in *Image, Music, Text* translated by Stephen Heath, New York: The Noonday Press, 1977, 32-51.

The Isabel and Agustín Coppel Collection features key figures of the Mexican contemporary art scene such as Francis Alÿs, Melanie Smith, Gabriel Orozco, Abraham Cruzvillegas and Damián Ortega, among many others. The exhibition not only departs from the work of these artists, but also expands diachronically in an effort to establish the possible influences and antecedents to their work. Therefore, next to the works of a younger generation of artists, we also find the more historical work of artists such as Gordon Matta-Clark, Lygia Clark, Ed Ruscha, Dan Graham and Hélio Oiticica. However, the exhibition also unfolds synchronically as it incorporates younger international artists whose works echo the conceptual concerns and aesthetic resolutions of the Mexicans. Such is the case of artists Tatiana Trouvé, Rivane Neuschwander, Pae White, and Terence Koh, among others. As the title indicates, *Mexico: Expected / Unexpected,* attempts to destabilize categories that one associates with concepts such as Mexican art, a Mexican collection, the local and the international, authenticity and copy. The Isabel and Agustín Coppel Collection and this exhibition project an image of contemporary Mexican art that is unstable, rich, complex and unpredictable in which tradition and innovation are in constant interplay. It resonates with what seems to be taking place in other areas of Mexican culture such as film and literature. The purpose of the exhibition is to engage and surprise audiences in areas where they simply would have expected the plainness of the cliché.

The exhibition is organized roughly in sections or rooms with no set trajectory and a constant interplay of works and spaces facilitated by the asymmetrical plan of La Maison Rouge. Here, we will highlight some of those exchanges to underscore the suggestive nature of the exhibition which insists on the relative position of works and artists and constructive quality of the narrative proposed by the collection/exhibition. Although, instead of a narrative of evolution and progress reflective of a monolithic idea of people and place, we propose short stories that echo each other with no aspiration to a climax or a conclusion.

In the opening gallery, neon works by Doug Aitken and Kendell Geers and an appointment schedule by Jonathan Monk, set a predicative framework in which chance more than causality determine their relationship to Mexico, or, better yet, to the unstable "Mexicanness" pursued in the show. The first work, entitled *99 Cents Dreams*, 2007 by Aitken relates to the dream of plenty and availability, as well as accessible consumerism that one dollar stores represent in the USA. In this context, and in relation to the works that follow, the piece displaces the economic model across the border, a model that at one point seemed within reach in Mexico under the auspices of NAFTA. A second neon piece by Geers introduces the notion of limits and borders—by these we understand the physical limits of the exhibition space as well as the geographical borders of the USA and Mexico—which have played so fundamental a role in modern and contemporary Mexican culture. The piece reads B/ORDER when the first letter is not blinking. When blinking, the word reads ORDER. A similar technical glitch can be detected in an adjacent neon by the same artist, that one reads *D/ANGER*, 2003. The play on words, and the instability of the sculptural signifier, can be directly related to the stressful political situations of Geers' native country of South Africa. However, the differential framework provided by the exhibition makes them a relevant comment on the border politics between Mexico and the USA. A work, entitled *Meeting 50* (2005-2007), and signified by text outlined in vinyl, is part of a series of meetings that the artist proposes in the distant future at a location, date and time of the artist's choosing. This one is to take place in Mexico City in 2017 between the artist and the collector. The rendezvous proposed by the artist is potentially fulfilled by the purchasing of the piece and somehow altered by its opening role in this exhibition. So as contingent as these meetings of Monk are, always dependent on another, so are the meeting of works, producers and aesthetic practices proposed by the collection and the exhibition. The viewing template is based on an aesthetic of displacement and a poetics of resonances that bypasses closed readings and defined structures.

A large section of the show links formally, through a series of resonating typologies and works realized in various mediums (painting, sculpture, video, installation). At the same time, it alludes, in order to undo, established notions of "Mexicanness" such as images of death, the relation between the city and nature, the poetics of craftsmanship and the precariousness of everyday life. Here we find the silent icons of Carlos Amorales *(Panorama)*: black, red and white outlined images of figures and shapes that accumulate in a nonsensical archive that aspires to an impossible comprehensiveness. Sublime vistas of flocks of birds in Graciela Iturbide's black and white photographs are also included. This lateral relation between the apparent order of Amorales' archive (deeply arbitrary when its logic is considered) and the chaotic dimension of nature is further elaborated upon in the juxtaposition of Ed Ruscha's serial but indistinct *Gasoline Stations*, 1962 (markers of in-between places, the road to nowhere, no man's land) and the localizable and lively photograph of Mexico of Helen Levitt (*Untitled, Mexico, D.F.*, 1941). Intersecting these opposing but complementary paradigms, we encounter an abstract work by Pae White (*Freeze Festoon*). It is a festive cascade of paper in a mobile configuration that repeats the theme of arbitrary accumulation while reminiscent of the cheap decorations that adorn popular celebrations in Mexico and elsewhere in South America. These unexpected resonances unfold adjacently to more predictable associations between Rineke Dijkstra's photographs of bullfighters (*Montemor, Portugal, May 1 A, B,* and *C,* all from 1994) and Terence Koh's performative skeleton (*Untitled (Skeleton Paintings*), 2006). Both are physically distant (in the exhibition space), but conceptually close to Manuel Alvarez Bravo's *Niño Maya de Tulum*, 1942 where the child and the wall-relief of a skull make natural companions.

Three other rooms, laterally connected to the main exhibition space, further repeat these associations. Starting with Maurizio Cattelan's *Untitled (Sitting Donkey, Trento)* 2004—a work that features an animal which is a humorous iconic reference to Mexico. It follows with Jack Pierson's *Si, Si, Si,* 1995, six three-dimensional found letters with the colors of the Mexican flag. It ends with Mexican artist Jorge Mendez-Blake's vinyl text work *Sin título (Sigue el llano en llamas),* 2007, an allusion to Juan Rulfo's 1953 novel *El llano en llamas (The Burning Plain)* about rural Mexican life during the epochal Mexican Revolution. A connected space is organized around the production of form based on (literal and stylistic) operations of Surrealism, popular culture and the contradictions of urban life. Here we can find works by Gabriel Orozco, Gordon Matta-Clark, Lygia Clark and Hélio Oiticica contrasting with works by Simon Starling and Manuel Alvarez Bravo. Lastly, central themes are reflected in the work of Francys Alÿs, Damián Ortega, Enrique Guzmán and Pablo Vargas-Lugo.

One could say that the backbone of the exhibition is a site-specific work, located centrally in the patio of La Maison Rouge, by Italian-French artist Tatiana Trouvé, which anchors those works that emphasize structural and constructive affinities, as well as the various iconographic resonances that probe notions of nationalism and belonging. This piece, with its Surrealist and pseudo-masochistic aesthetic, its openings and closures, its material ramifications and expansive nature, further dislodges the claims to represent identity that would drive a geo-graphically-bounded exhibition and collection. Instead, it suggests that Mexico is an elusive image to foreigners as well as locals. Belgian artist Francys Alÿs (one of Mexico's most prominent artists) also addresses this elusiveness of place and identity in his video *Zócalo*, 1999, created in collaboration with Mexican artist Rafael Ortega. It is a 12-hour documentation of the passing shadow of a flagpole in the main square of the city, considered one of Mexico's most historic and important sites. It is also the place where public manifestations and propaganda take place. Alÿs' video portrays people simply protecting themselves from the inclement sun by standing under the shadow of the rising structure. The video comments on the contingent nature of public encounters, public space, monuments and historical spaces (those congregating here are simply seeking protection from the sun). Alÿs, a foreigner who has made Mexico City his homeland, unveils the fragile nature of those institutions and the infrastructure that gives visibility to the concept of nation (here the undulating flag is an afterthought, a fragment that no one has come to honor). His working process summarizes it quite well:

> "...I spend a lot of time walking around the city... The initial concept for a project often emerges during a walk. As an artist, my position is akin to that of a passerby constantly trying to situate myself in a moving environment. My work is a succession of notes and guides. The invention of a language goes together with the invention of a city. Each of my interventions is another fragment of the story that I am inventing, of the city that I am mapping." [2]

Traveling and mapping, the construction of place through imagination; these have been powerful metaphors in the artistic production of the last 25 years. And their currency well into the twenty-first century only underscores our exacerbated condition of permanent travelers open to migrant ideas, permeable borders, and displaced certainties. To ignore the vulnerability of the constructions of nation, culture and identity is to ignore the fundamental link between modern and contemporary art, center and periphery, self and other. Furthermore, it is also to ignore the contextual foundation of art objects: their relationship to institutions, to the market and the compelling issues they address. It is up to artists to invent stories and reinvent the city, up to exhibitions and curators to narrate these trajectories, and up to collections and collectors to relinquish nostalgia and forge new, inconsistent, and ever-incomplete archives of contemporary culture.

Mónica Amor (Exhibition Curator)
Carlos Basualdo (Project Advisor)

---

[2] http://www.postmedia.net/alys/zocalo.htm. Accessed September 12, 2008.

Interview with Isabel and Agustín Coppel

by Mónica Amor and Carlos Basualdo, February 15, 2008, Philadelphia, PA

IC: Isabel Coppel
AC: Agustín Coppel
MA: Mónica Amor
CB: Carlos Basualdo

MA: How did you start collecting and what was the first piece you purchased?

AC: I visited some exhibitions in Culiacán, and I became the friend of an artist who has now passed away. With him I started to know a little bit more about art. Actually, I feel that the first piece we bought for the collection was a painting we got in L.A., at the Tere Iturralde Gallery. It was a 1940s piece by Cordelia Urueta, where a woman in a white dress dances before a mirror, and it has the aesthetic of Diego Rivera. Isabel and I loved it, and we still have it in our dining room.

MA: What was the name of the artist who introduced you to the art world? Do you remember?

AC: His name was Miguel Esparza Blancas. He was an artist who knew well what was going on in New York and he somehow tried to interpret it from Culiacán. He was a great follower of the work that De Kooning made in the 1950s. He aspired to develop his own language in a Mexican style, but he never really succeeded.

MA: And later on, as your interest in collecting developed, were you influenced by anyone in particular? Is there a collector or an artist who has been or is important for you?

AC: There is a collector in Culiacán, Mrs. Vita Podesta, who has been collecting for a long time. About 25 years ago she bought a body of work by very important artists: Picasso, Diego Rivera, Juan Gris. She really enjoys her artworks, and they also turned out to be a very good investment; they are something very meaningful in her life. She is a charming lady, and we are her friends; she invites us to her house and we talk about different subjects. She has always had a very modern and youthful spirit.

CB: I would like to know, why art? And also, if it was a decision both of you made, where does that decision come from?

AC: We both liked art a lot, and we found enormous pleasure in seeing artworks and discovering new museums, to get better insight into art.

MA: In the artistic context of Culiacán, any particular museum?

AC: There is a museum in Culiacán, the Museo de Arte de Sinaloa (MASIN), which has artworks from the 1950s and 60s in Mexico, as well as some by turn-of-the-century artists. But rather, we started to search on our trips. I was always involved with issues related to communication, philosophy and organization. I was interested in trying to understand complex matters, and to understand why there was an art market. Why a certain object was valued so much was a challenge. For me, understanding the meaning of these things was some sort of intellectual mystery: what were other people seeing that I could not see?

Along the way, we started to buy Modern Mexican artworks, not by the great masters like Tamayo or Rivera—except for an Orozco that we bought many years ago— but by peripheral Mexican modern artists, artists who are very good, but not so well known internationally.

MA: Do you still have those works?

AC: We still have and enjoy those works, all of them. But at some point we stopped that process and started to see the subject of art and what was happening in the world with more amplitude. We directly passed, with full conviction, to collect international contemporary art. I remember very well an afternoon at the beginning of the 1990s, in the Zona Rosa of Mexico City, at the Arvil Gallery with Armando Colina and Victor Acuña. Armando was very convincing. He said: "Warhol is what you have to look for, he is the most important artist, he changed aesthetics in the world, he is the real creator of Pop Art, and an artist with an enormous body of work." The first international contemporary artwork we bought was a very large installation by Gary Hill, *Learning Curve*.

CB: When? Could you give us a date?

AC: It was around 1991 or 1992.

IC: Your interest in art also comes from the time when you lived in New York, after you graduated from university.

AC: Yes, I was living in New York for ten months.

MA: When?

AC: In the mid-eighties. I had the chance to go and see some amazing exhibitions, to really enjoy them as just another visitor. I went through the city, and visited galleries and all of the museums.

MA: With a guide or on you own?

AC: Alone, by myself. I had an Argentinean friend that came along, but I haven't heard from him lately.

CB: But, how do you pass from a situation where there is not so much art, in which art is something relatively remote, to one in which going to galleries is something familiar? How did that transition happen? What made you feel curiosity at first?

AC: I believe that the first time I went to Europe with my father, a summer when I was already in college, was very transcendental. We visited the Prado and the Louvre, with him as a guide. I was fascinated. It was a great experience.

CB: Your father liked art?

AC: He liked classical art: Goya, Velázquez, Rubens...wars, heroic history painting and epic subjects in general.

CB: Were there any paintings in your house?

AC: There were paintings, but the kind you buy in the streets of Paris—Parisian landscapes, and an interesting portrait of my mother—that's all there was, it wasn't an issue. That summer, when I traveled with my father, I was about 19 or 20 years old, we spent three weeks going through the main European capitals. I visited the great museums for the first time, and then I started feeling curious, and wanted to know more about Expressionism, Impressionists and art history in general.

Now I remember that when Isabel and I went to Tahiti for our honeymoon, I took a very old version of Somerset Maugham's *The Moon and Six Pence* which had belonged to my father. It is about Gauguin's life. The whole trip was a very beautiful experience.

MA: And going back to the work of Gary Hill, what made you buy it?

AC: I was certain that Gary Hill was the best video artist of that moment, and I thought that it was important to buy something totally conceptual, very historic and meaningful. I remember I made a broad analysis of who the video artists at that moment were, and which were their most interesting works. Isabel liked Hill's work and we decided to buy it.

MA: But at that moment you did not own any video art, you were collecting Mexican painting. Then, how did that jump happen? Did you see that work during one of your trips? Who introduced you to it?

AC: I saw a similar work called *Learning Curve (still point)* for the first time installed in a darkened room at the Museum of Contemporary Art San Diego. The work is made of a long table with a chair at one of its ends. The table becomes wider and it ends in a little monitor that shows a wave continually breaking. In the version we bought, there is a very long flat-screen at the end of the table showing the same picture.

CB: It would seem that, from the start, you were thinking in terms of historical importance—of the position of the works in a wider context, as if there would have been a programmatic intention in the collection. It doesn't seem to be a matter of living with things you like, rather it looks like a matter of bringing a whole together. Did it happen that way?

AC: Always, but especially with the second part of the collection, where there was more thinking involved. Yes, I wanted to have a body of work that made sense, and would be interesting for me in the future, not just at the moment when I liked it.

IC: There was more studying involved in contemporary art, since it is not so easy to know where you're going, what you want, or what you are interested in, unless you study. And Agustín studies a great deal!

MA: In that learning process, in your studies, with whom do you think you have a more systematic dialogue? Is it with institutions, with collectors, with artists, with curators or critics? Are there some particular persons you have engaged with or some specific institutions?

AC: New ideas and very different perspectives arise all the time. They are very new, and they are often unimaginable and surprising. And there are many different levels amongst those who have opinions on art, those who know about art.

Eventually we talked to many different people, and we have had a continuous dialogue with those who we believe are more enriching for us. There are many people who constantly talk about art, but they don't seem to have a very good idea of what it's all about. Of course, at the beginning it is hard to understand how this works. Probably one of the most important things to learn is that there are many things that you know nothing about. This is very valuable: knowing that you don't know, and assuming that matters of art are multilayered, that they have many levels.

Meeting Carlos, and you too Mónica, has been a very interesting phase for us, because you have a perspective on art that includes trends that were not familiar to us—things that happened in Italy and Brazil—as well as a more global vision, that considers the importance of each piece in an international environment. Usually galleries have a very narrow perspective, and they don't realize how limited it is. Some museums also get married to the period they work with, and they end up being obsolete. Good art tries to ask questions and to generate ruptures.

In Mexico, for instance, the artists that came before Gabriel Orozco—artists who were very successful—don't really like him. They believe that his works are nothing but pranks. We have been told many times that they will fall to pieces, that they have no future. Then you realize that artworks by Orozco are valuable precisely because they are provocative. Other curators, like Pedro Alonzo and his wife, Lane Coburn, have a very youthful and open vision of art. We have had a good relationship with him in particular.

We have also had contact, for a very long time, with gallery owners like José Kuri, Mónica Manzutto, Enrique Guerrero, Jaime Riestra, Patricia Ortiz Monasterio, Marian Goodman, Andrea Rosen, Stephen Friedman and other very important gallerists whom we would like to get to know better; as well as with collectors like César and Mónica Cervantes, Patrick and Mariana Charpenel, Jose Noé and Marcela Suro and with some curators such as Yvonne Force, Taiyana Pimentel and Ana Elena Mallet.

MA: The relationship you have with them is based on an international perspective on art?

AC: Yes, we bought the work by Gary Hill with Pedro Alonzo—he has been a very good advisor. And we've also had an on and off relationship with Yvonne Force, but it has lasted for many years. She has helped us to understand other ideas and artists.

We have tried to choose with whom to have certain kinds of relations, with whom to establish more lasting ones.

A very important part of this adventure has been Mireya Escalante. We have worked as a team with her in the development of the collection, in choosing our advisors and relationships and in our studies and acquisitions.

MA: Do you live with the art you buy? Obviously, I guess, not with all of it, but maybe you make an effort to rotate the artworks. How do you systematize this effort to somehow experience the works?

IC: Yes, we live with the art. In Culiacán we have the modern Latin American art that we bought at the beginning and in San Diego we have more of the contemporary work. As a matter of fact, contemporary art feels better. We want to rotate the pieces continuously.

When you find the right piece something amazing happens—you like to see it every day, and every time you pass it by you see something different. That's what we enjoy the most.

AC: Actually, if we analyze it, the houses are art galleries. We want to re-structure our Culiacán house, which is an interesting process.

When you have a collection like ours, you need real curatorial work to exhibit the pieces, even if they are in your own house. We can no longer place the works because they look nice here or there. When you really curate the works, you find connections that make it difficult to move each work from its place. We need to have works to replace them—because we make loans— but yes, the houses end up being small galleries with temporary exhibitions.

MA: Of course, that is why I'm asking if you have systematized it in any way. It is difficult to replace works one by one.

IC: It isn't easy. The overall meaning needs to be reconfigured. You change three or four pieces, or you can't change them at all.

MA: What kind of interaction do you have with the artists you have bought? Is there any effort on your behalf to meet these artists?

AC: We have met a few, we have talked with some, and we have been pleasantly surprised most of the time. I feel that, at this moment, collectors perceived sympathetically by artists; that is, they are very open, they try to explain their ideas and pay attention to us. We have had a good relationship with those we have met.

I am not particularly fond of being overly influenced by the artist's personality, because it works better to have a certain idea of an artwork and some references. You have to see what artists do and be tolerant with their lives because we're not looking for role models but for other things.

MA: Is there any artist with whom you have a more personal relationship?

AC: We get along very well with Sofía Taboas, as well as with Pedro Reyes, Miguel Calderón and also with Gabriel Orozco. We are very glad that we got to meet them.

MA: How was your perception of art changed by collecting?

AC: Well, the perspective you develop as a collector is a lot more interesting. They are two different things, the appreciation of art in itself and the natural quest of collectors, whether they are old records, shoes, or whatever it is. The collector is active as part of the scene, and there is a special interest in looking for that unique piece and being able to recognize it right away. When we went to the Frida Kahlo exhibition in Philadelphia, we saw works that were available at one point, and it was hard to understand that they were masterworks. Something like that can be happening in many situations, not just in art, but also in business, in relationships, in friendships. There are situations and moments that turn out to be very important for something, but you can't tell they are at first sight. It is some kind of education you receive in learning how to see and appreciate things; and that has a value for your life as a whole. I belong to the world of business one hundred percent—art is really a change of mentality, a rest, a space of freedom, a great passion that I have been able to apply and use in many things—in working with groups, in human teams, in different strategies, in having an eye to know what is worth something and what is not.

MA: Have you ever seen a work that, as you say, you immediately perceive as something valuable, as something worthwhile, but then you say "no, it's not for the collection?"

AC: Yes, I believe we have never bought something we don't really like, even if we are certain that it is very valuable. Besides, the works have to be seen for their importance first, and then in the context of the collection.

MA: So, the matter of taste is very important

AC: Well, yes. We only bought something we believed to be a good investment once or twice, but we ended up selling those works. Somehow, having things we do not like deep down just because they are a "must" contaminates the collection.

MA: At the beginning, what was the focus of the collection, how did you choose it, and why was it important for you?

AC: I believe we don't know. It really is some sort of enigma. Even if I would have defined a perspective beforehand, I believe that with the show that Mónica is curating she has found a very interesting and different sense, something we had not yet seen. I believe that if you try to define the collection too tightly, if you try to explain it, and only confine it to a medium or a period, the process loses its depth and the pleasure it gives you. And it also takes coherence away, because coherence is in the works themselves. We believe in the message of art itself. For instance, this exhibition that is being shown in Paris gives us a series of very interesting new relations that we are just discovering. This is what is unexpected about the collection, that it has a potential to be read in different ways.

MA: Other works could have been chosen, or the same works could have been read in some other way. Maybe this heterogeneous spirit is the one that allows for this openness. Now, what determines the incorporation of a new work? What are the elements that determine that a work can be incorporated to the collection?

AC: It is very subjective, sometimes we are looking for something from a certain period and we end up buying something else. At a certain moment, a piece or an artist makes sense for the stage of the collection at that point. For instance, we had been looking for a Nauman for a long time, and well, we did not have the piece or it wasn't the time, but we finally found something that could be adequate for the collection and we bought it. It is also related to the reality of available resources, as we don't have unlimited resources; but if we had an unlimited amount of money collecting would loose its appeal, because then it would only be about buying the top, the most expensive work you can find anywhere, and we would be buying a *Celebration* piece by Koons. I don't believe that would be the best for the collection, but that's another story; anyway I wish we would have done it some years ago, at least the balloon puppy.

MA: The experience of curating this exhibition, the experience of working with the pieces, of looking for similarities. Do you feel there is a reflection or a parallel in the way you establish a relationship between works and they way in which you incorporate an artwork to the collection?

AC: Yes, for instance the works by Gordon Matta-Clark that are included in the show became very important. I didn't believe that Matta-Clark would go so well with a soccer ball by Gabriel Orozco, but you see the ball and the work by Matta-Clark and it makes a lot of sense.

IC: Seeing our collection from another perspective has allowed us to find new connections. We have learned to relate things that we had not thought of before, and that is very interesting.

MA: What sort of dialogue do you believe you are looking for between the works of Mexican and international artists, or the artists from other countries and how do you try to establish that dialogue?

AC: I believe that there has always been a dialogue. At some point, I was very interested in the dialogue between Rufino Tamayo and Siqueiros on nationalism. Rufino exhibited more outside of Mexico, and his work never had a political message, and back then that wasn't considered to be something good, but actually you feel that Tamayo's work is both Mexican and international. I was always a liberal, advocating Mexicanism like Rufino Tamayo did. Today, more than ever, Mexican artists are very successful when they get involved at an international level, they have a Mexican fiber, they are not obviously folkloric, but they are Mexican in a deeper way. I believe this is very valuable for Mexico, now that it is taking part in international competition in all fields, as other countries are. I believe that there is a message of globalization in these new artists. And the same is happening in architecture, in film. You see how new directors are having so much success by showing a particular vision that the world is appreciating and that is a source of great pride for Mexico.

MA: So local resonances are incorporated into ways of seeing in a more structured way, in the way materials are used. In this exhibition you can also appreciate how these local resonances might reverberate in other contexts.

CB: That reminds me of what Jorge Luis Borges said in his 1936 essay, *The Argentinean Writer and Tradition*, "there are no camels in the Koran."

MA: Do you think there is a sense of mission in your activity as collectors?

AC: I believe that there is always a will to give a mission to art, some sense of social responsibility, and many are constantly looking for it. At the moment when you start looking for that mission, everything is affected by that quest, even social responsibility itself, since the works themselves are the main value in matters of art.

If we have these works in the collection it is because they are from very good artists and they are also very good pieces, or, at least that is how we value them. If there is any mission in the collection, it is a quest for talent and real creativity, and not the attempt to help a group to do well. We wouldn't like to cheat anyone. What we want to include in the collection—the kind of works we look for—are those that make you vibrate, that are worth it, that have talent in them.

MA: Are you interested in sharing the collection with an audience? Have you thought of ways in which that could happen?

AC: Of course we would like to have these works shown to an audience. They were not bought not to be shown. We will find adequate places and times to do so. Now, there is a project!

MA: Tell us a little about that, I think it would be important.

AC: There is a beautiful garden in Culiacán; it is a space that belongs to the state government, a public space. And there is an association of which I am the president called *Sociedad Botánica y Zoológica de Sinaloa, AC (Botanical and Zoological Society of Sinaloa, A.C.)*. I had a very good relationship with the man that came up with the idea of the Botanical Garden, Engineer

Carlos Murillo, who passed away some time ago. I worked with him for about 15 years, trying to improve the space. We did a very good job and at some point, because of my interest in art, I thought it would be a good idea to start incorporating some artworks into the space. Then we started to talk to some Mexican curators and we made the decision to invite Patrick Charpenel to work on the project. He made a very interesting proposal, a very deep one, as to how to turn this Botanical Garden into a space where contemporary art could be discovered by incorporating site-specific works to the garden in Culiacán.

IC: Here, as well as with the collection, Mireya Escalante has worked with us in a very professional way. She has coordinated the projects, the acquisitions and the public relations; she has formed a team of analysis, study and work. Her participation in the collection and in other projects is very valuable, and at the same time it is the reason and the cause of many of the things that happen.

MA: And is there any indoor space within the garden that could be used for the works that need a more conventional kind of space?

AC: There will be some sort of gallery that is being designed by Tatiana Bilbao, but it has small rooms, just enough for a small art exhibition. Everything else is integrated to the garden. The installations are permanent and they will need maintenance. There are works by James Turrell, Gabriel Orozco, Dan Graham, Francis Alÿs, Julian Opie, Olafur Eliasson, Pablo Vargas Lugo, Simon Starling, Teresa Margolles, Rikrit Tiravanija, Tino Seghal, Diana Thater, Richard Long, Mario García Torres, Sofía Taboas, Kyoto Ota, Fernando Ortega, Pedro Reyes and so on.

MA: When do you think the project will be ready?

AC: In about two years. Some of the works are already being finished, and the garden itself needs a lot of improvement. It is an endless space when it comes to maintenance and you need to make aesthetic decisions all the time.
MA: Do you think that there can be other kinds of cultural activities around these installations?

AC: Yes, as a matter of fact, it is an ideal space for that. Many activities are already taking place at the Botanical Garden, such as school visits. It is a very special place and I believe it will be very important for Culiacán.

CB: It is interesting that on one hand, you say that the work itself is the most important thing for you and that it has to be strong, but I feel there are two other things. There is also an intention to assume a social responsibility, something that would be called "giving back to the community" in America, because there is nothing one could think of that would be further away from a vanity project than the Botanical Garden. It is not about making a palace and showing master works totally out of context, but working with a garden that has a relation to nature.

MA: And to the city.

CB: Yes, to the city. That has a series of connotations related to how it is used and to the people who use it—to an integration of art in such a way that people will be allowed to discover it. I believe it is a very meaningful project if you think about it as social responsibility. On the other hand, I feel that your discourse—your way of working—always involves an intention to support the talented people that you find, whether they are artists, architects or writers. For this project there are two Mexican writers. I've noticed that you are always interested in making a connection with their fields. It seems as though in some way the collection has also inserted itself within a project that supports improving the living conditions of the place you live in and which you have also helped create.

AC: Yes, I am conscious of that, even though I do not think about it so much, because I am rather focused in making this thing work, which is already a challenge. I believe that if we manage to get it right, each of the visitors to the Botanical Garden will enter the experience of the garden itself with its natural charms, and will have an unexpected contact with contemporary art, which is almost non-existent in Culiacán. This will open their minds and generate interest. It will be an unforgettable experience for all the young people, and in general for all visitors. Certainly that is a genuine interest.

IC: But that has always been your interest—promoting a taste for art, so there is a change in the way people think, so they have the opportunity to see other things, to see how that change and that flexibility that comes from seeing art applies to their lives.

CB: And that is what you feel regarding any anonymous person, like the potential visitor to the Botanical Garden, but also in relation to your friends who are motivated by you and with whom you usually travel to see art. I believe there is a very clear attempt on your behalf to promote the art you are interested in, the one you collect.

IC: They are like nets that intertwine and that arrive at different places that you may never have imagined. Especially the people in Culiacán who feel they are participating in a very direct way with this project.

AC: When I went to walk through the gardens with Engineer Murillo to supervise the work, everyone greeted us as though we were running for office. The Botanical Garden is very important for many people in Culiacán; they go there for a walk every day, they meditate, reflect, and witness the transformation of that space. It has been something very special.

MA: What is the future of the collection?

AC: To further channel the collection as a collection, to find pieces and artworks that help to make it stronger, and to make it more interesting and more coherent in different ways. To go on buying artworks that are relevant for the collection itself.

Of course, a very important goal is to finish the Botanical Garden. It is a very complicated work—very complicated—and we have invested a lot of time in that project, not only because of art issues, but also because of the botanical part of the project, building each piece, having the artists visit the site, and so on. In the end it is a very big collective effort. Now they are working with landscape advisors from Mexico and abroad. In this life it is better to do one thing very well, than to do a hundred things not so well.

MA: And that experience will be the one to determine what other projects you embark upon, or what line you will take regarding the future of the collection in relation to an audience.

AC: Yes, at the moment we are here. If we manage to carry out the Botanical Garden project successfully, we will come up with other projects.

IC: Indeed.

17 GLOBAL MEXICANS

Sabina Berman

EXILE

SAM ZYMAN composes his music in New York, where most of his compositions have been played for the first time, but he is a Mexican. I reiterate, he is Mexican.

He studied medicine in Mexico, even if he always played music. One day, his wife, Nancy Carrasco, showed him a call for entries to a composition contest. Samuel composed music for the first time, an octet. Even if he did not win the contest, at that moment he knew what he wanted to do for the rest of his life. Soon, he immigrated to New York, to study at the Julliard School. And now, from Julliard, where he teaches and rehearses his new compositions, his music is becoming known around the world.

Once again, Samuel Zyman is a Mexican.

He cannot stop being Mexican, and he doesn't want to. You can feel his "Mexican-ness" in his music, but in a novel and singular way. If critics are not familiar with his biography, they do not notice certain inflections in particular rhythms. If they know it, they soon point at to its "Latino" flavor.

In 2007, his *Suite for Two Cellos* opened at the Palacio de Bellas Artes in Mexico City, performed by two of the most important cello players in the world: Yo Yo Ma and Carlos Prieto. When both musicians were standing on the stage, bowing to thank the audience, Yo Yo Ma, with a gesture, called to Zyman. Sam walked down the aisle between the seats towards the cello players with the intention of shaking their hands from there, and then Yo Yo Ma pulled him up saying:

"Come up Sam, I'll help you"

"Not very elegant," noted Sam, and thus—holding the hand of a Paris-born Japanese that lives in America—he went on stage to receive the applause of an audience that didn't really know that he was also Mexican.

ALEJANDRO GONZÁLEZ IÑÁRRITU was educated as a filmmaker in Mexico. He worked as a radio DJ and programmer; he made hours of images for Televisa's ads and filmed his first feature film, *Amores Perros*, while he worked directing TV commercials. He did all that in Mexico.

Then, he decided to move to Hollywood, that is to Santa Monica, a residential area of Los Angeles where Hollywood is not a dream, just part of the film industry that scatters all throughout the city.

He left Mexico with his wife and children, and in changing home, he suddenly became nobody, whereas in Mexico people already recognized him on the street. He was a nobody in a city where Julia Roberts shops and is followed by a multitude of photographers. He was a nobody in a city where Spielberg goes in a coffee shop and 16 hands are raised to greet him and where—one afternoon—when El Negro (as his friends call him) went into his house through the backyard, a neighbor called the police believing he was a thief.

But according to Iñárritu, the hardest part was accepting that he was putting a distance of 3,000 kilometers between his children and their grandparents. Their grandparents, their uncles, their cousins: the family.

Isn't that the homeland? The place where our loved ones live, and isn't that exile? Not being able to get in a car and arrive at your grandparents house.

"Never mind" answers Alejandro to himself with a thoughtful attitude. "For better or for worse, they are my children." He and Maria Idalia, his wife, often take their children to Mexico so they can spend some time with the family. "But it is not the same," says Alejandro.

Iñárritu struggled for three long years to create *21 Grams*—his second feature film—while living in L.A. The film was made with a cast of American English-speaking actors, although many in the creative staff where were Mexican or Latin American. The script was written by a Mexican, the score was composed by an Argentinean, and the editing, the camera, and the art were made by Mexicans.

Like Zyman, Iñárritu considers himself absolutely Mexican. In his films there is an emotional intensity, a set of values, and an almost surrealist freedom to imagine—and all of that is very Mexican. In addition, Iñárritu is very active within the Mexican community in L.A. and supports their causes.

Famously, when he received the Golden Globe Award for his film *Babel* from the governor of California, Arnold Schwarzenegger, El Negro made a little joke: "Search me, I have my papers." Thus, he compared himself to the millions of illegal Mexican immigrants. The governor grimaced at this remark.

One morning, I received a call from **ALFONSO CUARÓN.** You can never really know where Cuarón is calling from. He has a dream house in the Italian countryside; he rents an apartment in London—where the studio where he has filmed his two last films is located; he spent a year working from an apartment in New York and until two years ago the offices of Esperanto—his production company—were located there. Although he usually meets with film studio producers in L.A., he often travels to Mexico, where most of his family lives, to take care of family matters.

I believe that Alfonso's home is his mobile phone with international roaming.

"Where are you Alfonso?" I asked.

"In an airport," he answered. "I'm off to Mexico to present *Children of Men*."

Alfonso wanted feedback on some of the things he was going to say to the reporters when he met them at the Mexico City airport. For instance, when they asked how he sees himself:

He said he was thinking of saying, "I'm a pirate. I come and go."

I told him, "Ha! That's romantic, but to me you are something more contemporary, just a luxury Mexican *bracero*." In Mexico, *bracero* is the name given to Mexican laborers who travel to the USA hired to work in temporary employment.

I said that, and Alfonso laughed.

The following day, I read in the heading of the entertainment section of the newspaper: "Cuarón, luxury *bracero*." The reporters also liked the moniker.

Just like Cuarón and Iñárritu, **GUILLERMO DEL TORO**—the director that completes the three aces of our emigrated filmmakers—feels that they are related (have an affiliation) to the other millions of Mexican migrants.

For ten years now, five hundred thousand Mexicans leave Mexico every year. Before, the flux was about two hundred thousand immigrants a year. Today, nine million Mexicans live illegally in America and 20 million legally. There are also considerable Mexican communities in Canada, Alaska and Spain, and there are also Mexicans living in the rest of Europe, although their numbers are smaller.

Just like those immigrants, and like many other Mexican artists born in the 1950s, these three aces of film were forced to abandon their home in Mexico looking for better work opportunities. Just like the other immigrants, they know about the restlessness of not belonging, about the daily longing for their homeland, about the resentment felt towards the incompetence of the Mexican government and they maintain a sentimental loyalty for the country. Just like the *braceros* of hunger, luxury *braceros* have helped friends across the border by offering them employment.

And just like them, they are faithful to Spanish and to Mexican culture. Cuarón is also informed about the latest important novel, the latest national film, the never-ending quarrel of our politics. Even if he is filming in London he reads *Letras Libres* and *Proceso*.

THE GLOBAL

GAEL GARCÍA BERNAL, the most active Mexican actor in world film, is thoughtful when I ask him if he believes he is a luxury bracero.

He tells me "Cuarón, Del Toro, and Iñárritu had to migrate to be able to do large projects. That was impossible in the Mexico where they lived (the one where they first started working). Besides, they would have never been able to achieve worldwide distribution from Mexico. So they were "luxury *braceros*." Instead, I never felt the need to migrate." And he emphasized the word "need."

But, just as in their case, your Mexican films did not get international distribution, I note. Today, it is still through London or New York or L.A. that a work of art gets international distribution. "Yes," agrees Gael, but he remains thoughtful. The truth is that he doesn't fully identify with the term "luxury *bracero*." It implies a condition of need, of scarcity, that doesn't really correspond to his experience.

Instead, he has experienced plenty of opportunities and extraordinary mobility. Gael has not immigrated, he goes in and out of Mexico, he comes back and leaves, and he does that several times a year, depending on the places where the films where he acts are being made. And for his Mexican projects, he has access to Hollywood funds, to Mexican and European money.

"Does 'global artist' suit you?" I ask.

"Yes" he answers more convinced, "it sounds better." But he adds something else, "I don't want to go too far structuring in thought something that, in reality, has no structure," he tells me.

"The globalization of culture has no structure?" I ask.

"Indeed, it's something that just happens day after day, and it is re-invented day after day."

It would seem that what Gael is actually saying is that giving it a structure would mean rushing into a tactical mistake. Too many vectors are moving within the phenomenon, too many players are involved.

Certainly, a part of Gael's success is due to this unplanned way of being in the midst of events created by the globalization of culture, open to whatever happens and willing to participate in yet-unheard-of ways which do not interrupt the flux of common creativity.

Gael is part of at least two international scenes: the global Latin American scene and the thirty-something global scene. With the former he has made memorable films such as Y *Tu Mamá También, Babel, Essay on Blindness*, and *Motorcycle Diaries*; with the latter scene, he has also made films such as *The Science of Sleep*; plays such as *Together*, and has even recorded a rock song "Cristóbal" which is also the title song of *Déficit*, the first feature film directed by him.

"How many languages do you speak?" I ask Gael.

"I can speak Spanish and English perfectly. But I can also chat in Portuguese, Italian and French." He says that he has heard that it is very easy for children to learn a new language, nevertheless, as someone in his 30's who travels between different countries, directors, and films, he is amazed at his own ability for picking up new languages.

"I just performed in a play in Iceland, and there were mornings when I could see myself speaking Icelandic. Well no, I merely spoke some words in Icelandic, but it happened just like that."

The second to the last time that I saw the artist **GABRIEL OROZCO** it was on a North American TV show on PBS which was being broadcast in Calgary where I was working in a theatrical production.

The program showed Orozco taking pictures of melons in a supermarket, and then of a pyramid of tuna fish cans that could have been found in the supermarket of any Western city.

Isn't that globalization too? In it ordinary events become standardized to the point that you shop for food in a supermarket that is identical to any other supermarket in the world. This is another sign of globalization, the tuna-fish-can pyramid is the equivalent of the oranges and apples in a Renaissance oil painting.

As a matter of fact, Orozco was in Paris. The following images showed him taking pictures of a paper bag being moved by a slight wind in an unmistakably Parisian sepia-colored street.

Orozco stood before a garbage container and took a picture of a ball made of shredded paper.

The last time I saw Orozco we were in a Mexican town. Malinalco, Chiconcuac, San Miguel de Allende? I cannot remember. In any case, it was in one of those well-preserved towns in Mexico which becomes flooded with amber light at dusk. I recognized him from afar at the end of a street. He was taking pictures of the steel rods that crowned an unfinished brick wall.

Indeed, as Gael said, there is no central power leading the globalization of culture. There is no Queen Ant, no Hugo Chávez or World Bank tracing a path or setting the rules.

I ask him "Is there some kind of plan for the global Mexican filmmakers?"

"Nothing." "A manifesto?" "Nothing." "Not even an informal manifesto?" "Nothing."

Nevertheless, some important features might still be highlighted amongst all of those that are involved in the globalization of Mexican artists.

1. The world is getting smaller, because of an intercommunication that would have been considered impossible in the times of our grandparents.

2. A global culture which holds a repertoire of aesthetic values and which appreciates two things that come naturally to Mexican global artists:

a. The ability to belong to global culture, which is the trademark of our times.

b. And the eccentric—whatever lies outside the central discourse of culture in the West.

3. The largest generation of millionaires known in history—scattered through the five continents—who may buy art. And who, as a matter of fact, are buying it, are creating a global market, especially for the visual arts.

4. The crisis of the arts in Mexico, where they live.

a. The largest generation (in numbers) of Mexican artists ever, artists educated in excellent public schools who manage to refine the gifts they've been given with the aid of all the available grants and subsidies.

b. A cultural policy that has failed in two areas: first, in promoting the creation of cultural industries; and second, in bringing the work created by Mexican artists closer to the society around them.

Thus, contemporary Mexican artists find themselves with their instruments well tuned, but with no audience or anyone to promote them. Incited by fear—a fear of isolation—and an ambition—globalization—hundreds of them have started traveling around the world.

TO BE OR NOT TO BE ECCENTRIC

Octavio Paz realized that regarding culture, Mexicans are eccentric Westerners. That is, culturally we belong to the West, but not to its center; our cultural tradition is attracted to the central Western tradition as if it were a magnet.

During the 1960s Paz worked in Paris. Back then, Latin Americans thought that it was the center of Western culture, and for him this eccentricity was an unavoidable condition for a Mexican. Things have moved on.

Today, no place is the main center of culture in the world. But the opposite is not true either: the world is not as horizontal as some observers of globalization optimistically and prematurely assume. No, opening a play in, let's say, Buenos Aires will not have the same effect as opening it in London. If it becomes a success in London it will go to 30 other cities; if it is a success in Buenos Aires its fame will remain locked in Buenos Aires.

Thus, the market for the arts has been expanded throughout the whole planet, but the decisions about the distribution of the arts worldwide are still made in a few cities, New York and L.A., and to a lesser extent, in London, Paris and other European capitals.

In this global culture, Paz's statement about the eccentric Westerners has become an option for every Mexican artist. Each one should choose how eccentric and how Western he wants to be.

As an artist, Gabriel Orozco follows in the footsteps of Marcel Duchamp and it would take a lot of nationalist faith to find a relationship between his work and that of Diego Rivera or Frida Kahlo. Mary-Anne Martin, the Latin American art gallerist based in New York, says that the buyers of his work don't know that he is Mexican and—if they do—they believe it is "just incidental information."

Instead, Samuel Zyman clearly acknowledges the Mexican influences in his work. "I am not a nationalist," he says. "I don't like nationalisms. But I am a Mexican, I speak Spanish, I lived in the Mexican reality, and it is a part of how I look at the world, of how I see everything. Being a Mexican is an essential part of who I am."

He remembers that, in his childhood, Mexican music came in from everywhere. "You could listen to it in a taxi, on the radio, on TV, or in the little plazas where bands used to play. I also was—and am—in contact with Mexican classical music, the music by the great composers. And I studied with Mexican composer Humberto Hernández Medrano."

He wrote two "deliberately Mexican" works because he was asked to do so. "I composed *Encuentros (Encounters)* to represent Mexico at the 1992 Expo in Seville; and my second symphony, that was written to commemorate the 50th anniversary of the National Institute for Nutrition."

"That was back in 1996, Mexico was in the midst of a crisis, and the peso had been devalued. Doctor Segovia, who was the head of the Institute, told me 'write a work that will bring the pride of being Mexican back to us, and call it *The Recovery of Pride*'. He was asking me to compose a nationalist work, and that's what I did. But still in the works that don't have that agenda, the Mexican part comes out, as well as the Jewish part."

Critics can immediately tell that Samuel Zyman's compositions are influenced by composers of the Western canon, mostly by Bach; as well as by Jazz. Next, they usually notice its Jewishness, which is often included even in the titles of the pieces, as it is in his *Kol Nidrei*. But usually the critics only notice that he is Mexican when they get to know his biography, and then they label him as a Mexican or Latino musician—depending on the cultural biography of the critic.

The case of choreographer **LUIS SERRANO** is different. Serrano has chosen the "Mexican" as an identity trademark that he can use to globalize Monterrey's Ballet Company.

Serrano was born in Cuba. As a classical dancer he developed a solid trajectory in first-rate companies in Cuba, Venezuela and America. When he assumed the artistic direction of the Monterrey Ballet (or the BdM, as it appears in its logo), Serrano and Yolanda Santos de Hoyos—the founder of the company—had the intention of internationalizing it. They found two ways to do so. On one hand, they improved the technical level of the dancers, and on the other they created new works with Mexican music.

"More classical identity at a formal level and more Mexican identity when it comes to the music," wrote Fey Berman about the paths that they traced for the BdM in 2007 and is which are bearing its their fruits in 2008 as they tour several capital cities around the world.

Each night, the program of the BdM closes with the *Huapango*, by nationalist musician Moncayo, "a fully Mexican piece that requires a lot of energy and forces the dancers to perform minutely complex and spectacular moves. Men leap audaciously and turn in the air. Women stand on the tip of their toes and look as if they were suspended in the air. Men stand up and make the women turn, so both attain unexpected and exciting poses."

"This piece" says Serrano, "is the company's trademark. With the *Huapango* we have created an easy way to identify a personality of our own".

Instead, **GUILLERMO GÓMEZ-PEÑA**, the well-known performance artist, has chosen to declare himself not being from here or there. Instead, he belongs to the place where borders cross. That is his art: portraying himself at the crossing of the borders, somewhere between established identities, capturing the hybrid that is born when this crossing of borders takes place.

Guillermo was born in Mexico City. I met him at the workshops in the Capilla Alfonsina when he was twenty-something. In those days I used to go there to work on my free verses, while he was working in an epic poem about an intergalactic trip. I though he was a very funny and dangerous kind of guy.

For instance, I remember one afternoon when we went to have some beers and talk about everything and anything in a small Argentinean restaurant. We were just killing time. Then, Guillermo noticed this elderly man reading a newspaper sitting at the table next to us. The newspaper covered his face and half his body, so he could not see the young man with the large moustache—Guillermo—approaching him and setting his newspaper on fire with a lighter, just to go back to his seat and appreciate the "event."

Still in his twenties, and "suffocated by a static and hierarchical culture," Guillermo crossed over and moved to California; and there he also crossed the invisible border between Latino immigrants and Chicanos. He started to hang out with the latter even if there was a taboo that forbade him to do so.

Now, in San Francisco, he is the leader of an artist group called La Pocha Nostra and he is one of the most influential players in performance art.

Mexican, Chicano, Mex-American, multi-cultural artist, eccentric westerner, an American covered with a layer of Chilango dust? What the hell is Gómez-Peña?

He is the devil that dissolves borders. He is the devil who shows his tricks, his political cruelty, his existential foolishness.

Lately he calls himself a Mexican whose identity does not depend on belonging to a territory or to a political entity i.e. "a post-national Mexican." And he also considers himself one of the heroes of a virtual nation called "Latin America of the North."

But as we have already said, Gómez-Peña really rebels against any fixed identity. His work transcends borders: cultural borders, gender distinctions, different languages, the limits between art and politics, practice and theory, the artist and the audience. Gómez-Peña famously expresses himself through performance art, but he also makes videos, installations and photos. He also writes essays and books, and in some of his aesthetic events, he does everything at the same time.

If Zyman lets his different cultural backgrounds intertwine and flow through his music, and leaves the definition to the critic-audience; if Gabriel Orozco is comfortable as a Western artist; if Luis Serrano chooses being Mexican as his distinctive trademark of Mexicanity (even if he himself is Cuban); Gómez-Peña—always in the process of becoming someone else—has made self-definition the territory of his art.

He is a citizen of change, and his homeland is movement...

MEX-AMERICAN SIBLINGS

Out of every three families in Mexico, one has a relative who lives in the USA. In my family, that is my sister **FEY BERMAN**. She's my Mex-American sister.

A good deal of what I have written in this essay is indebted to her articles, interviews and the long conversations we have on a daily basis via Skype. What I say and write about Samuel Zyman, about Mary-Anne Martin, about Luis Rubio and Mex-American films is based on the articles that Fey wrote about them.

Fey is fascinated with the luck of Mexican artists whose exposure in New York is giving them global recognition. She also writes about the nascent Mex-American culture, and about the everyday life of Mexican immigrants.

Fey tells me to notice that the life of Mex-Americans and the art of Mex-American or Mexican artists hardly come into contact. In general, the artists have not considered themselves spokespeople for the latter. Nevertheless, they have done so in exceptional moments, and the pieces they have made already constitute a considerable body of work.

In film, there is a whole genre informally called "migration film." Amongst the films and documentaries in this genre, Fey points out two. She has chosen one because it is unconventional, and the other because it has been the one which has portrayed the feeling of migration more faithfully.

Sleep Dealer by **ALEX RIVERA**—a New Yorker of Ecuadorian descent—imagines that, in the near future, there will be a *"cyber-maquila"* (cyber-sweatshop). It is "the dream of the American Right turned into a sci-fi film: they have an abundant labor force of Mexican *braceros* and they have no social obligations towards them: in *Sleep Dealer* the workers stay on the Mexican side, with their nervous system plugged to a computerized program, so it is they who—long distance—do the hardest jobs for the American metropolis and even fight their wars on other continents."

The second film mentioned by Fey is *La misma luna (The Same Moon)*, one of the largest Spanish-language blockbusters.

La misma luna was born of the collaboration of two women, each on opposite sides of the border. **LIGIA VILLALOBOS**, an American with Mexican parents, who wrote the script (in English, by the way) based on her childhood memories. And the other, a Mexican, **PATRICIA RIGGEN**, who directed the film.

La misma luna captures the feeling that according to Ligia Villalobos predominates throughout all the events related to migration: abandonment. When one crosses a border, a country is abandoned. When new friendships are made on the other side, one abandons the previous ones. When one becomes established in a new homeland, one renounces the original homeland.

On the roaring success of *La misma luna*, Patricia Riggen has said "that everything that has happened is a miracle." Ligia Villalobos, more of a Saxon, with her feet more firmly grounded, has said that "this little film will open the door for the directors and script-writers of upcoming Latino films."

Fey has also written about **MAX LIFCHITZ**, a piano player, composer, orchestra director, and head of the musical ensemble *Consonancia Norte/Sur (North/South Consonance).*

As an interpreter, Lifchitz is a virtuoso. As such, he demands virtuosity in those who interpret his music. His music is brilliant, impetuous, passionate, post-modern and often political. And it has been very influential for contemporary music.

So far, *Yellow Ribbon*—a series of short works that is still being developed—comprises 46 short pieces which have been written over 26 years. This series celebrates the political and artistic freedom of the West. Each work is devoted to each of the 54 Americans abducted in Tehran in 1979, and it also talks about the prohibition the Ayatollah Khomeini imposed on the radio.

Tlatelolco de villancicos rebeldes (Tlatelolco of Rebel Christmas Carols), a piece that commemorates the massacre of Mexican university students back in 1968, roars with overwhelming sadness.

Elegy recalls the Vietnam War. *Still Life* is a piece for twelve female voices that was composed in memory of the victims of the terrorist attack on New York's Twin Towers on September 11, 2001.

One of Lifchitz's CDs, on Mexican piano music, was considered by *Fanfare* magazine to be "probably the most interesting piano CD recorded in 1996." His latest CD was released in autumn 2008.

"How is it possible that no one in Mexico talks about Lifchitz?" asks my Mex-American sister, scandalized, almost protesting.

Her embarrassment is fair. It is as if a family did not acknowledge one of its most prominent members. And even more because Lifchitz feels he is a member of the Spanish-speaking culture, and an active one when it comes to reflecting this membership into in his own works, and has been self-appointed as his own promoter. *Consonancias Norte/Sur*—the group he founded—has played about 800 compositions by Latin American composers for the first time in the USA and some of that music has been recorded in more than two dozen CDs.

I ask Fey if everything that is happening in the Mex-American culture is something new. She confirms that it is something new. To begin with, this cross-over of artists from one side to the other may only uncomfortably be called Mex-American, and it is also hard to separate the phenomenon from the one involving Latin American artists. To continue, this creative effervescence does not have precedents and it had never had so much visibility in America.

On April 8, 2008 I went to a gala at Lincoln Center in New York. On stage, a hundred local children who were Italian, African-American, Asian, Jewish, Irish—that mixture of origins that characterizes New York—were dancing the *jarabe tapatío*, *quebraditas*, and singing songs from Veracruz. Every now and then they cheered, "Me-hi-co, Me-hi-co, ra-ra-ra!"

This ceremony closed a year when two-and-a-half million children devoted their art classes studies to learning about the customs and dances of Mexico.

The initiative came from the National Dance Institute and the private Mexican organization **CONARTE**, and it was complemented with a parallel program implemented in Mexico.

Specialized dance teachers from New York came to Mexico, so local teachers were able to provide dance education in elementary schools in downtown Mexico City.

THE FUTURE OF THE GLOBALS

Gael García Bernal feels that it is not wise to structure that which flows better without a structure, the increasing participation of individual Mexican artists in the global art game.

Instead, Guillermo Gómez-Peña sees in that absence of a common project the abandonment of the Mexican State. As he has said many times, the Mexican State simply hasn't articulated a reaction to the "immense phenomenon of Mexican migration."

We should add that it hasn't been able to react to the immense phenomenon of cultural globalization either.

In 1990, Carlos Fuentes—who spends most of the year in London and works there—wrote an article inviting the Mexican government to seize the opportunity opened by a world that, suddenly, was interested in the Spanish language. He warned that there should be Mexico Houses everywhere, places where Spanish could be taught and that could serve as portals into our culture.

In 2000 Lourdes Arizpe—at the end of her term as the head of culture at **UNESCO**—declared, "Mexico should cash in on its cultural leadership in the Spanish-speaking world."

In the end, it was Spain who seized the opportunity foreseen by Fuentes and Arizpe. Today, the Instituto Cervantes created in 1990 by the Spanish Ministerio de Relaciones Exteriores has 58 centers throughout the world.

In that context, every global Mexican artist still flies the wide heavens above the globe as a lonely bird: they have no choice. But maybe, for a while, it may find a few other birds to form a Mexican flock. And that is why isolated initiatives, which are undertaken at a very personal level but still transcend individual Mexican artists, such as the collaborative project between the New York National Dance Institute and **CONARTE**, or the exhibition of the **COPPEL COLLECTION** are so exceptional.

The Coppel Collection is the map of the love for art felt by **ISABEL** and **AGUSTÍN COPPEL**. The Coppels have immersed themselves with pleasure and interest in art, the best possible guides. The first pieces they bought were Mexican and Modern. More recently they have acquired international and Latin American contemporary works.

One of the most positive features about this exhibition is that it preserves the traces of that eccentric map and keeps "Mexican-ness" at the core of their global collection.

It is an eccentric map that was shown in Europe, first in Paris, one of the centers of the West.

It is a happy idea.

THE MUSIC OF TWO LONELY CELLOS

One afternoon after they had been playing duets, Carlos Prieto and Yo Yo Ma laid down their bows and left their two cellos aside, on their steel bases at the center of a room and went out to have a chat with composer Samuel Zyman.

Carlos Prieto made a joke, "let's see what the cellos do if we leave them all alone, maybe they'll have little cellos or something."

They went on talking, and then, in a serious tone Prieto told Zyman that he should compose "something" for the two cellos.

That was the origin of *Duo for Two Cellos*, a piece that Prieto has interpreted with other cello players in different American cities. But it took nine years for Yo Yo Ma to extend his hand and invite Zyman to climb, from the seats, onto the most famous stage of his country of origin, the Palacio de Bellas Artes, where he received the applause of the Mexican audience.

That is how mobile the art scene has become.

CARLOS REYGADAS planned the story for a film that was to be called *Luz Silenciosa (Silent Light)* from his house, and then he went out to the world to find a landscape that suited it. He decided that the place was the desert in the north of Mexico—where the Menonite community lives—because it was an almost empty space with almost no buildings and a very scarce population. There, his story acquired the flavor of an essential drama.

Guillermo del Toro wrote the script of *Pan's Labyrinth* so it would be filmed in Mexico. Nevertheless, he decided to move the story to Spain because of financial difficulties in Mexico, even if he had to make some changes to the script.

Certainly, the sign of the global culture is mobility.

A gunshot in the Sahara desert affects the life of a Japanese teenager as well as impacting other lives in California and Mexico. That is the myth built by Alejandro González Iñárritu and the writer **GUILLERMO ARRIAGA** in *Babel*, filmed in four languages, that presents itself as a metaphor for the times we are living in.

In his latest book, *El nuevo border mundial (The New World Border)*, Guillermo Gómez-Peña writes about a "New hybrid culture emerging in all the world," "a fusion culture," a culture "of multi-syncretism," of "sampling," "of pastiches," "of juxtapositions," "of cultural interconnections."

It is an emerging culture, one which appears without central command or master plan, and which will acquire a new level of organization on its own.

How will this global culture acquire a "new level of organization?"

Ah! The suspense created by that question is called the present.

Unexpected

Elmer Mendoza

A Man and his shadow were the ones who thought that a city was not a group of buildings erected upon a few low hills, but a human space on which the sun never set. Nevertheless, the shadow left without saying goodbye. Some say it opened a map factory in Cairo and others that it bought an island in Sweden and that no one could get it to leave.

The Man without a shadow did not believe in ghosts, or in a value scale from one to ten, nor in the purity of forms. He then became nothing more than a sedentary traveler.

It took some time before the Man stopped feeling confused, before he got his balance back and got himself believing that there is a reason for everything, knowing that reason is not always important. Soon, people no longer noticed him due to his lack of resources. Years later, everyone wanted to meet him because they suspected that he owned a valuable collection.

He lit his cigar. He was in his garden with three other people who wanted to know about his collection. There are several things that impact me about Gabriel Orozco, he said: the way in which he ironically uses materials, life and memories, those that have accumulated through the years and which make you be yourself. I see one of his works and I meditate, as if I were a Phoenix reborn from those depths of the world where nothing seems to have a coherent explanation. He smoked. The smoke that he expelled got filled with little witches flying upon their brooms. It is an intense feeling that stays with me for days. I even dreamt of a scarecrow parade led by Alfred Hitchcock. At the begining I remember he had an enormous crow on his head and another on his shoulder. He lit his cigar again. Several little sorcerers solemnly withdrew.

I worry about the city, he confessed, and he developed interesting arguments on the trace of the streets, the avenues, the squares and on the ten thousand and forty two colors that inhabit the planet. Your collection, demanded the three fellows, tell us about your collection, is it really made up of Etruscan art? And he added that a group of architects drafted several plans that he never finished studying: What do you do with a temperature of forty degrees Celsius? Paradise had fountains, lush gardens, streams and that's that. We have too many hills but it couldn't be otherwise, isn't the world round? One of the guests, a prestigious sheik who wanted to buy the collection because he thought it was comprised of Marlene Dietrich's films, left the place bewildered. This man speaks of painters and projects as if there was nothing else in his life, he exclaimed, before he got on his helicopter and disappeared. He was not offended and missed his shadow, a companion who had an explanation for everything, even if he did not understand how it could live on a small island without him. Well, he concluded, if I can live without it, why wouldn't it live without me?

Toledo is a thorn, he is many thorns. Fish bones, maguey or cactus thorns. He commented enthusiastically. There is no way to get a grip on his figurative art because it floats and it is tradition, esotericism and mannerism. You change your vantage point and enter the dark side of the universe and you jump from delirium to tranquility as if you were on a swing and the night was simply a soup. His work is a thick shadow. The nature that leaps upon the canvas falls down entangled with its mystery and in the fingers of a man of few words. Of course, he is dressed in white. They drink wine. The witches in the cigar smoke engage in impossible leaps while he looks at them, amused.

He tells them: this square is for the girls in their prime to go about, explained an architect who was showing me a project. The floor is made of marble and we will install some fans so they all think they are Marilyn Monroe. I watched, calculated and realized that no one would ever talk about the city because of that. No—I pointed out—we need something else: a human city, a city where people like themselves because of the place where they live. I want a city that is one of a kind…expected/unexpected. A city where every tree and every room are self-assured voices. I want our visitors to ask where they are, and I want them to be unable to answer that question at first.

I like art because I see the hidden, I listen to the unsaid, I feel the life in my body; that is why I am interested in art. It is that strong feeling which enables a new anticipated life because it knows that nothing will be as it was yesterday. Everything shall be new. Color, shapes and space rule the universe. Each perception becomes a vehicle that operates in the opposite way: it becomes a new way to see the world. This cigar is too dry, it is not meant to be smoked at sea level, or at 41 meters above, like we are here. Let's see, would you like one? I have another box with softer ones. The guests declined and he lit his. The witches jumped off his chin, into the puff that came out of his mouth.

Perhaps they only founded the city because of the rivers and the farming basin. It grew around them. There are one hundred and three bridges in this plan. An architect told me so. All sorts of them: some are covered, others are made of wood or concrete, there's a replica of the Golden Gate and another of Saint Michael's. I did not interrupt him. Well, let's leave some of them, those that are not a copy of something else, but I want two imaginary ones. I want people to get there and assume there must be a bridge and I want them to get soaked in the river if they try to cross. I want them to know that there is a bridge over there and that it is worshiped by the city. It could be a bridge that can only be admired by people who have a good heart. The architect rolled up the plans and left. I thought that perhaps he had never read "The Emperor's New Clothes."

The guests nervously listened to him and he answered their questions. Collecting is a way of life, explained the Man—who did not like to be on TV or answer to reporters. It is a force that always induces you to think, the next day, of the things you must do in order to earn the moments of glory given by artworks. A man makes his own story whether it rains or snows, and—in the end—there are not so many transcendental moments; those days are like great works and they are the ones that make you think that life's worth living. They are also akin to the poet who becomes immortal because of one of the thousands of poems he wrote. We should all create those moments. Please sir, we have come from afar, they say that you have a collection you will not negotiate on. No one knows what it is made of, but that doesn't matter, we believe that if it comes from you it must be endearing. The Man watched the smoke and he drank.

He did not know why, but he missed his shadow deeply. He did not want to reject his guests even if he was at the limit of discretion. One of them encouraged him to continue. I am no longer interested in your collection, but I still want to listen to your words, I would like you to go on. He thanked him: I know that you sponsor a very important museum, I congratulate you. For me a museum is the most vivid example of everyday humanism, the one which expresses the ways in which life goes by, that which is breathed, and however small, no visitor is bound by its walls. There is a revolving air that places us in time and space. Another guest insisted: are there only twentieth-century artworks in your collection or...He moved his head in denial.

He answered to his most attentive listener. Art, like feelings, has no nationality. I am not always able to explain the attraction, slight or overwhelming, of a painting. He stood up to open a bottle.

The little ones got merry and started playing again. They flew and flew. Then, someone rang the bell softly. He became silent. He thought, it is someone else who is searching for my collection, or perhaps that Chinese man whom I have not wanted to receive. The witches went to see who was looking for him and were magnetized by the visitor and came back with it. It was his shadow softly sliding into the room along with the witches who fluttered around. Astonished, the Man stood up. Do you know how to hug a shadow? Well, he didn't know either. He thought of several questions, but decided not to ask them. The newly arrived shadow looked around into the space and nodded approvingly. The visitors experienced an acute strangeness but did not move.

He accepted the presence of the shadow which kept itself amused with the witches. He poured the wine and went on talking with absolute precision, "Artworks only become artworks by denying their origin," said Theodore W. Adorno during the short instant when he stopped being Julio Cortazar's cat. I love that expression because it escapes nationalism. What is the origin of an artwork? He smiled and brought a cracker to his mouth, drinking from his glass. What does it deny? He brushed away a crumb. His joy became palpable. Even the witches smiled standing on the shadow's face, who sat in the chair that had been occupied by the sheik before he left.

A collection is an endless path. And he was a pilgrim who escaped any explanation, even the one provided by *The Little Prince* who was a frequent traveler on a planet where only one person lived. How do you sell that?

Sometimes you cannot see all the objects in your collection, but you feel well knowing that you have it, that it is well kept somewhere. They thought that he was eclectic; that his passion had no limits; that he risked too much. He smoked. The witches looked for the smoke while they flew on their brooms. You know that nothing will happen to it, and that the place that each piece has in your heart is well occupied. The shadow made a gesture of approval.

After a long smoke: Sirs, my collection is not for sale, it is almost me. How could I sell it? But—a nobleman from a ruined country insisted—no matter how valuable it is, it must have a price, would you take a shadow as payment? No one spoke. Sirs, it has been my pleasure. Think about it, insisted the Man with a threatening look about him. I don't need your shadow mister, can't you understand?

He smiled at it as soon as they were left alone; he was back in his chair. The witches stood still. Did you feel like seeing me? It nodded. I hope that you have not been disappointed by the city; it is not the one we dreamt of. The shadow made a neutral gesture. Where have you been living? He felt he received the answer in his mind: in Rapa Nui. On that island, why? I like the horizon. The shadow looked relaxed and the witches restlessly flew from one side to the other. What is that racket about your mysterious collection? I don't know, I am about to show it, it is a collection of contemporary art and I really hope it is something unexpected. You are still delighted by the surprise factor. They had a lively conversation while he finished smoking his cigar. I must go back. What? Do you mean you're not staying? Some Men do not need their shadow, you are one of them. You only came to tell me that? I don't know; shadows have no memory. They said goodbye. He reacted after a few minutes; he felt really cheerful, relaxed and totally self-possessed.

And the witches, where did they go?

The following is a selection of works from both exhibitions listed in alphabetical order

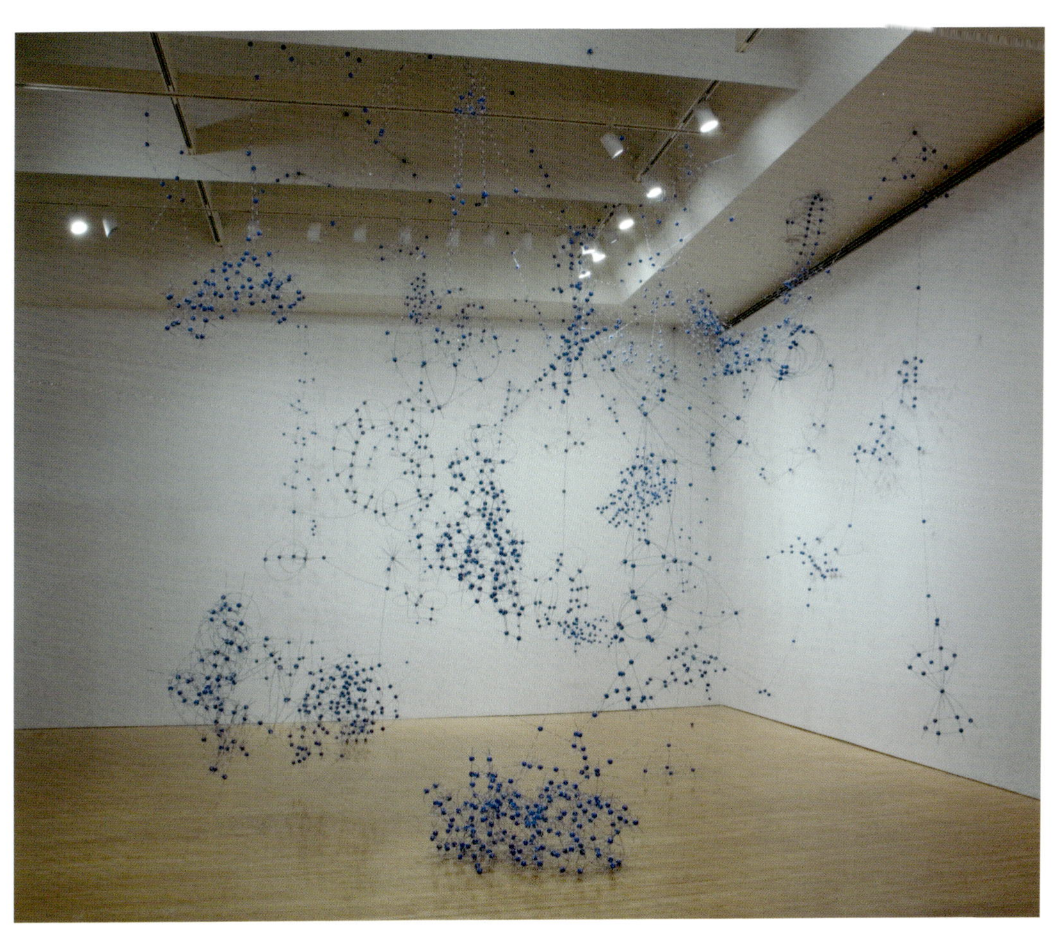

EDUARDO ABAROA (b. 1968, Mexico)
BCIN (Node in a Corner) / BCIN (Nódulo en la esquina), 2007

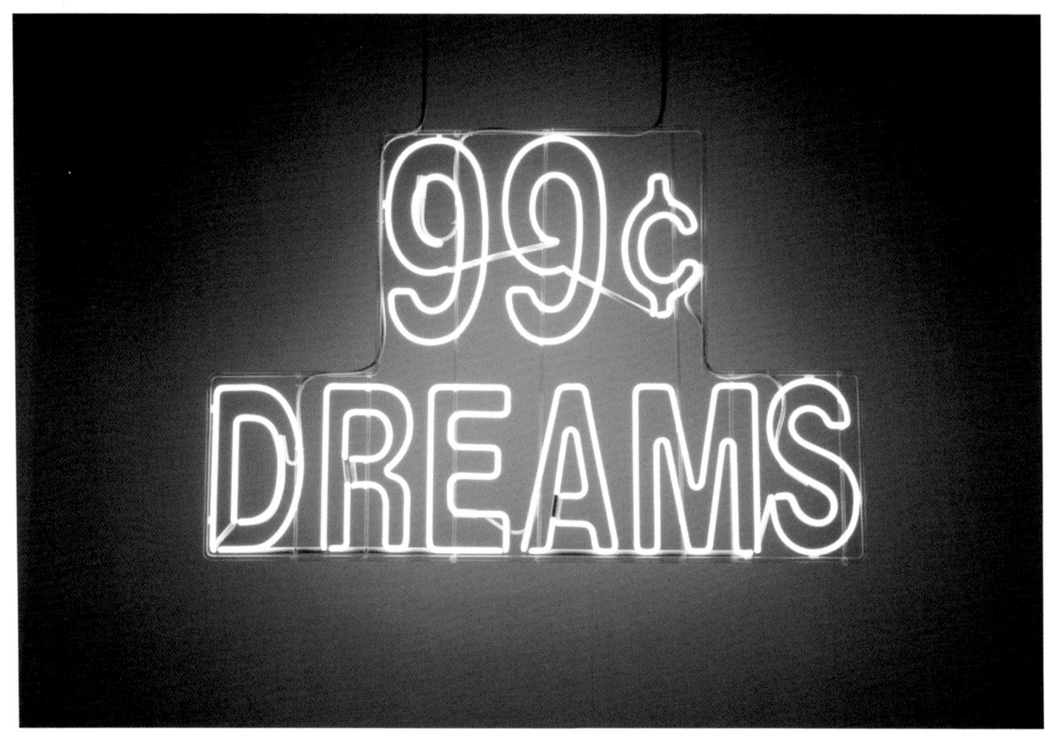

DOUG AITKEN (b. 1968, United States)
99 Cents Dreams / Sueños de 99 centavos, 2007

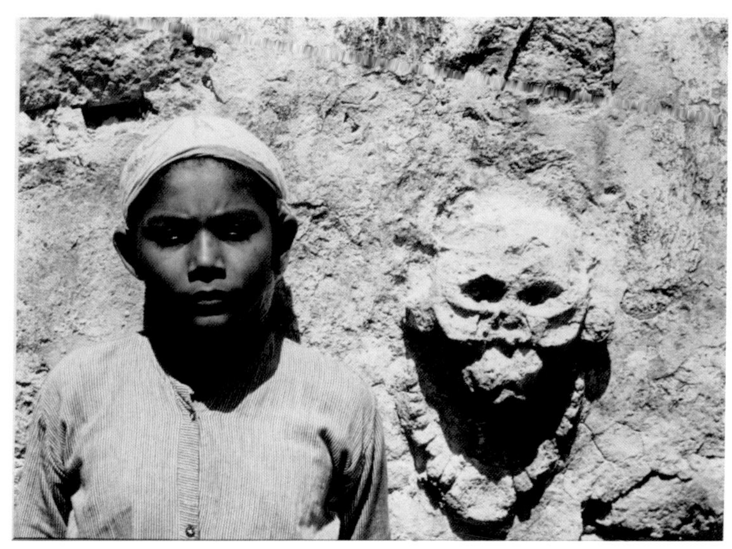

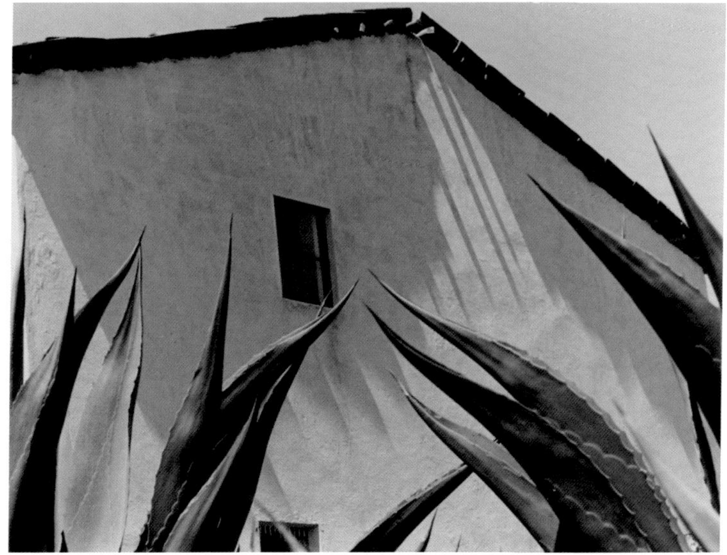

MANUEL ÁLVAREZ BRAVO (1902-2002, Mexico)
Niño maya de Tulum / Mayan Child from Tulum, 1942
Ventana a los magueyes / Window Looking at the Magueys, 1976

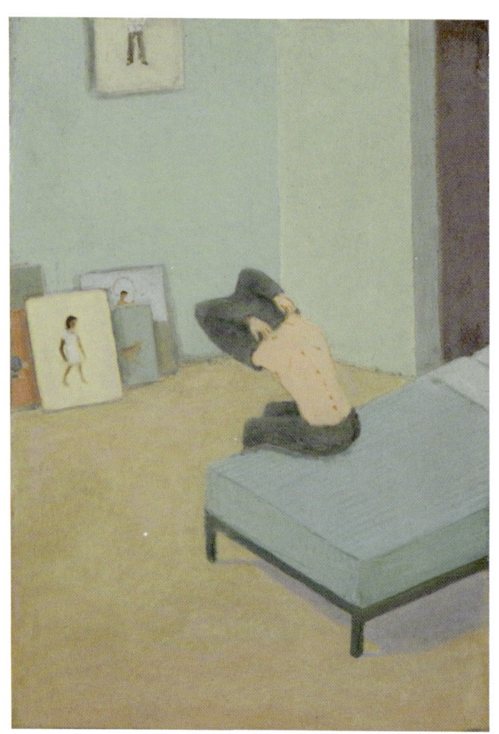

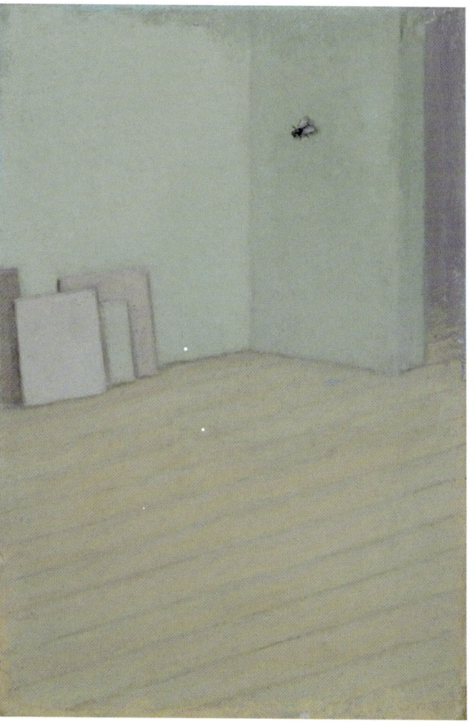

FRANCIS ALŸS (b. 1959, Belgium)
D- El jersey y la mosca / About the Sweater and the Fly, 2003

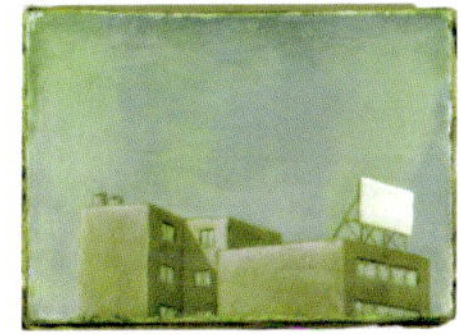

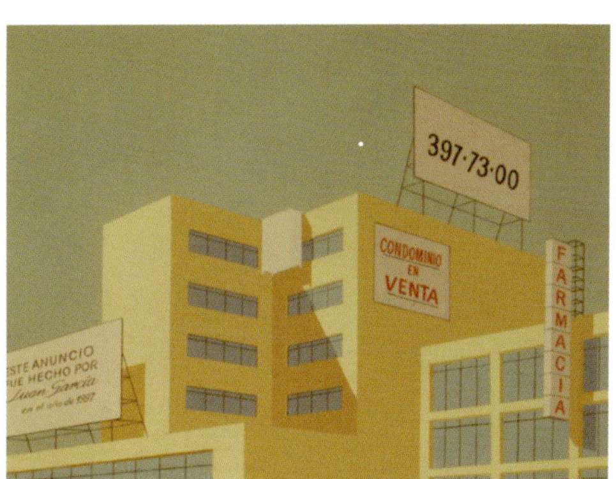

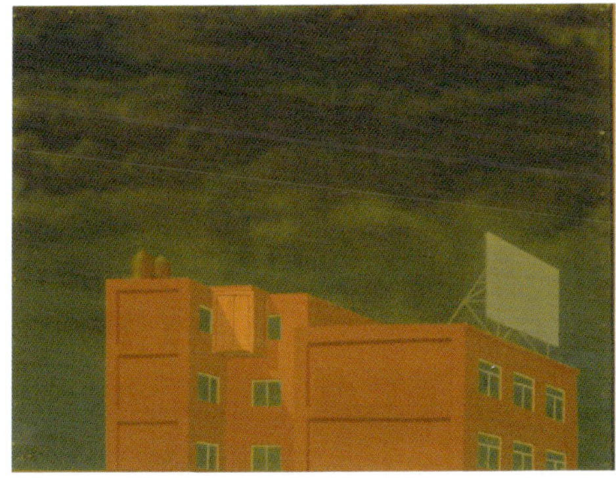

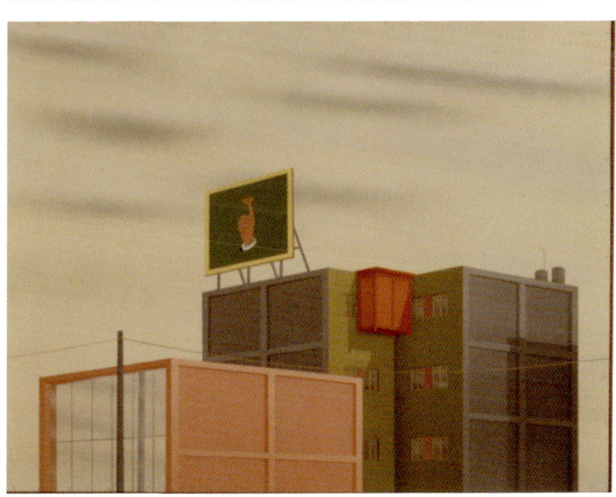

FRANCIS ALŸS (b. 1959, Belgium)
Untitled (Cityscape) / Sin título (paisaje urbano), 1995-1996

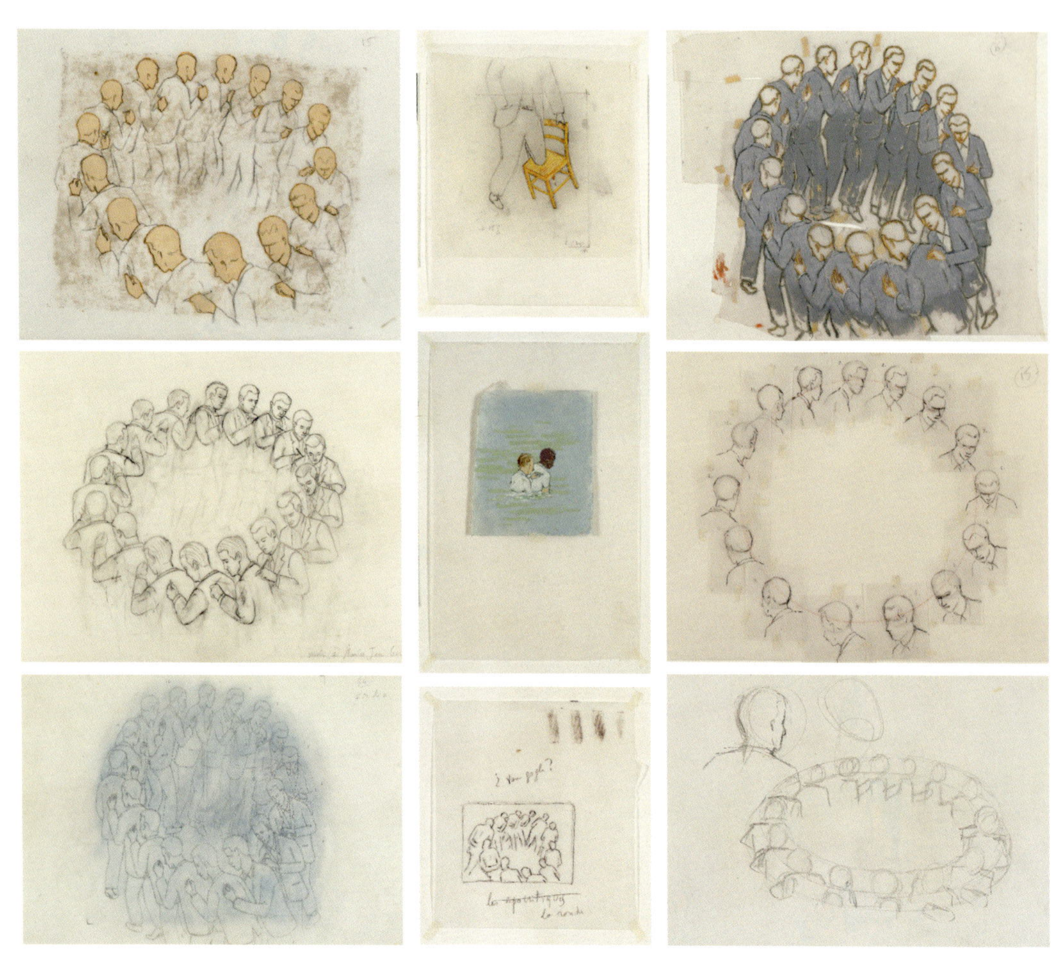

FRANCIS ALŸS (b. 1959, Belgium)
La ronda / The Round, 1998-2006

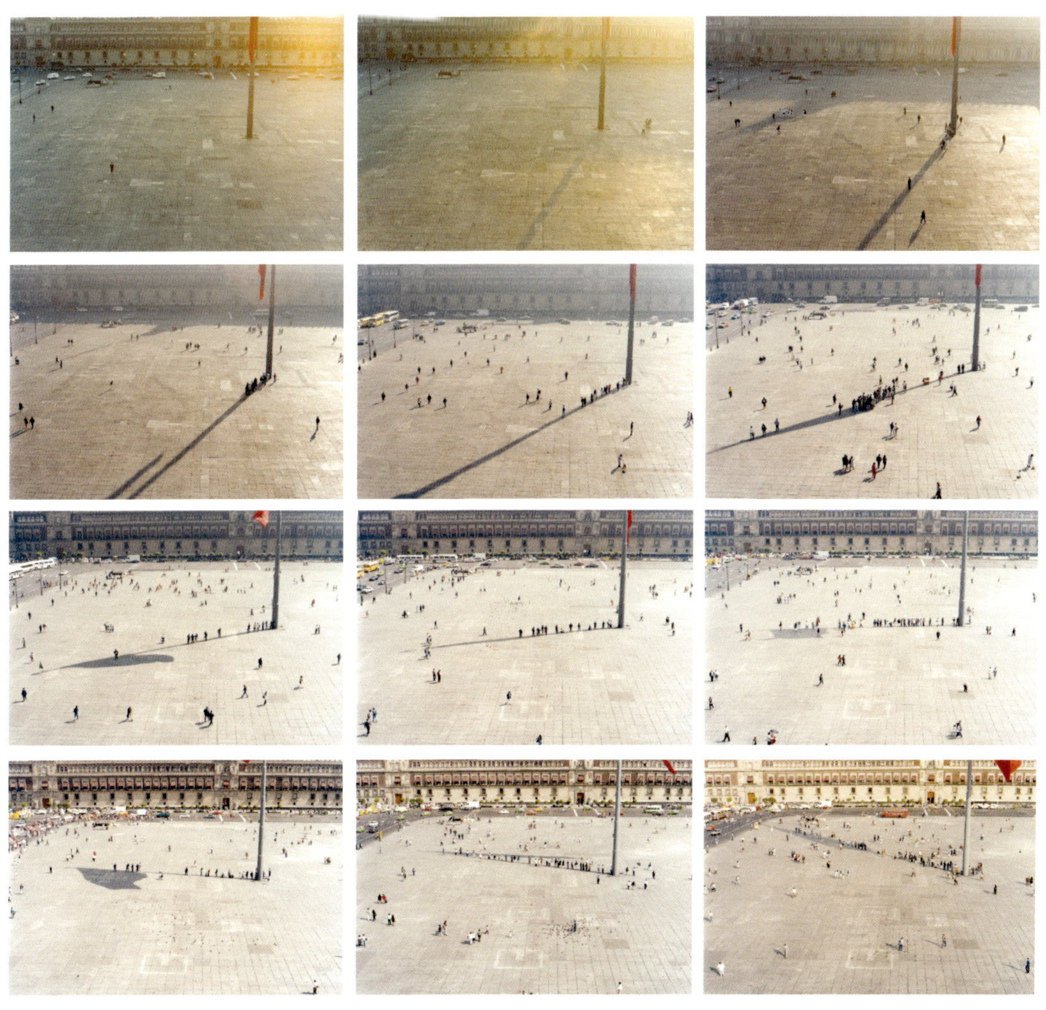

FRANCIS ALŸS (b. 1959, Belgium) In collaboration with Rafael Ortega (b. 1962 Mexico City)
Zócalo, mayo 22 1999 / Main Square, May 22 1999, 1999

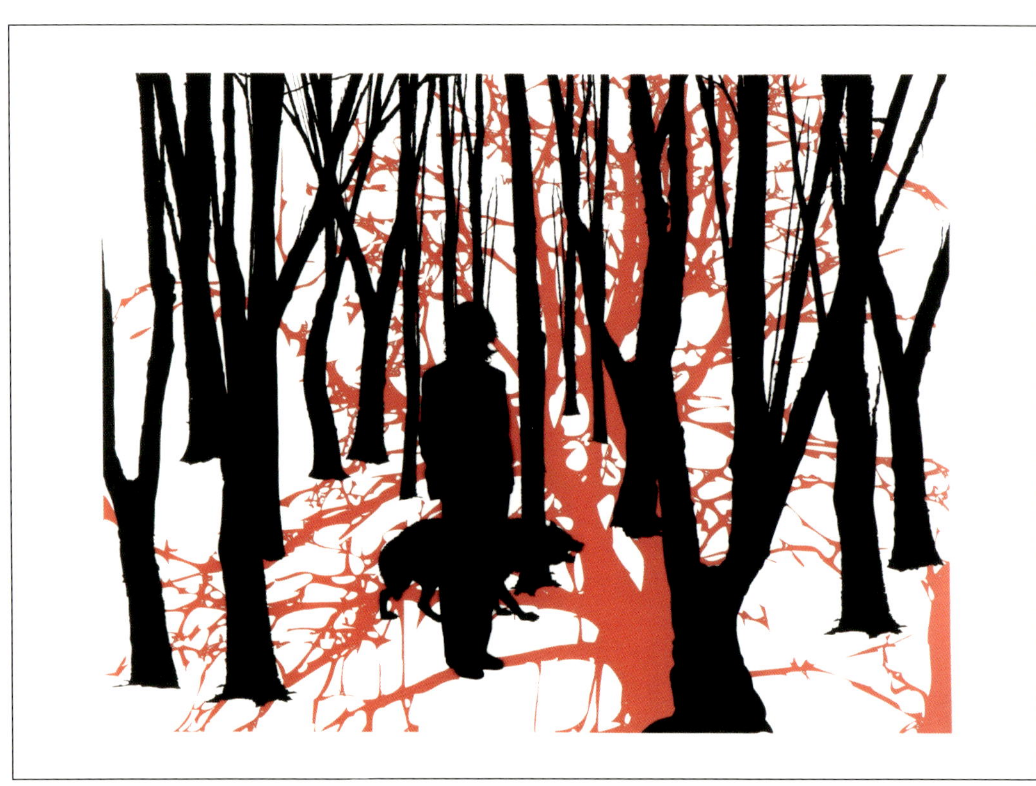

CARLOS AMORALES (b. 1970, Mexico)
Panorama, 2007
From the series of thirty collage drawings

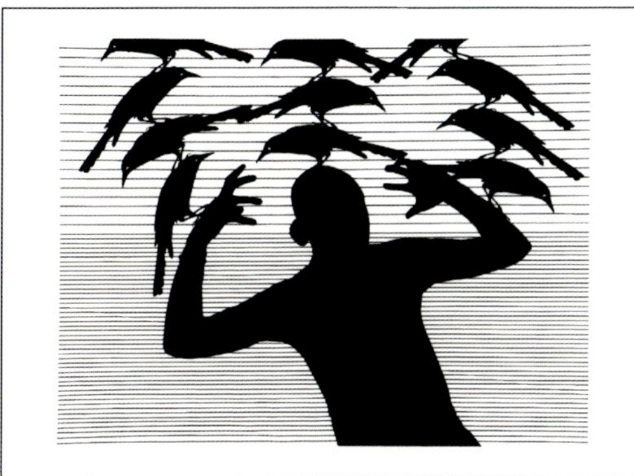
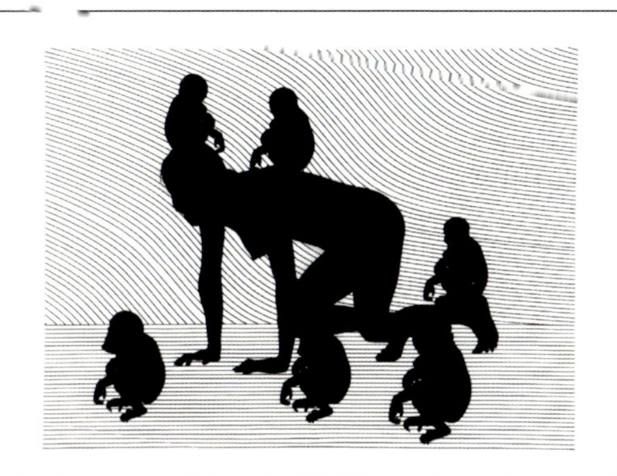
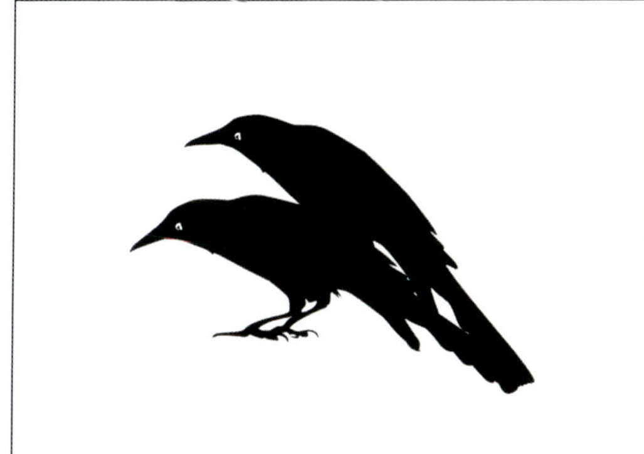
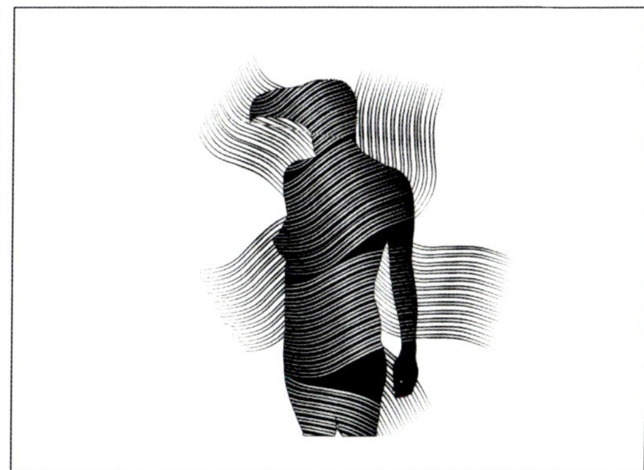
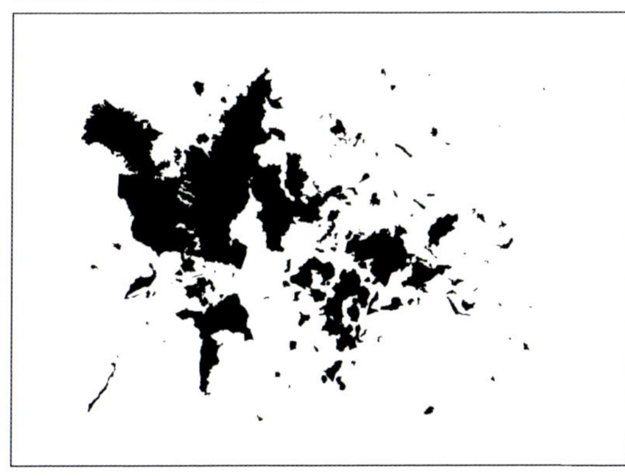
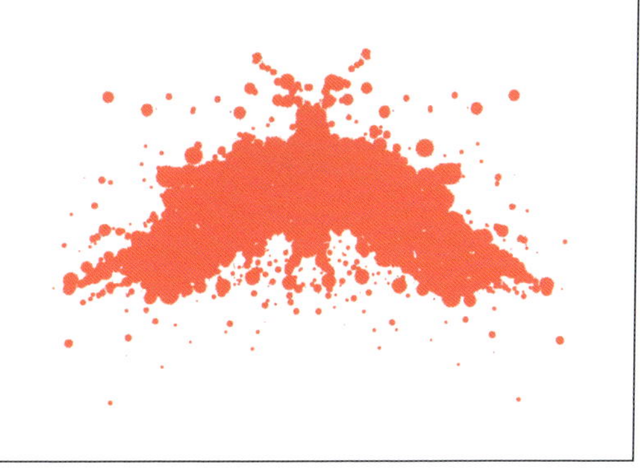

CARLOS AMORALES (b. 1970, Mexico)
Panorama, 2007
From the series of thirty collage drawings

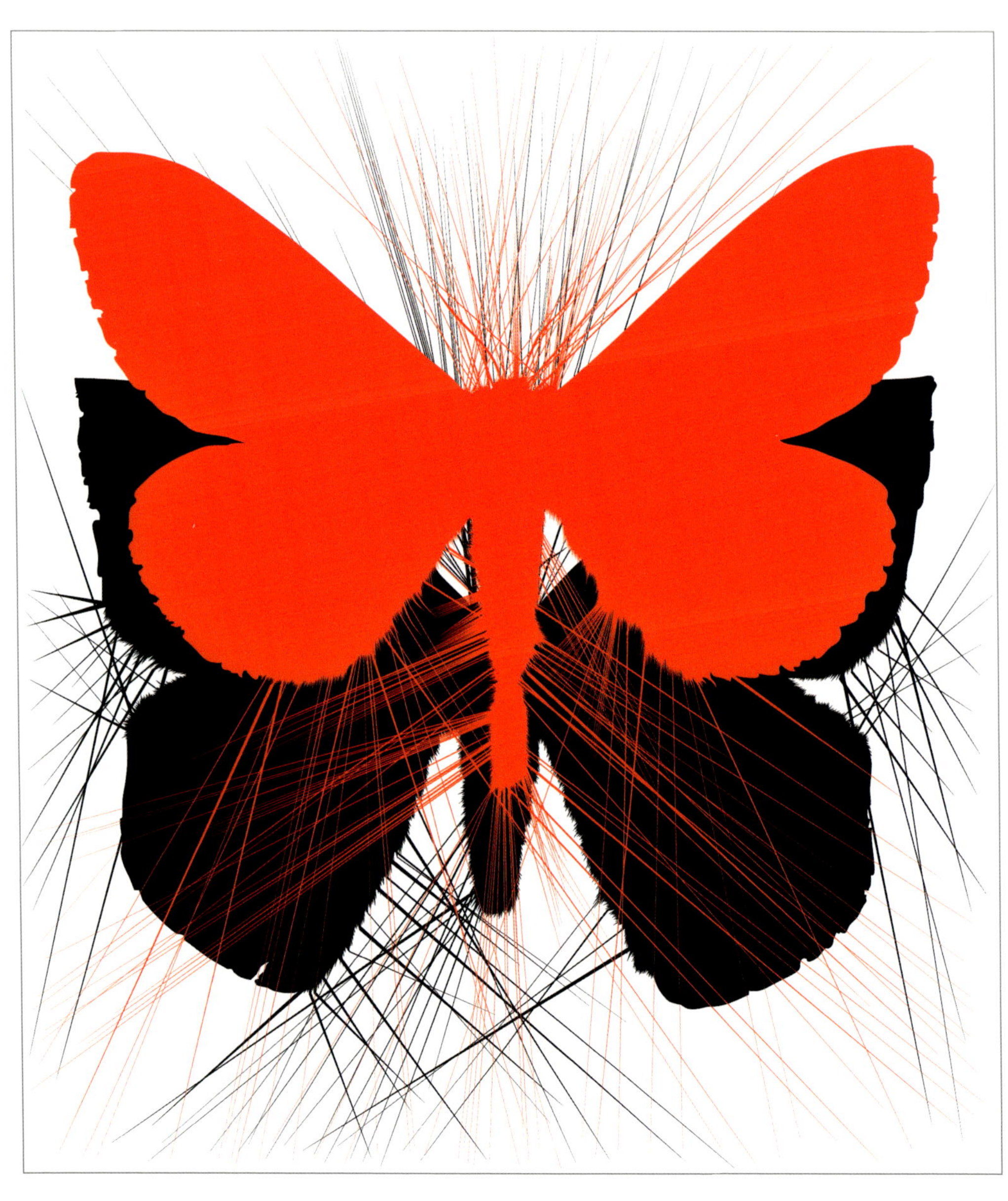

CARLOS AMORALES (b. 1970, Mexico)
The Horny Ghost 07 / El fantasma calenturiento 07, 2007

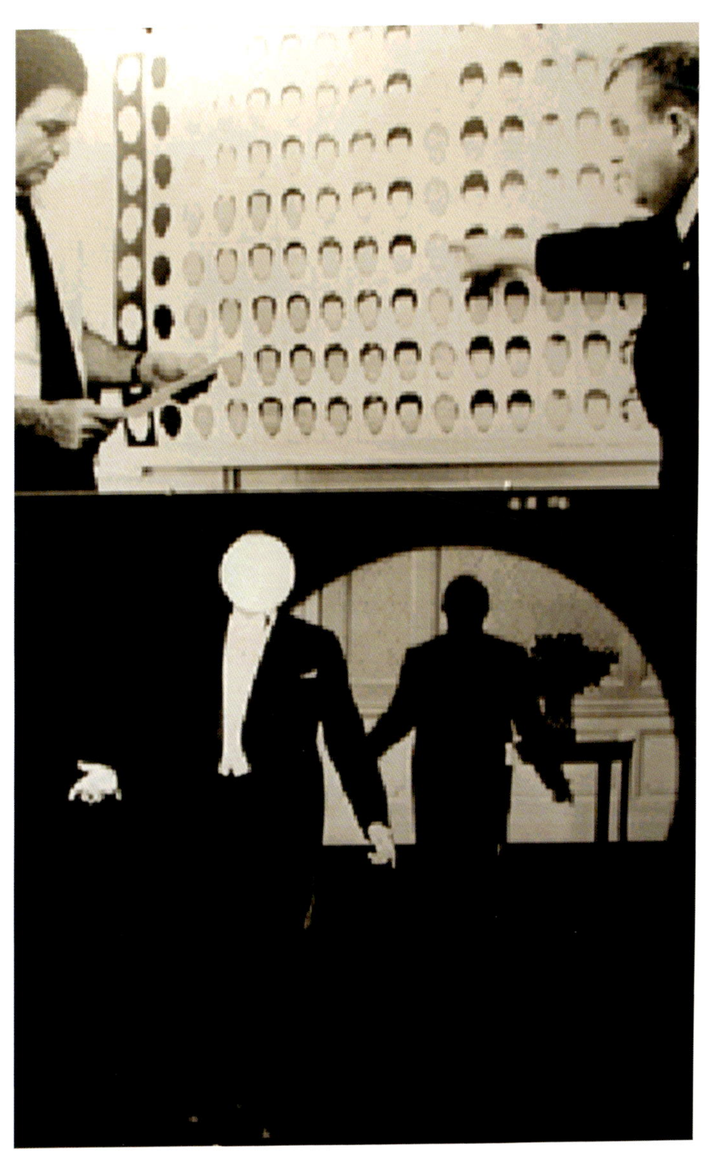

JOHN BALDESSARI (b. 1931, United States)
Two Faces: Three Figures; One Shadow (Version #2) /
Dos rostros: tres figuras; una sombra (version #2), 1988

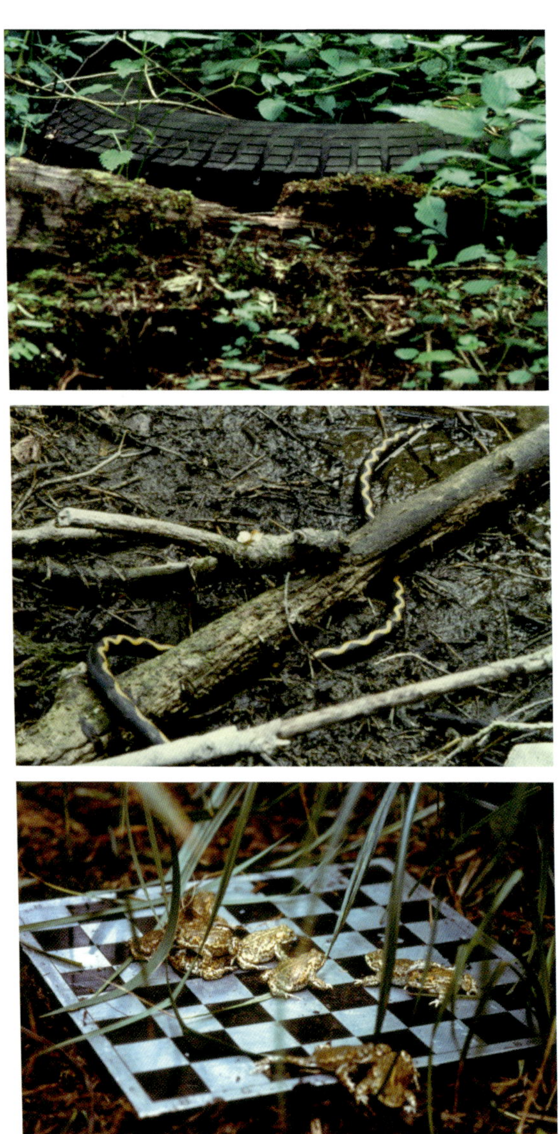

LOTHAR BAUMGARTEN (b. 1944, Germany)
Antizipierte Gürteltiere (Anticipated Armadillos) / Armadillos anticipados, 1969
Äskulap / Asclepius, 1971
Conquista Rochade / Rochade Castling, 1971

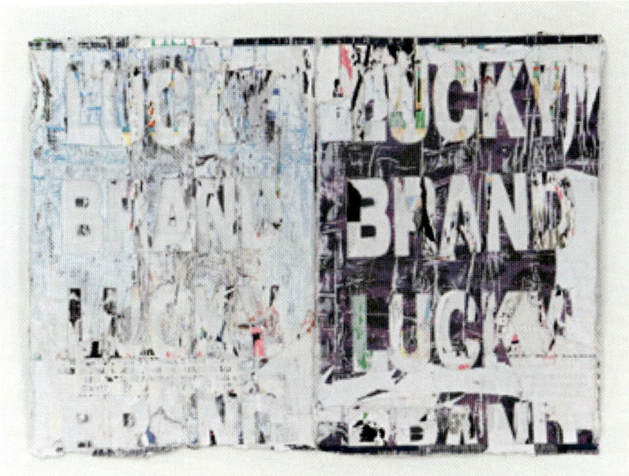

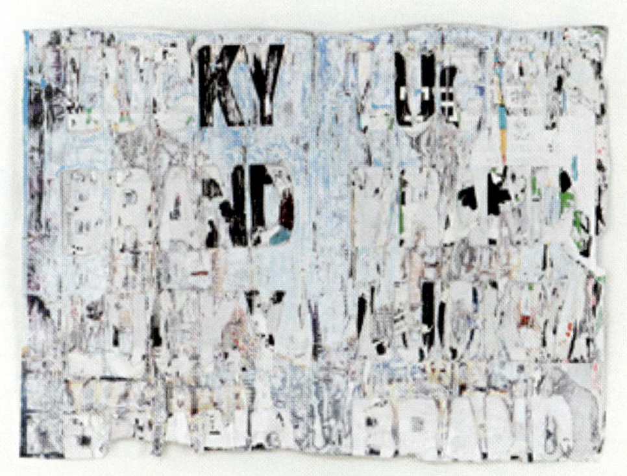

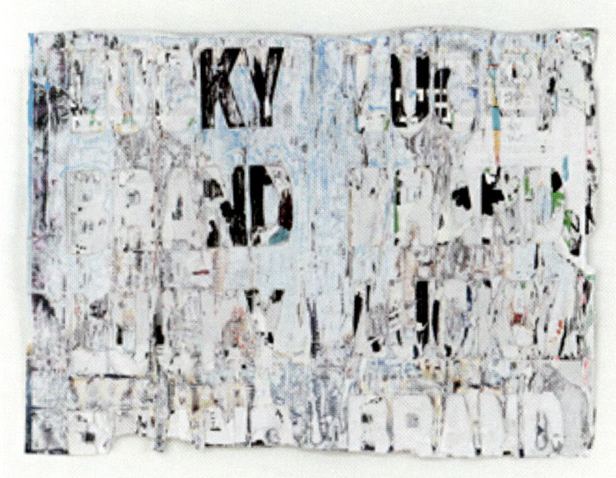

MARK BRADFORD (b. 1961, United States)
Untitled / Sin título, 2007

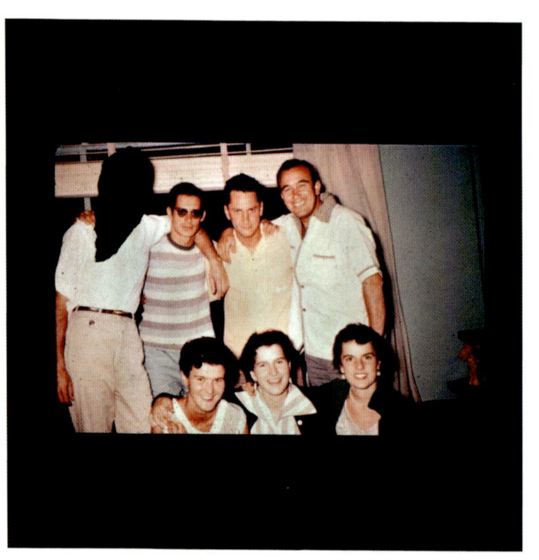

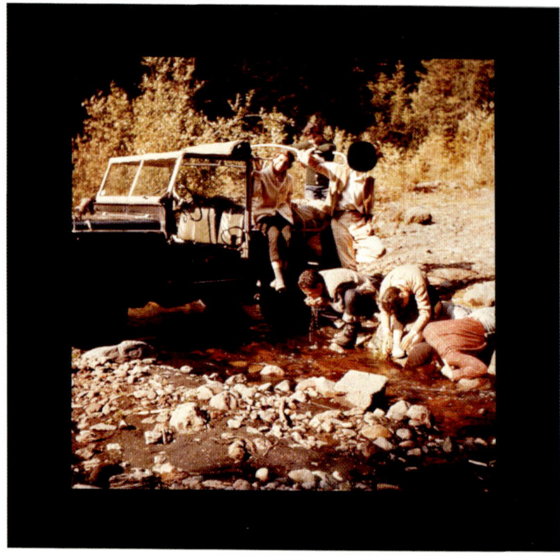

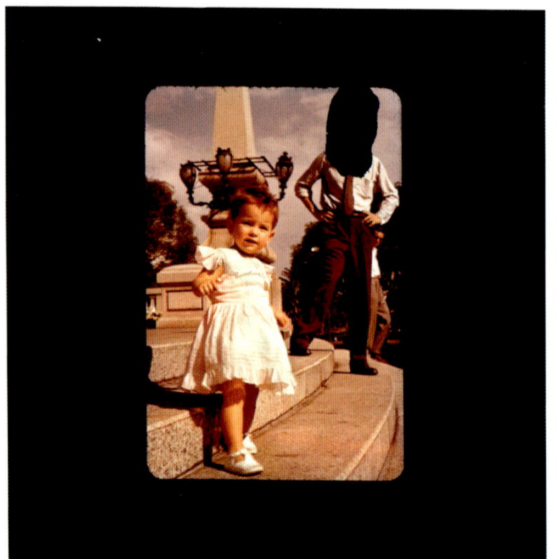

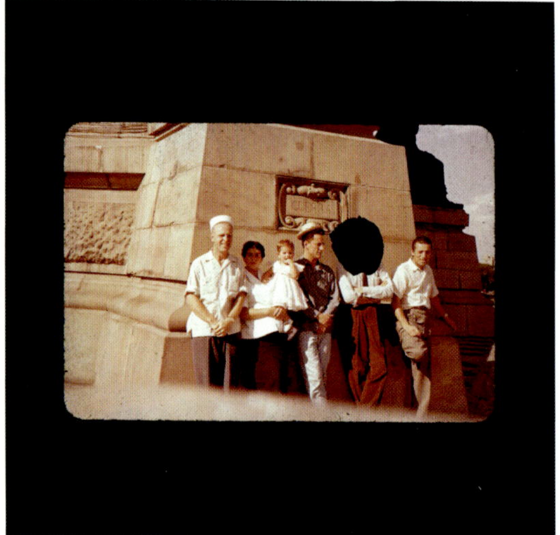

IÑAKI BONILLAS (b. 1981, Mexico)
"Casa Fernando" de la serie *Martín Lunas* / *"Fernando House"* from the *Martín Lunas* series, 2004
"La cabaña 01" de la serie *Martín Lunas* / *"The Cabin 01"* from the *Martín Lunas* series, 2004
"Angel 01" de la serie *Martín Lunas* / *"Angel 01"* from the *Martín Lunas* series, 2004
"Angel 02" de la serie *Martín Lunas* / *"Angel 02"* from the *Martín Lunas* series, 2004

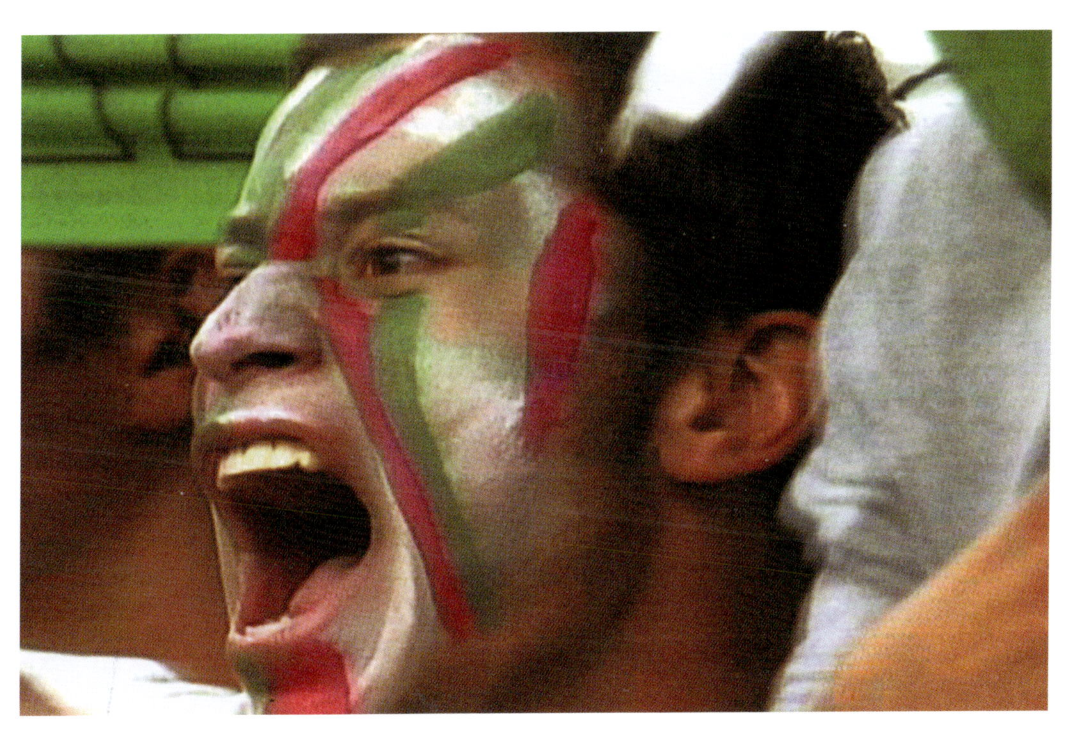

MIGUEL CALDERÓN (b. 1971, Mexico)
Mexico vs Brasil, 2004

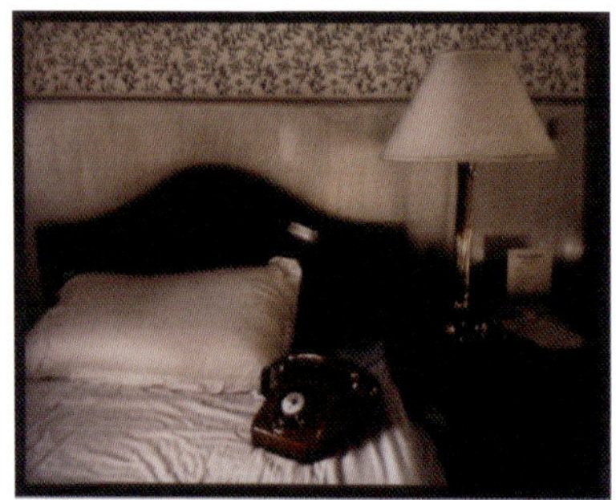

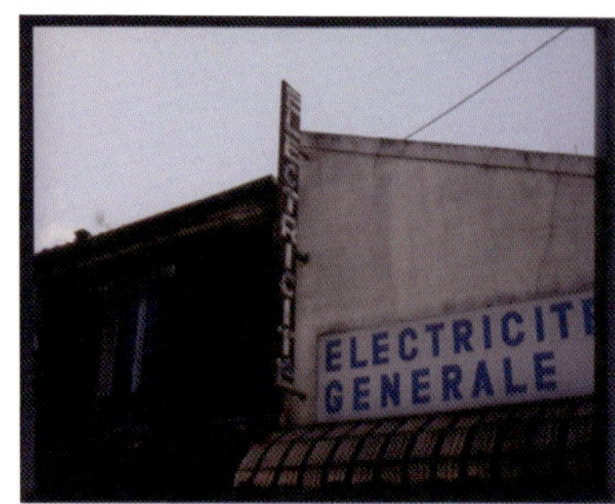

Fifty days ago, the man I love left me.
By phone. It was January 25, 1985 at two in the morning. I was sitting on the bed in room 261 of the Imperial Hotel in New Delhi. A dreary, dusty room with a gray moth-eaten carpet and bright red telephone. I had just dialed his number in Paris. It was a brief exchange.
"Sophie, I wanted to come and take you in my arms and explain a few things."
"Have you met another woman?"
"Yes."
"When?"
"Twenty days ago."
"Is it serious?"
"I hope so."
"Poor me."
I hung up. And that's how it all finished. A banal love affair with a pathetic ending. Nothing more.

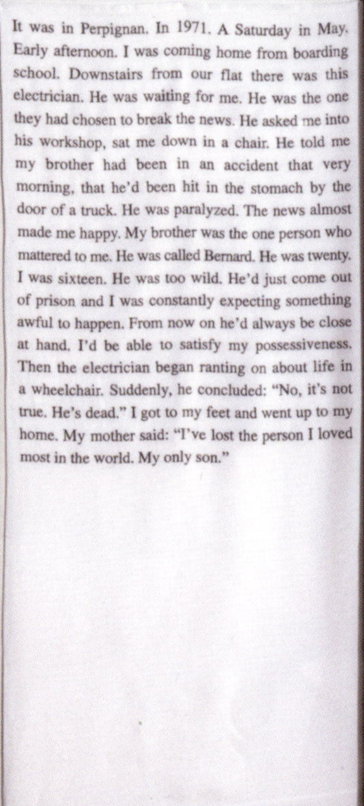

It was in Perpignan. In 1971. A Saturday in May. Early afternoon. I was coming home from boarding school. Downstairs from our flat there was this electrician. He was waiting for me. He was the one they had chosen to break the news. He asked me into his workshop, sat me down in a chair. He told me my brother had been in an accident that very morning, that he'd been hit in the stomach by the door of a truck. He was paralyzed. The news almost made me happy. My brother was the one person who mattered to me. He was called Bernard. He was twenty. I was sixteen. He was too wild. He'd just come out of prison and I was constantly expecting something awful to happen. From now on he'd always be close at hand. I'd be able to satisfy my possessiveness. Then the electrician began ranting on about life in a wheelchair. Suddenly, he concluded: "No, it's not true. He's dead." I got to my feet and went up to my home. My mother said: "I've lost the person I loved most in the world. My only son."

SOPHIE CALLE (b. 1953, France)
Count Up to Unhappiness: Day 50 / Cuenta hacia la infelicidad: Día 50, 1984-2003

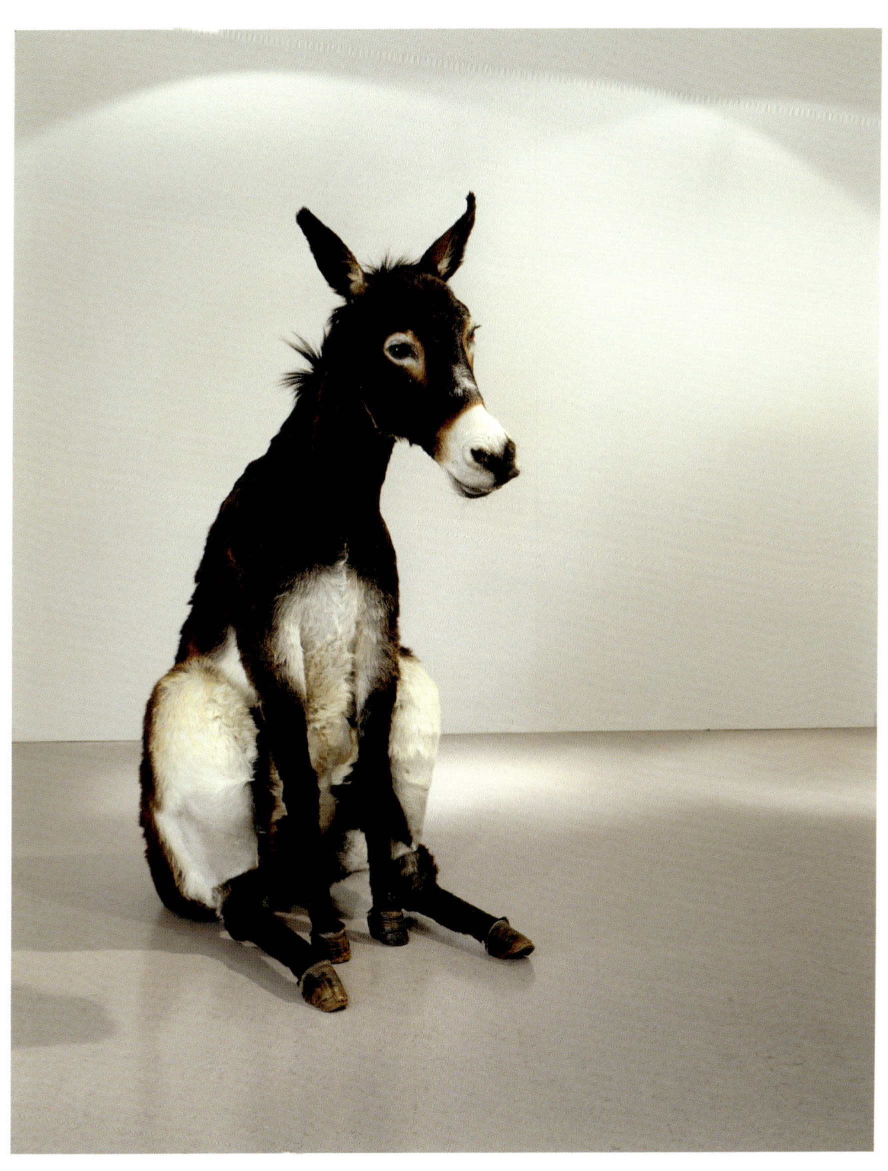

MAURIZIO CATTELAN (b. 1960, Italy)
Untitled (Sitting Donkey, Trento) / Sin título (burro sentado, Trento), 2004

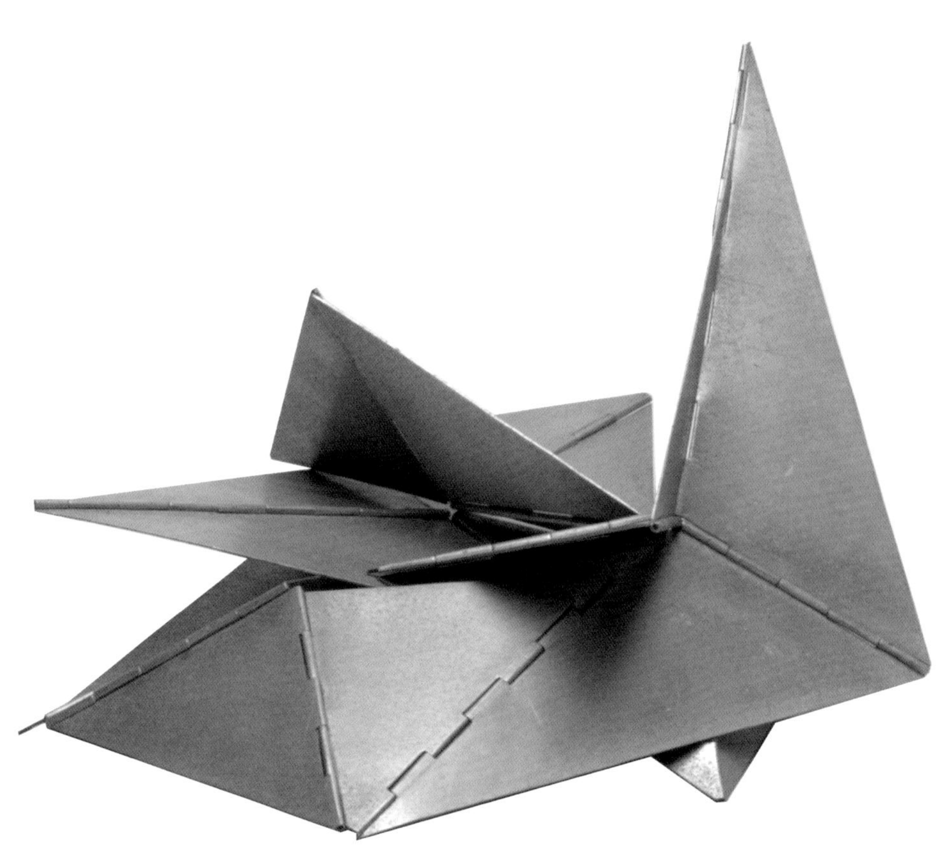

LYGIA CLARK (1920-1988, Brazil)
Bicho / Bug, 1960

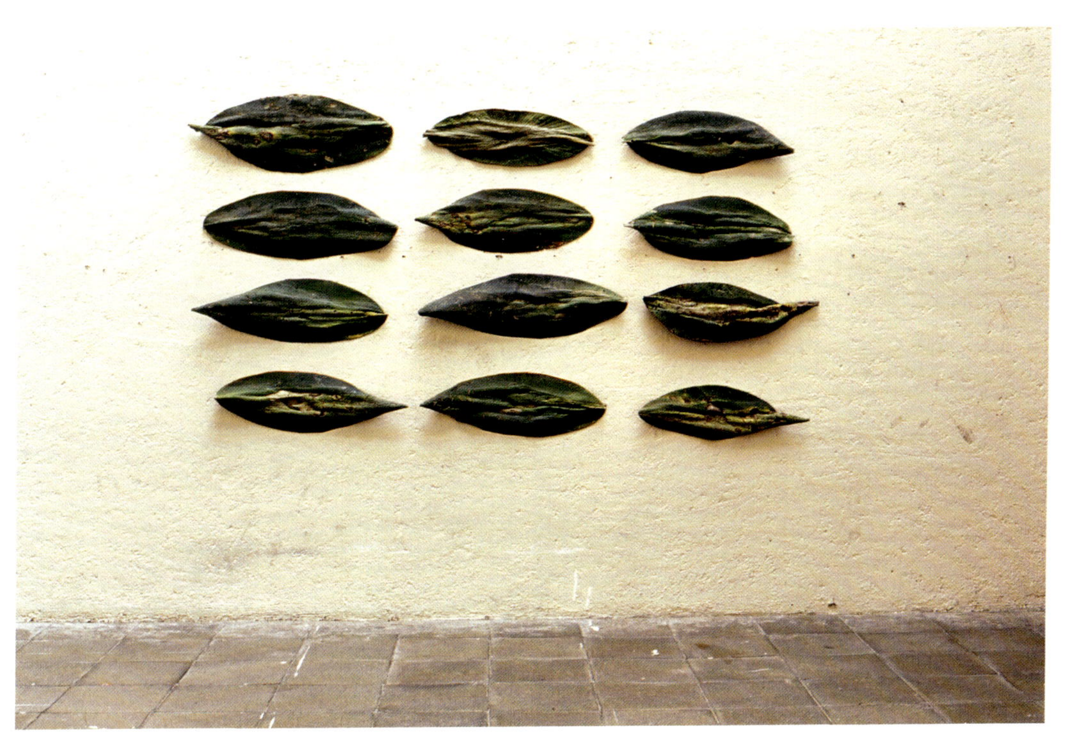

ABRAHAM CRUZVILLEGAS (b. 1968, Mexico)
Las Guerras Floridas II / Florid Wars II, 2003

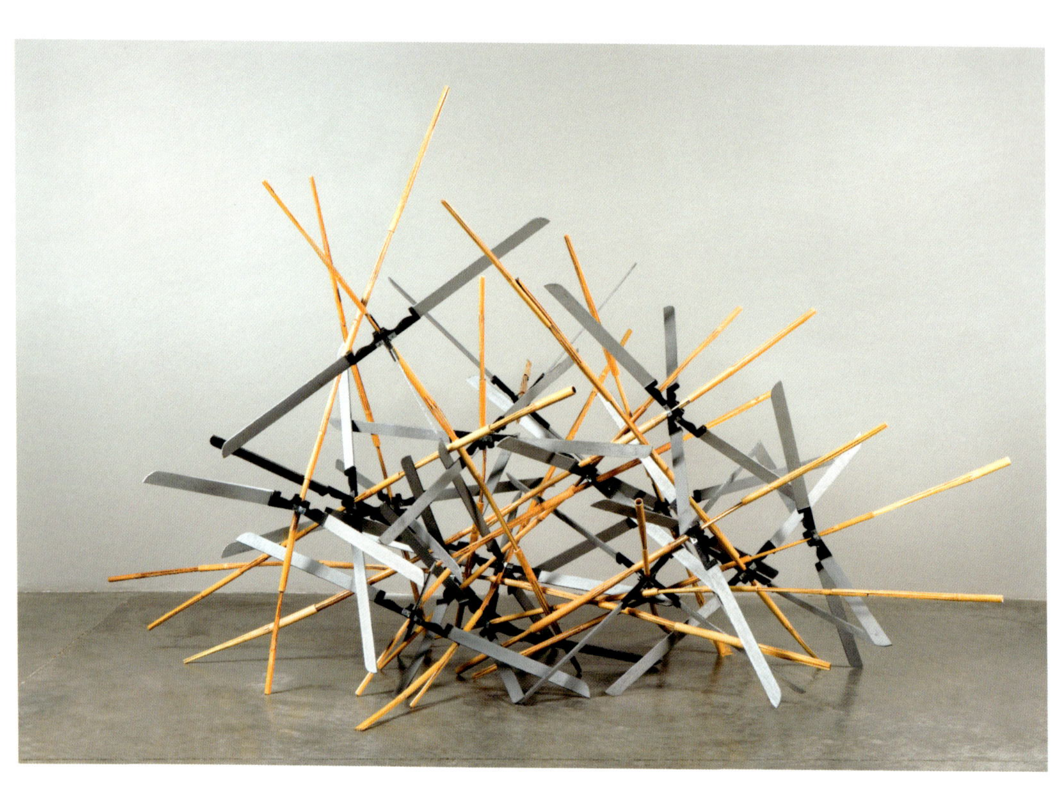

ABRAHAM CRUZVILLEGAS (b. 1968, Mexico)
Martí, 2003

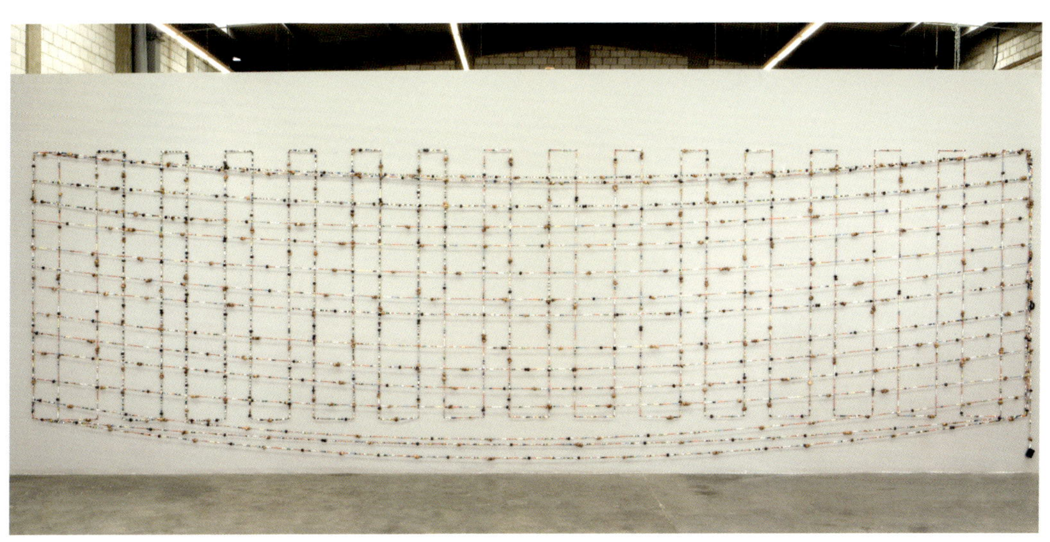

ABRAHAM CRUZVILLEGAS (b. 1968, Mexico)
Unión / Union, 2003

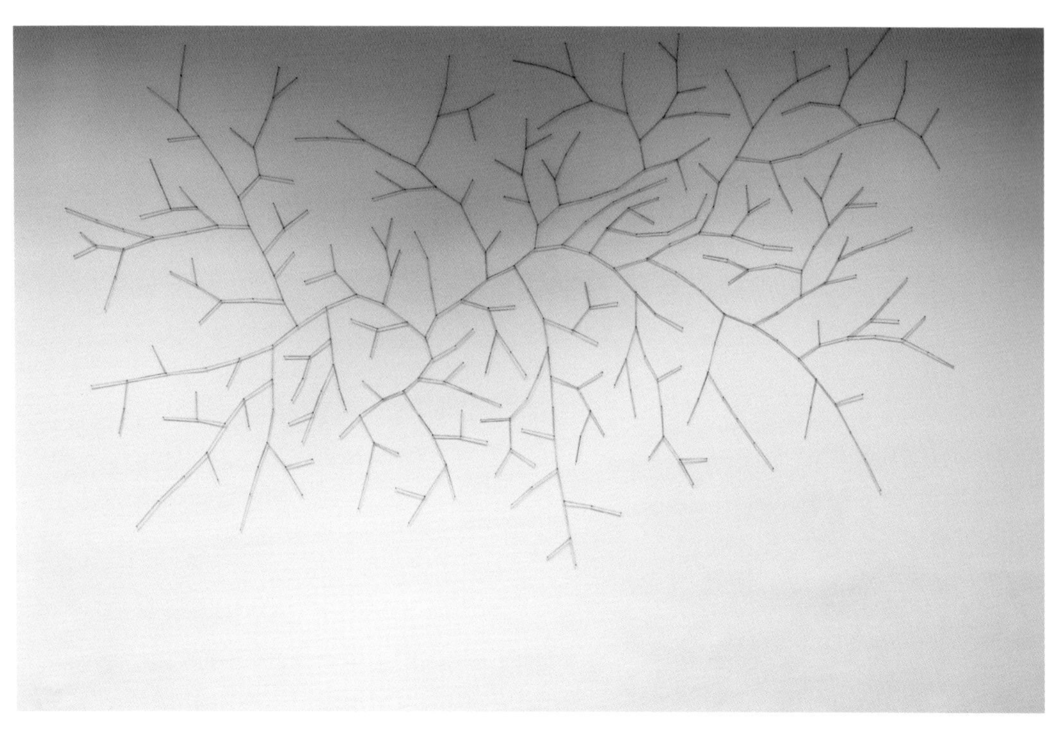

JOSE DAMASCENO (b. 1970, Brazil)
Cinema Elastico / Elastic cinema, 2009

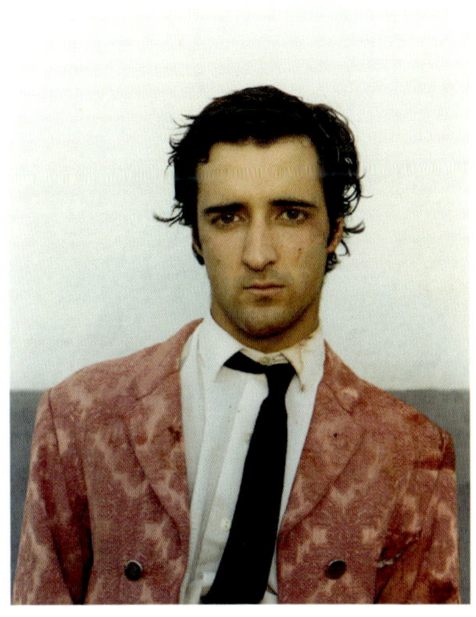
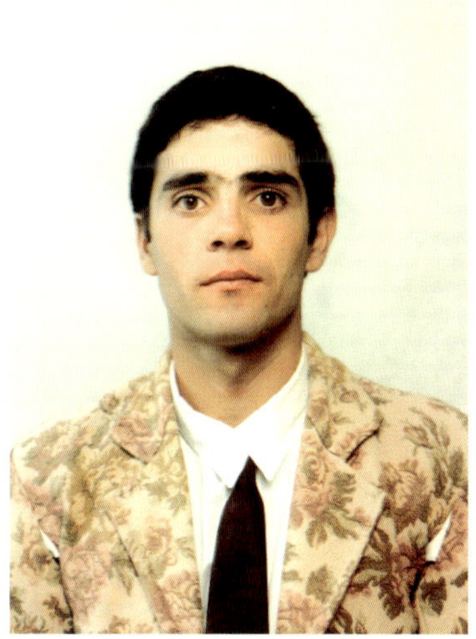
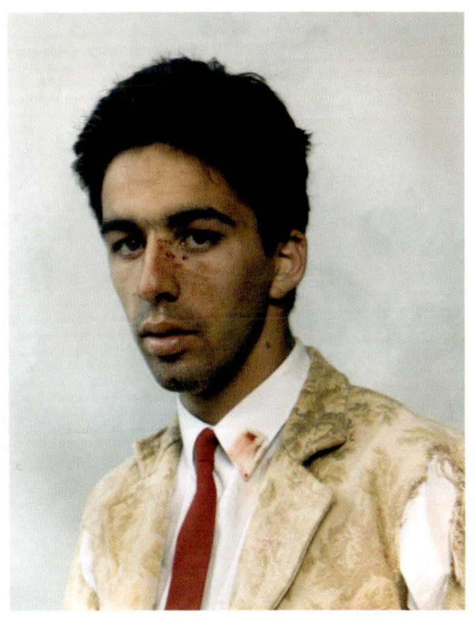
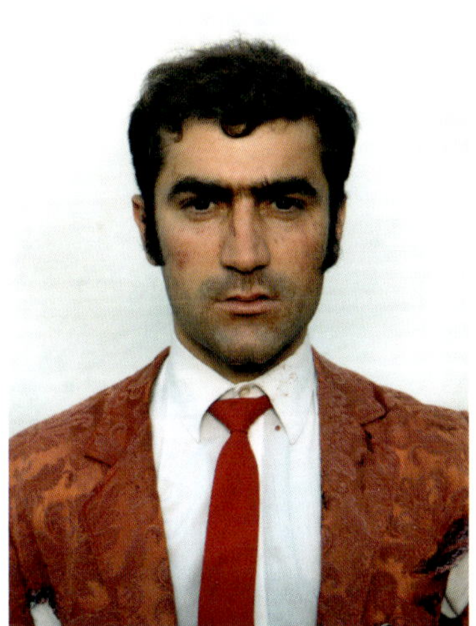

RINEKE DIJKSTRA (b. 1959, Netherlands)
Montemor, Portugal, May 1 B / Montemor, Portugal, mayo 1 B, 1994
Montemor, Portugal, May 8 A / Montemor, Portugal, mayo 8 A, 1994
Montemor, Portugal, May 8 B / Montemor, Portugal, mayo 8 B, 1994
Montemor, Portugal, May 1 C / Montemor, Portugal, mayo 1 C, 1994

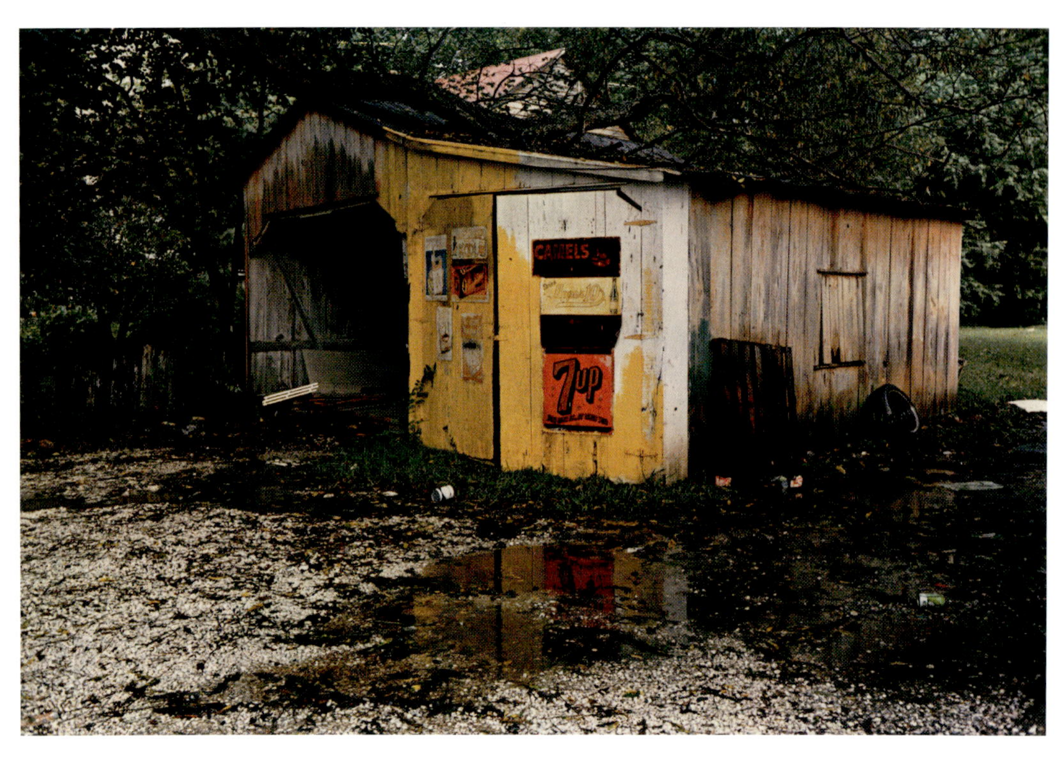

WILLIAM EGGLESTON (b. 1939, United States)
Untitled (Shack with Yellow Door) (from the *Los Alamos* series) /
*Sin título (choza con puerta amarilla) (*de la serie *Los Alamos), 1965-1973,* printed 2002

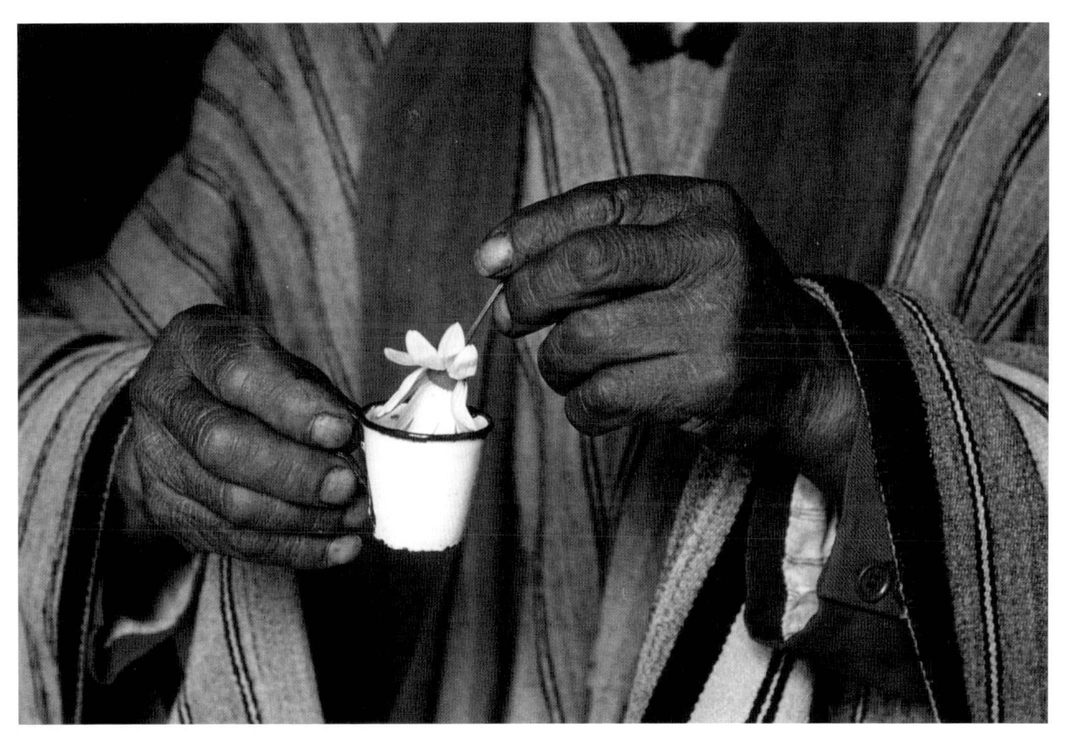

FLOR GARDUÑO (b. 1957, Mexico)
La Bendición. Isla del Sol. Bolivia / The Blessing. Isla del Sol. Bolivia, 1989

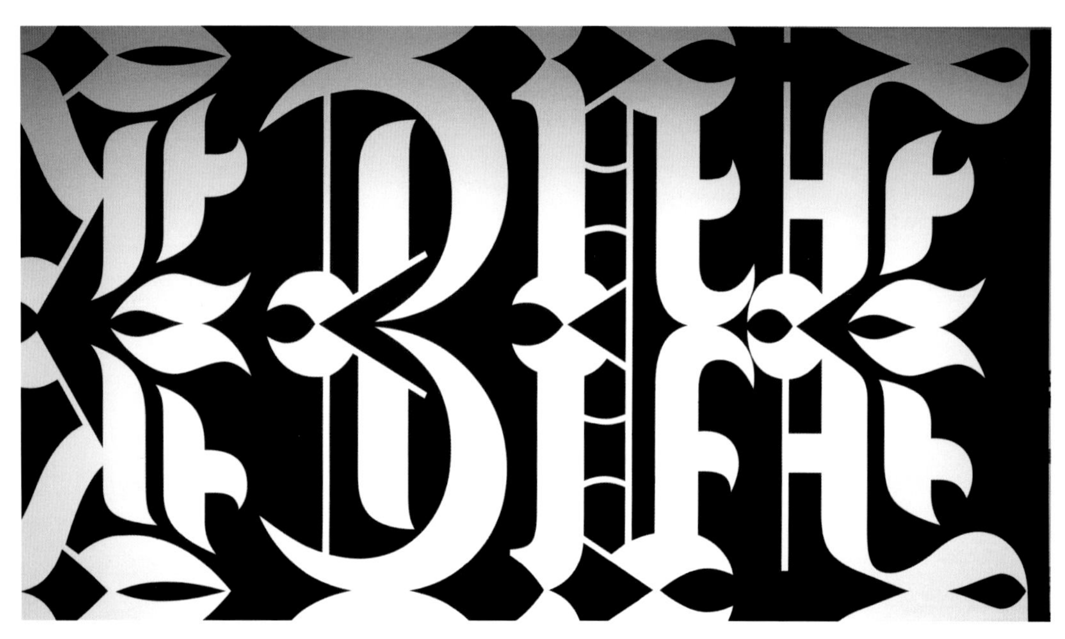

KENDELL GEERS (b. 1968, South Africa)
Post Pop Fuck 22, 2006

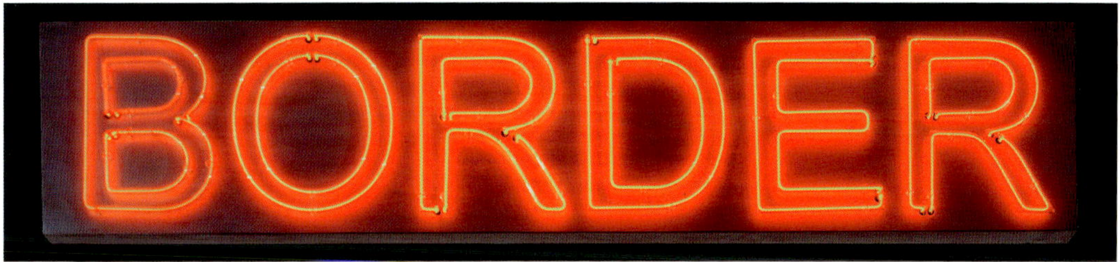

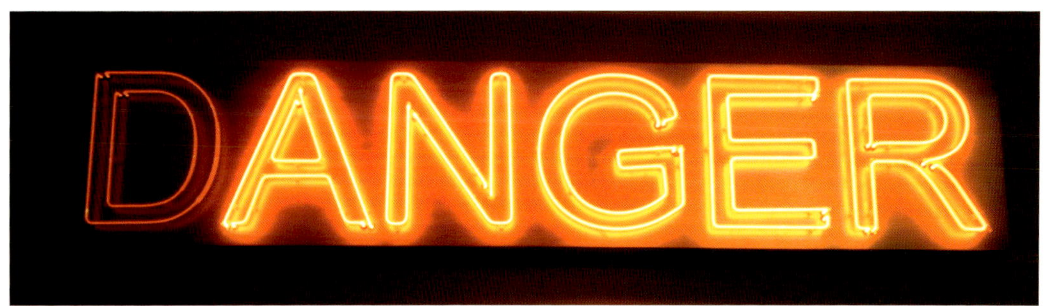

KENDELL GEERS (b. 1968, South Africa)
B/Order, 2003
D/Anger, 2003

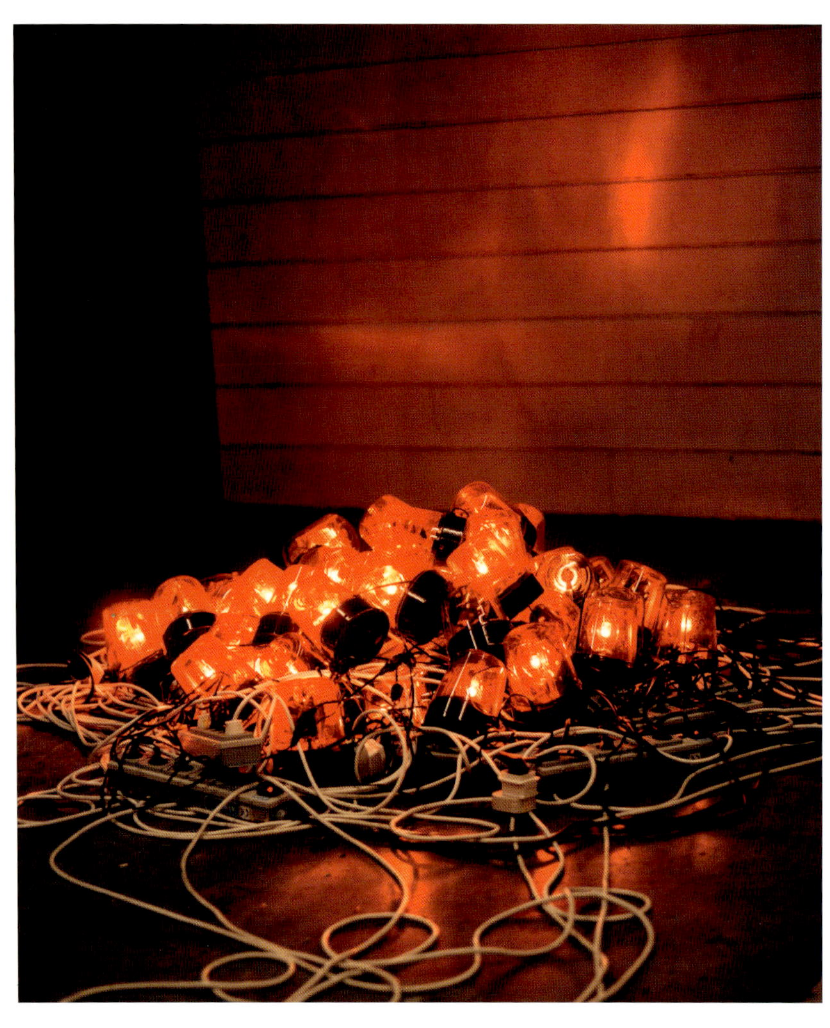

KENDELL GEERS (b. 1968, South Africa)
Cry Wolf / Falsa alarma, 1999

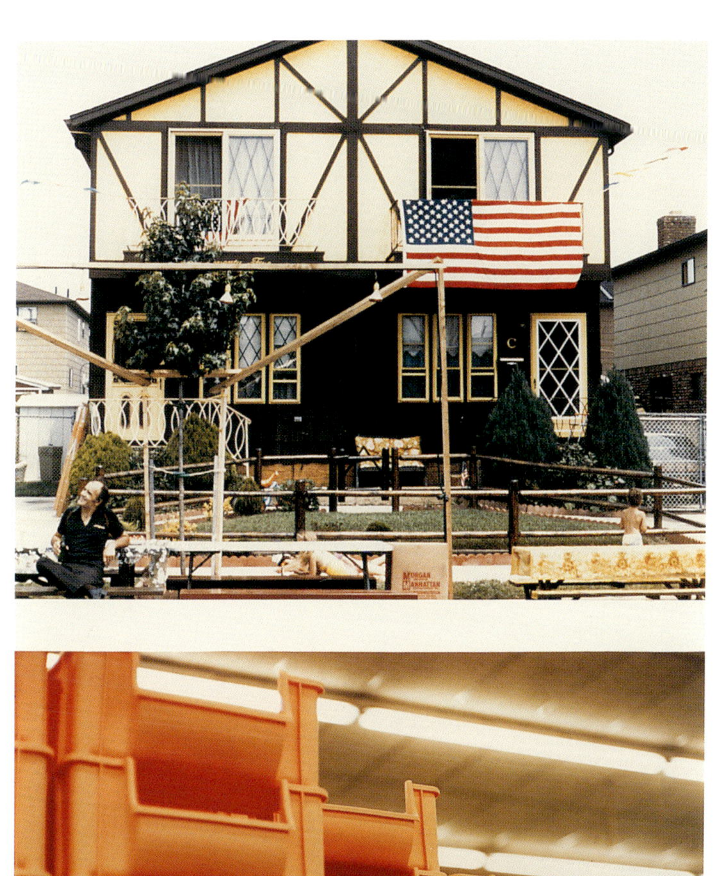

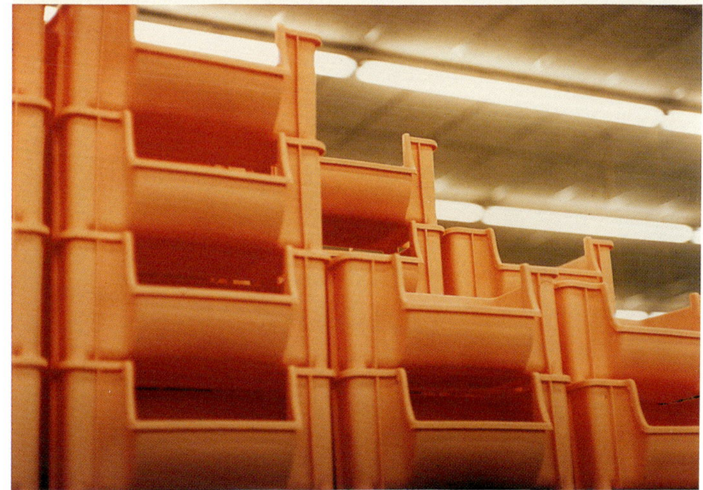

DAN GRAHAM (b. 1942, United States)
Pseudo Tudor Style Housing, Staten Island; Kitchen Trays, Bayonne, New Jersey /
Casa en estilo pseudo-Tudor, Staten Island; Charolas de cocina, Bayonne, Nueva Jersey, 1978-1966

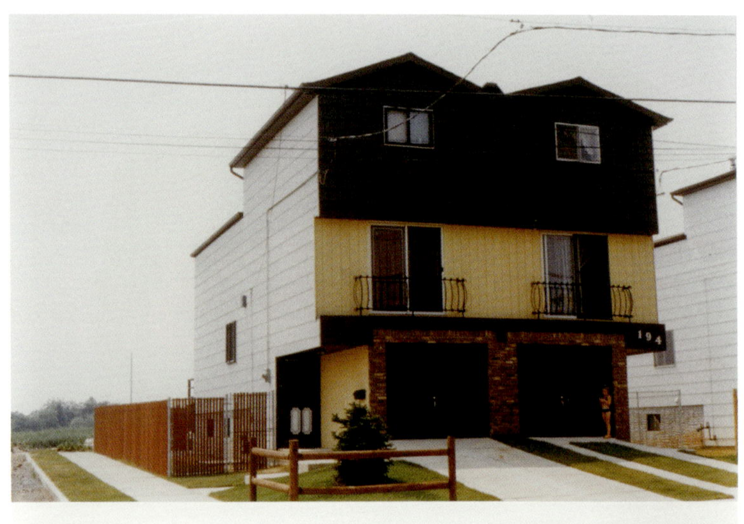

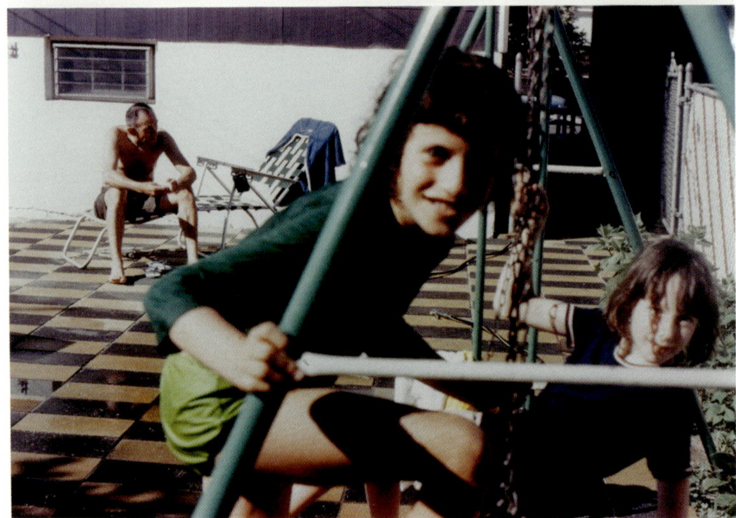

DAN GRAHAM (b. 1942, United States)
Two Homes Housing for Two Families and Family in Backyard /
Desarrollo habitacional de dos casas para dos familias y familia en el jardín trasero, 1978-1969

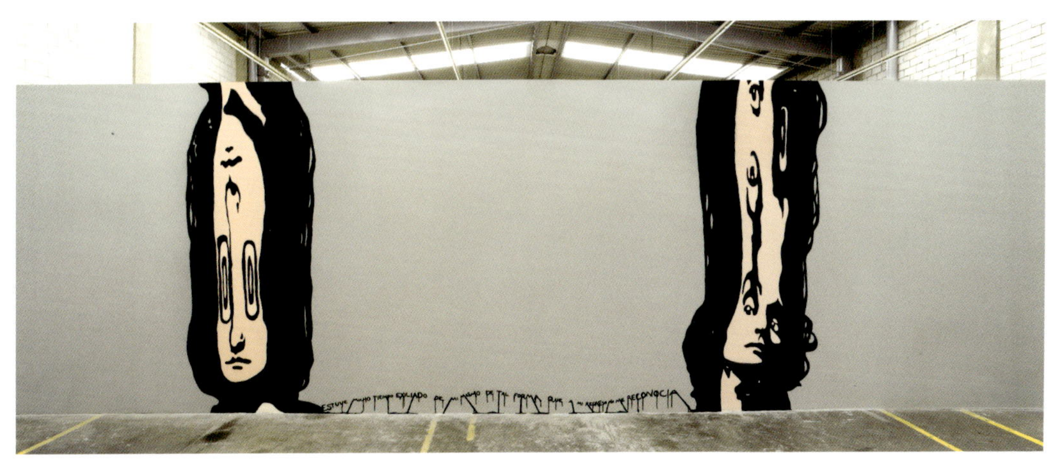

DANIEL GUZMÁN (b. 1964, Mexico)
Exilio / Exile, 2006

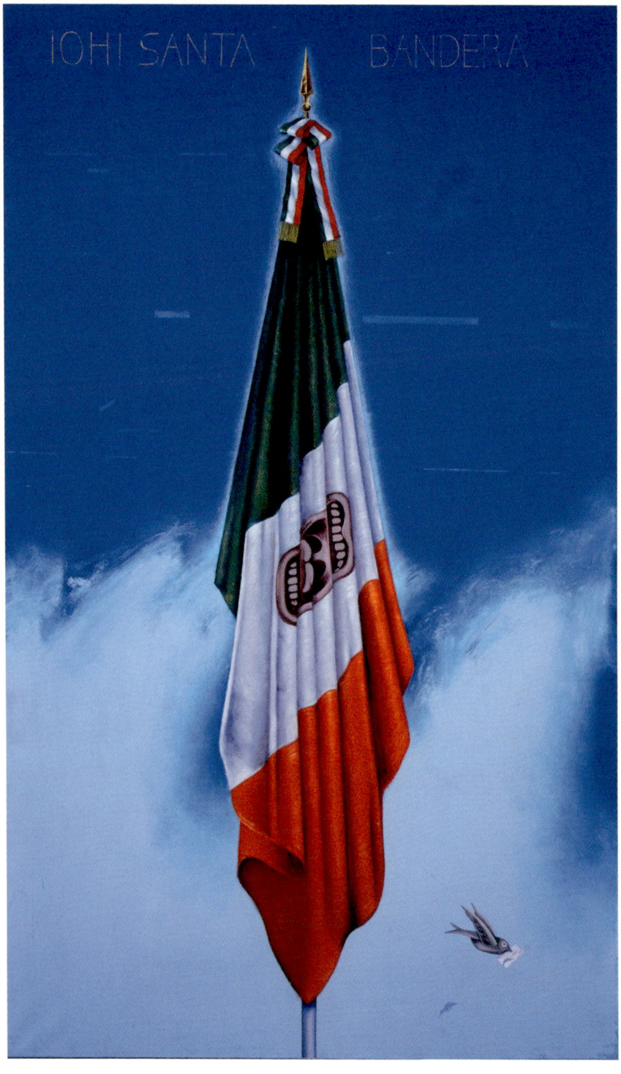

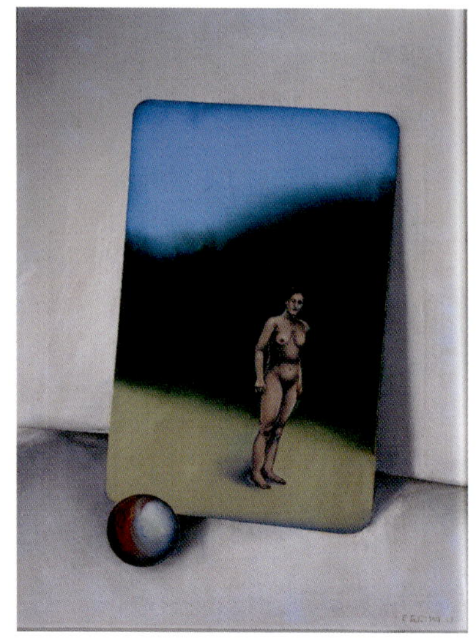

ENRIQUE GUZMÁN (1952-1986, Mexico)
¡Oh! Santa Bandera (Serie*: Su destino secreto) / Oh Saintly Flag! (Its Secret Destiny* Series), 1977
Postal con canica (Serie*: Su destino secreto) / Postcard with Marble (Its Secret Destiny* Series), 1977

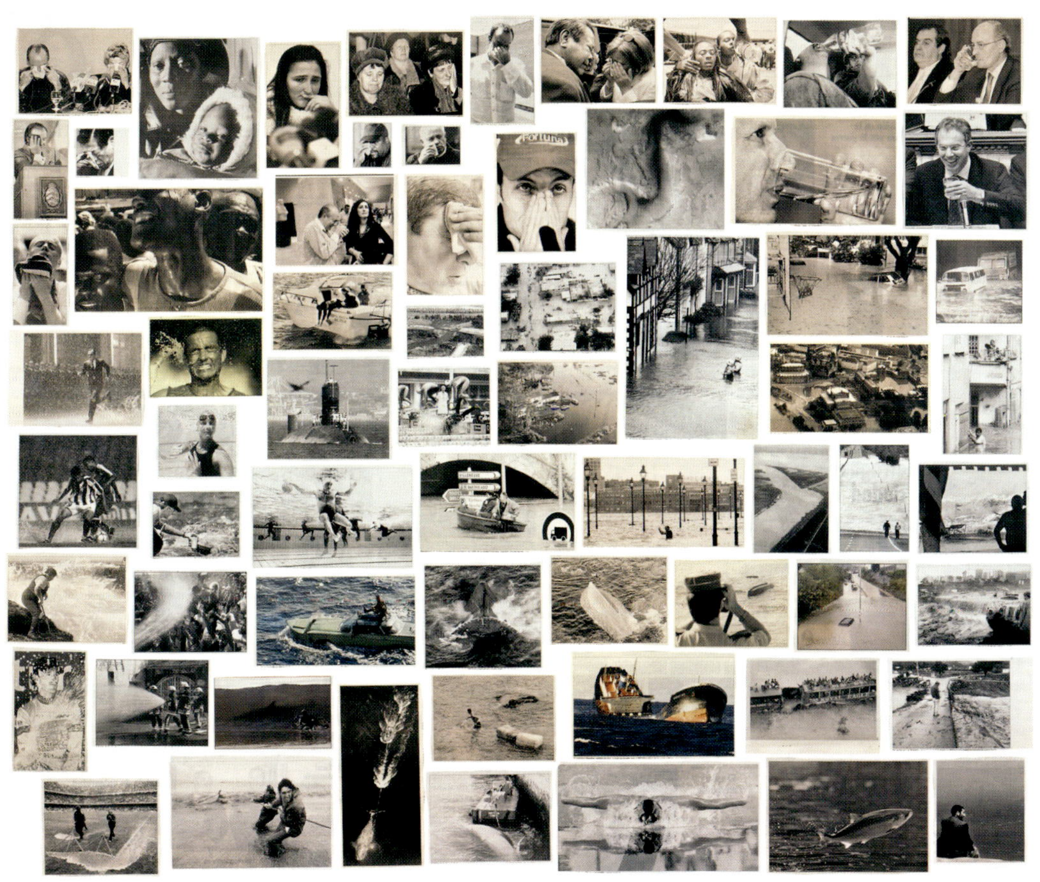

JONATHAN HERNÁNDEZ (b. 1972, Mexico)
Vulnerabilia (agua, fuego, masa, ruinas) / Vulnerabilia (Water, Fire, Mass, Ruins), 2005

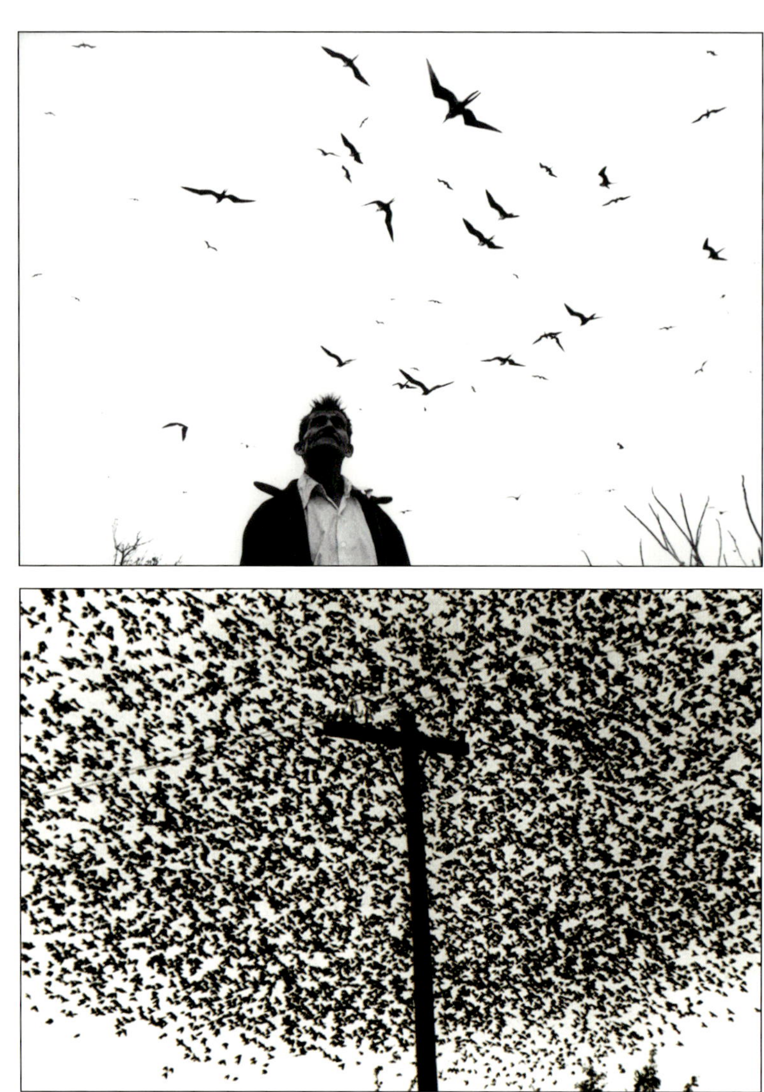

GRACIELA ITURBIDE (b. 1942, Mexico)
El Señor de los pájaros. Nayarit / Man of Birds. Nayarit, 1985
Pájaros en el poste de luz. Carretera a Guanajuato / Birds in the Light Post. Road to Guanajuato, 1990

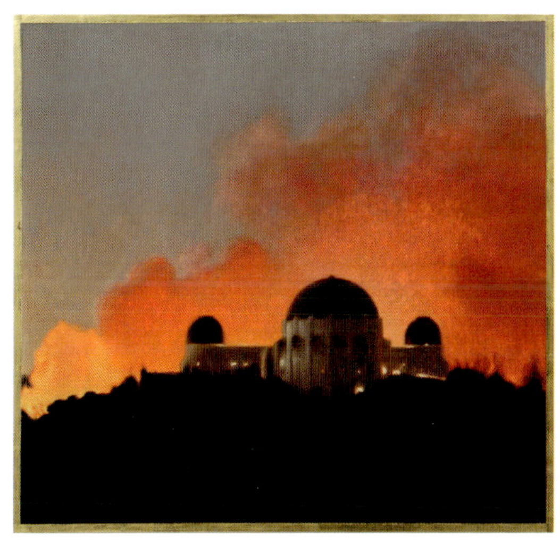
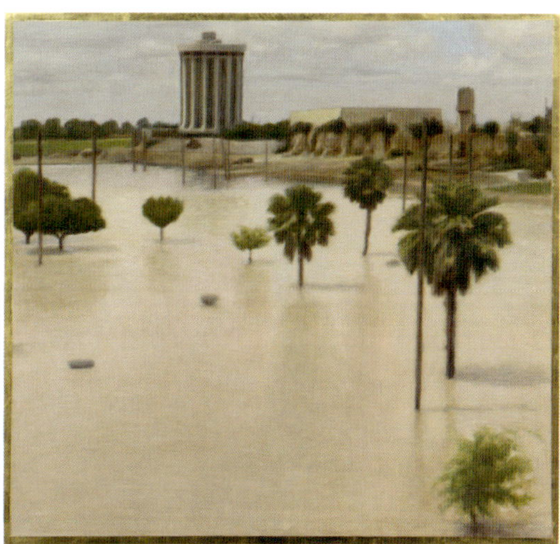

YISHAI JUSIDMAN (b. 1963, Mexico)
The Economist Shuffle #15 / Juego del The Economist #15, 2007
The Economist Shuffle #16 / Juego del The Economist #16, 2007

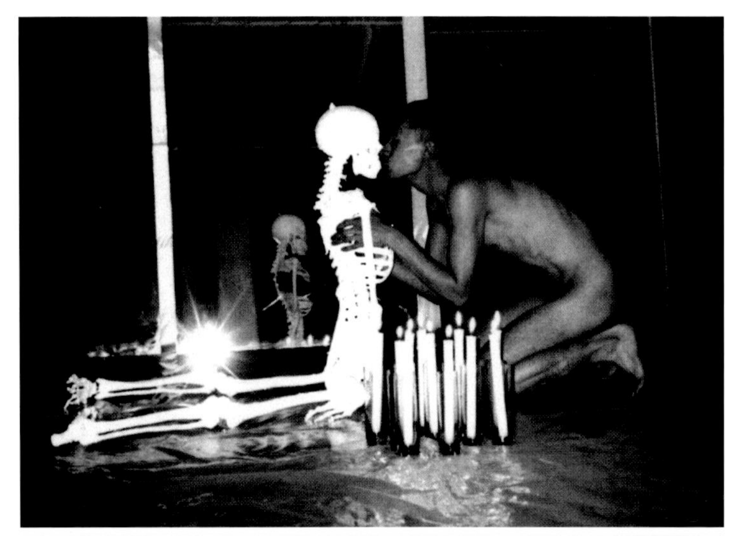

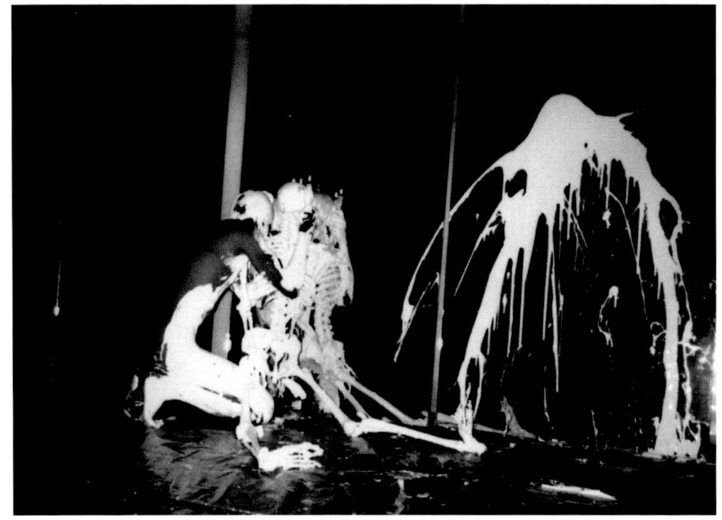

TERENCE KOH (b. 1977, China)
Untitled (Skeleton paintings) / Sin título (pinturas de esqueleto), 2006

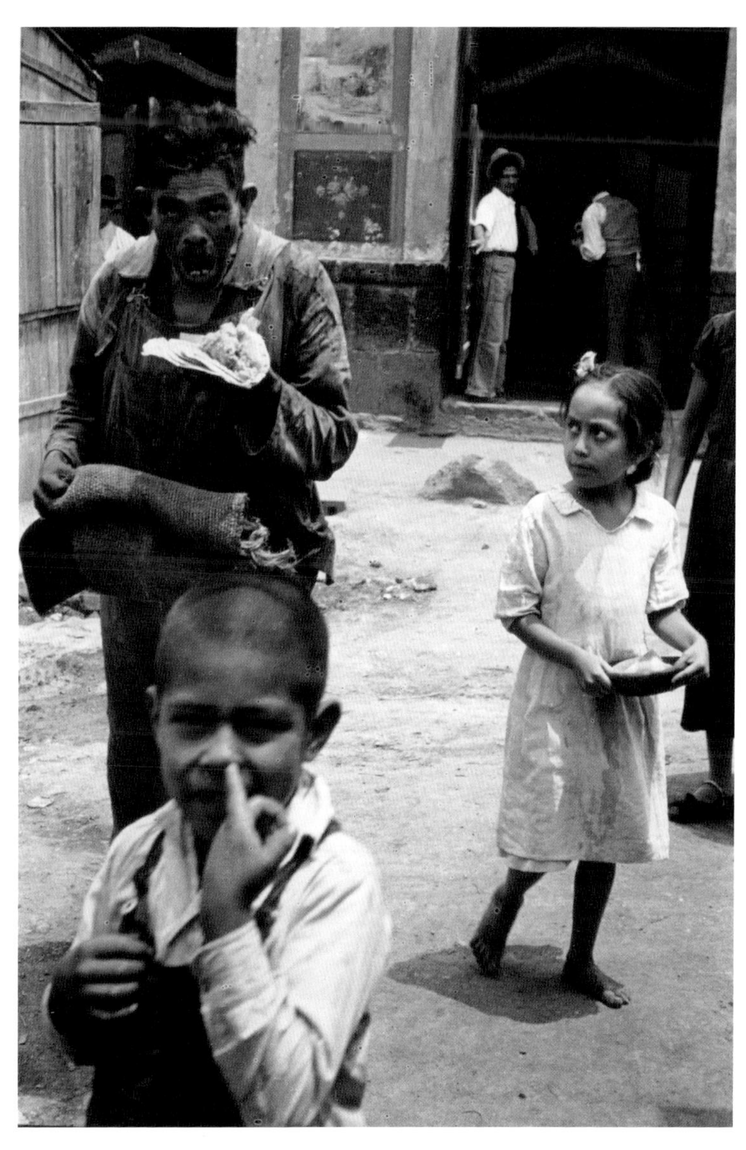

HELEN LEVITT (b. 1913, United States)
Untitled (México, D.F.) / Sin título (México, D.F.), 1941

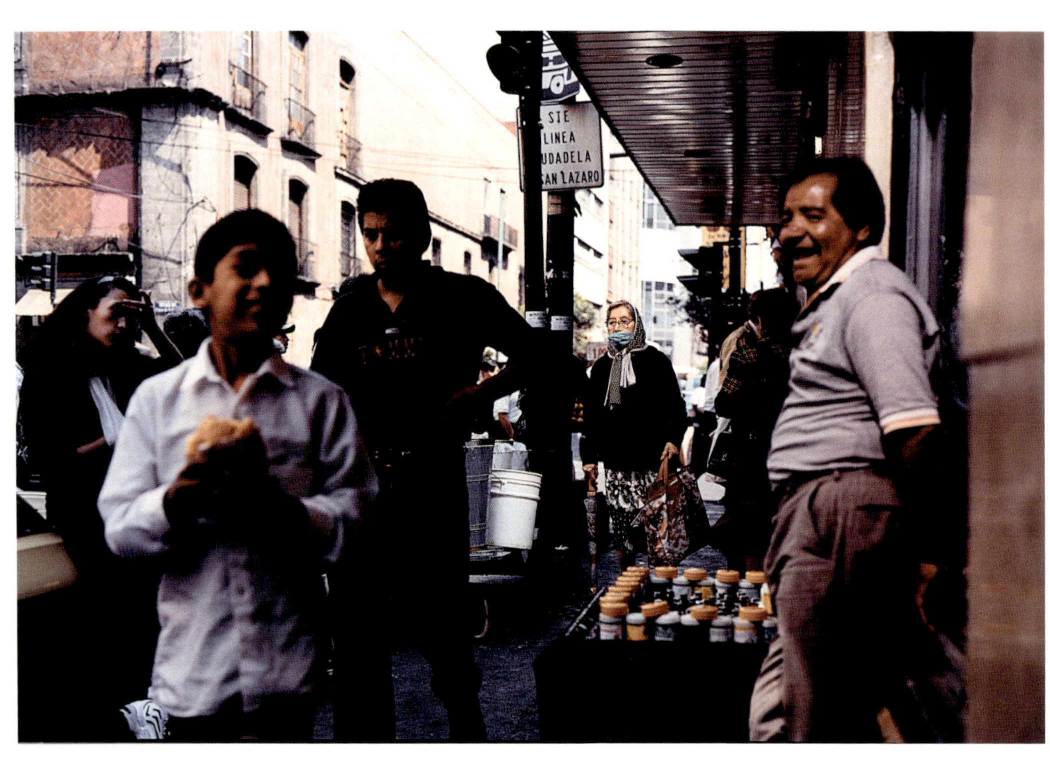

PHILLIP LORCA DICORCIA (b. 1953, United States)
Mexico City / Ciudad de México, 1998

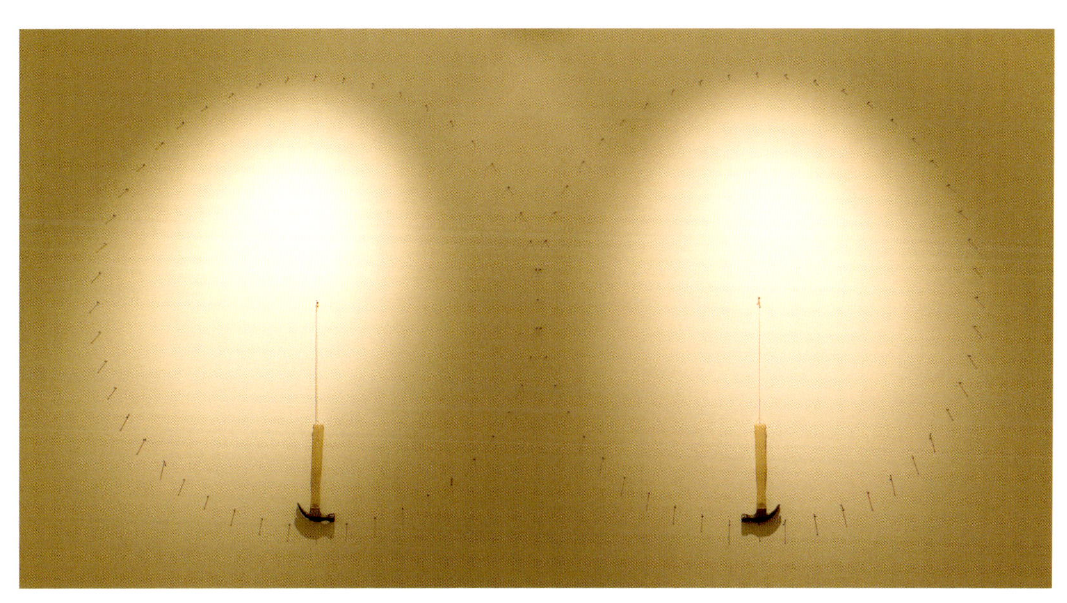

JORGE MACCHI (b. 1963, Argentina)
El beso / The Kiss, 2005

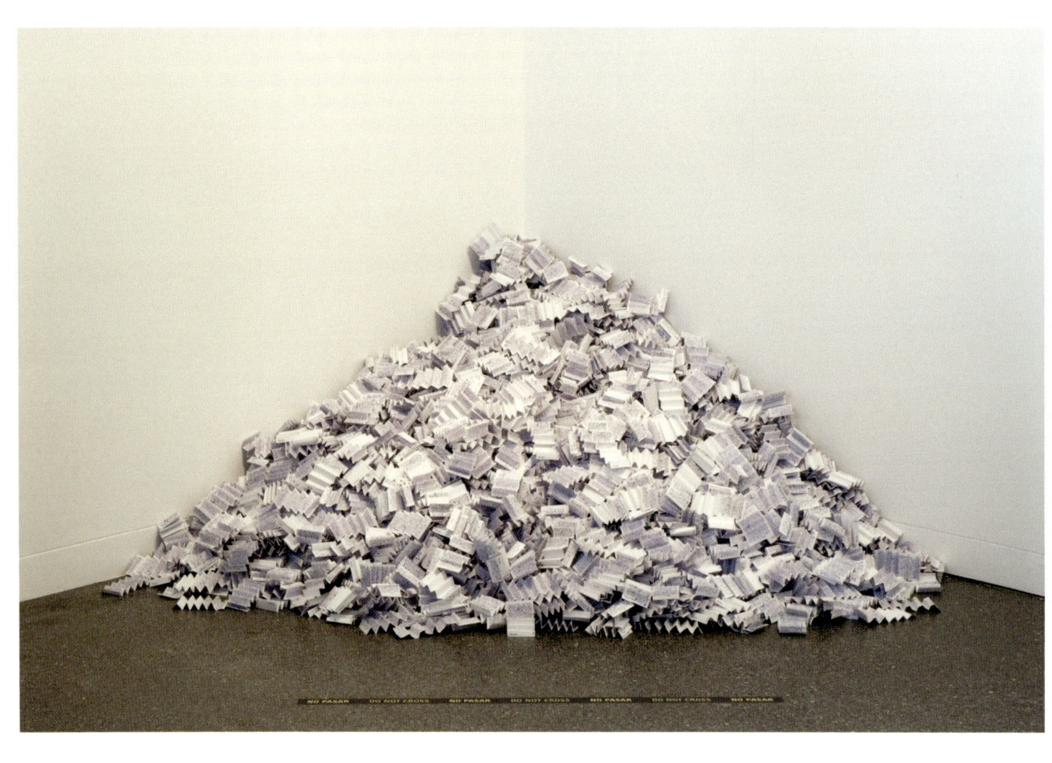

MAREPE (b. 1970, Brazil)
Sanfoninha, 2006

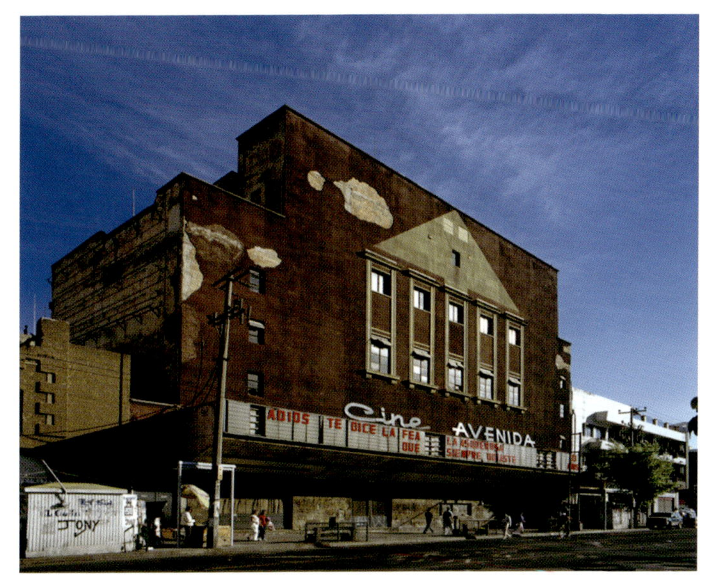

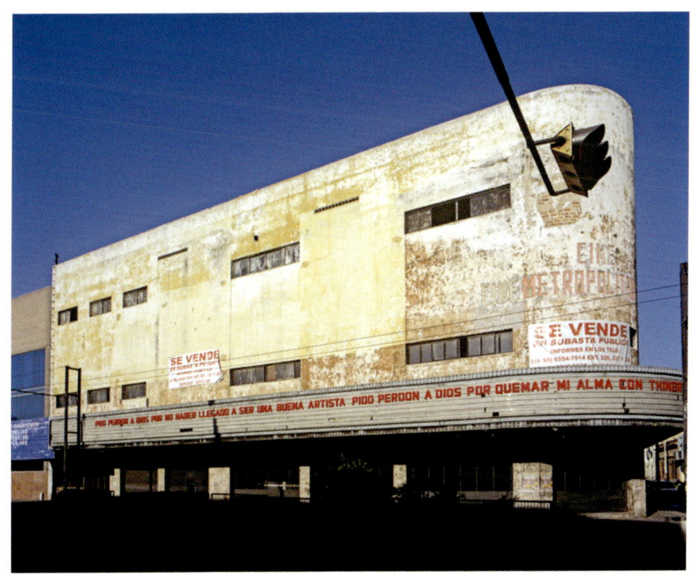

TERESA MARGOLLES (b. 1963, Mexico)
Recados póstumos (Cine Avenida) / Posthumous Notes (Avenida Movie Theatre), 2006
Recados póstumos (Cine Metropolitan) / Posthumous Notes (Metropolitan Movie Theatre), 2006

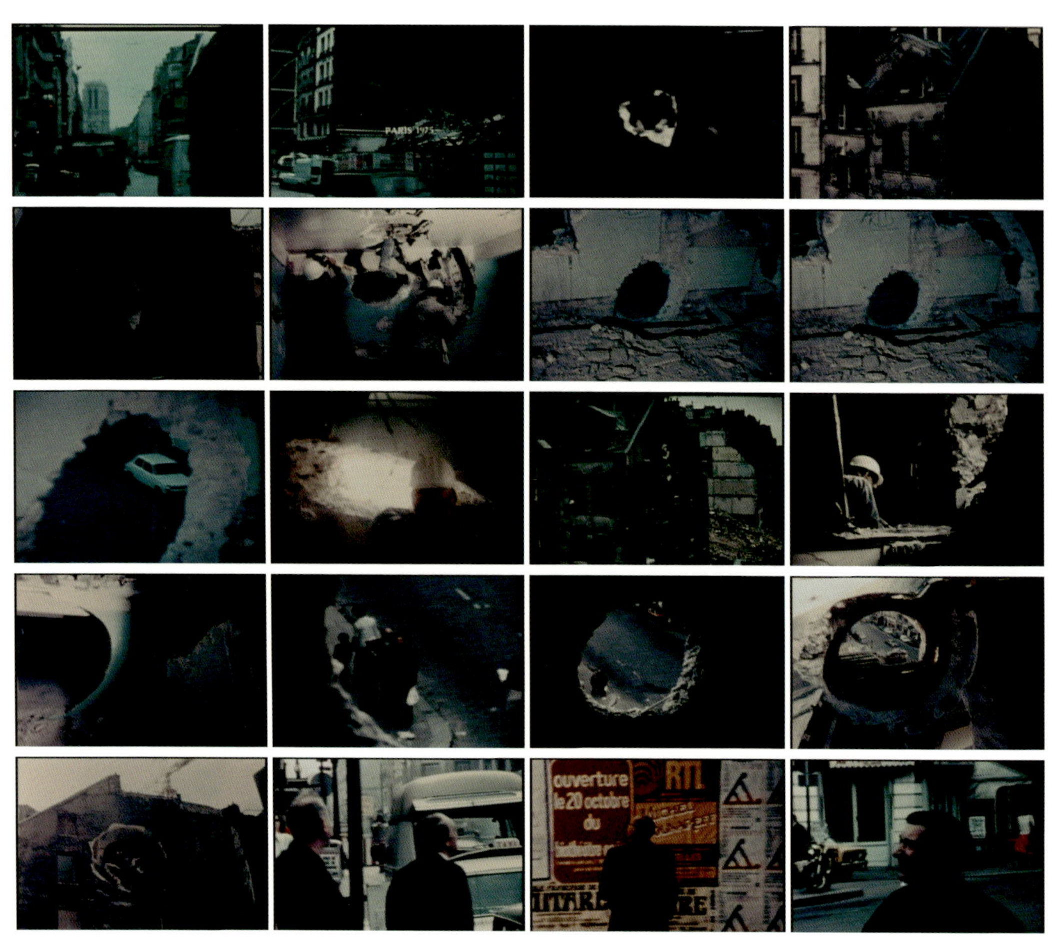

GORDON MATTA-CLARK (1948-1973, United States)
Conical Intersect / Intersección cónica, 1974

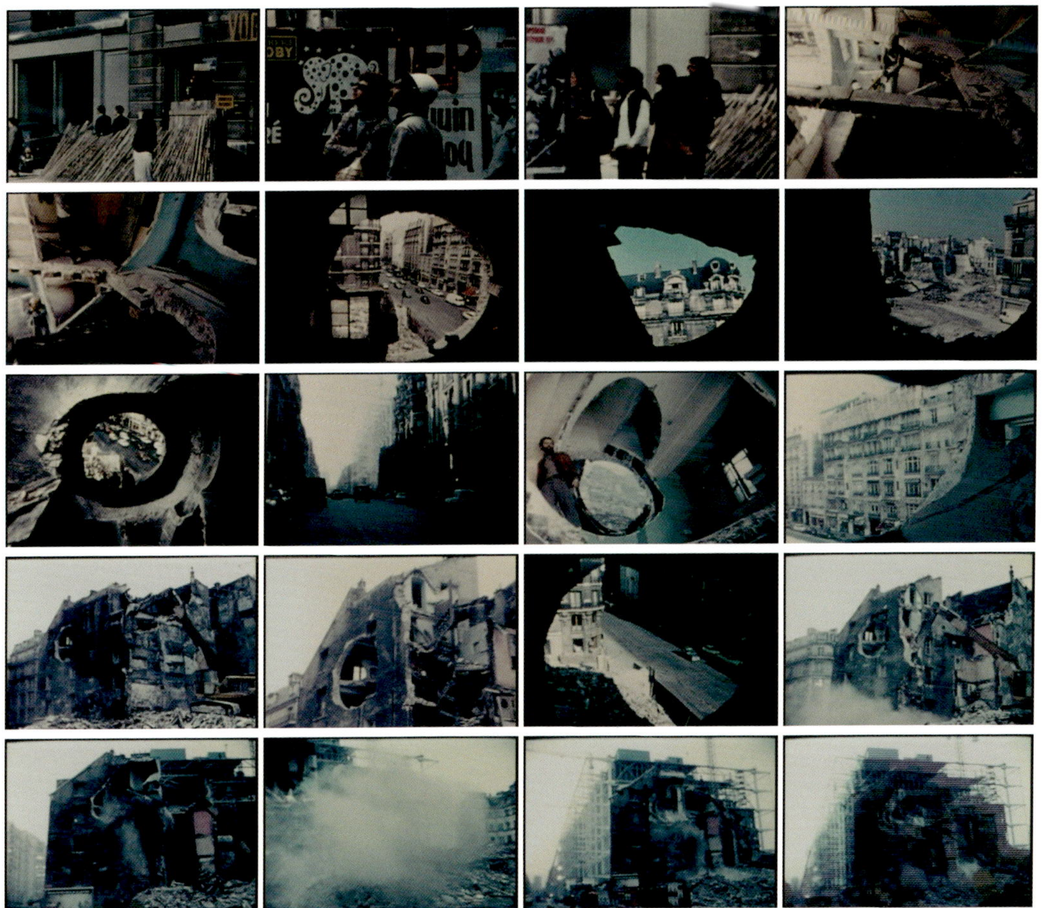

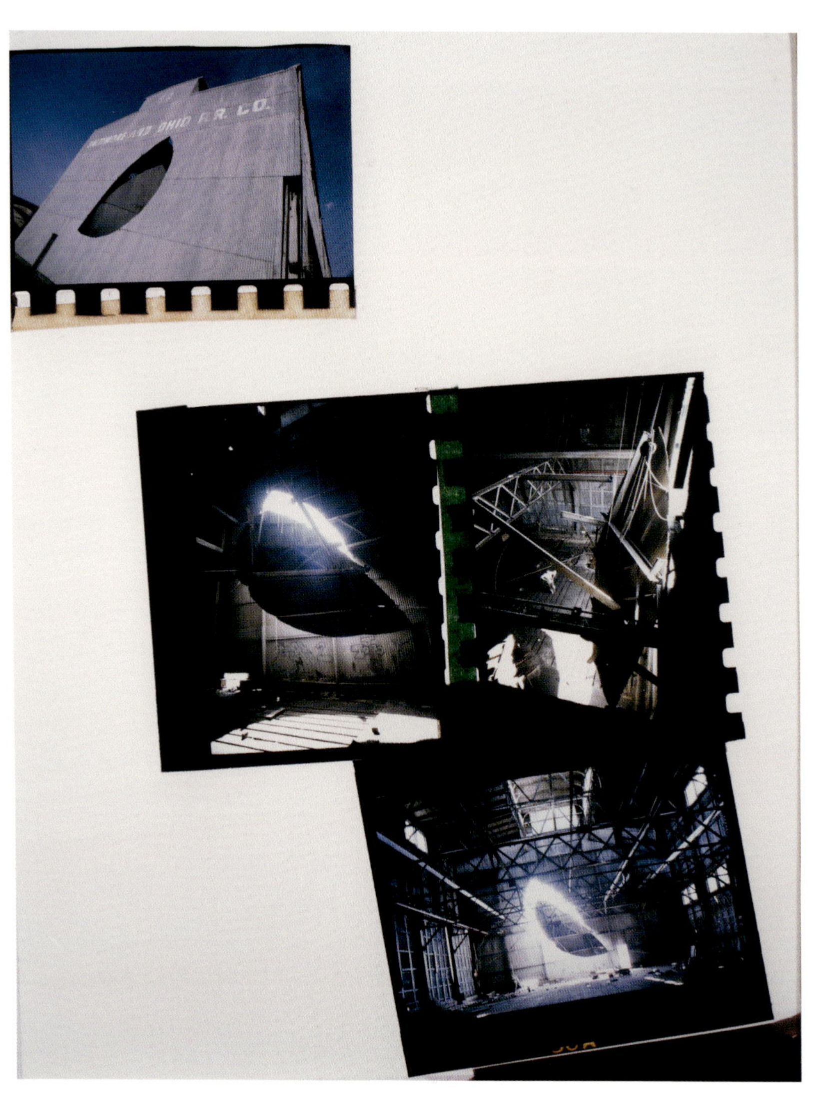

GORDON MATTA-CLARK (1948-1973, United States)
Day's End Pier 52 / Final del día en el muelle 52, 1975

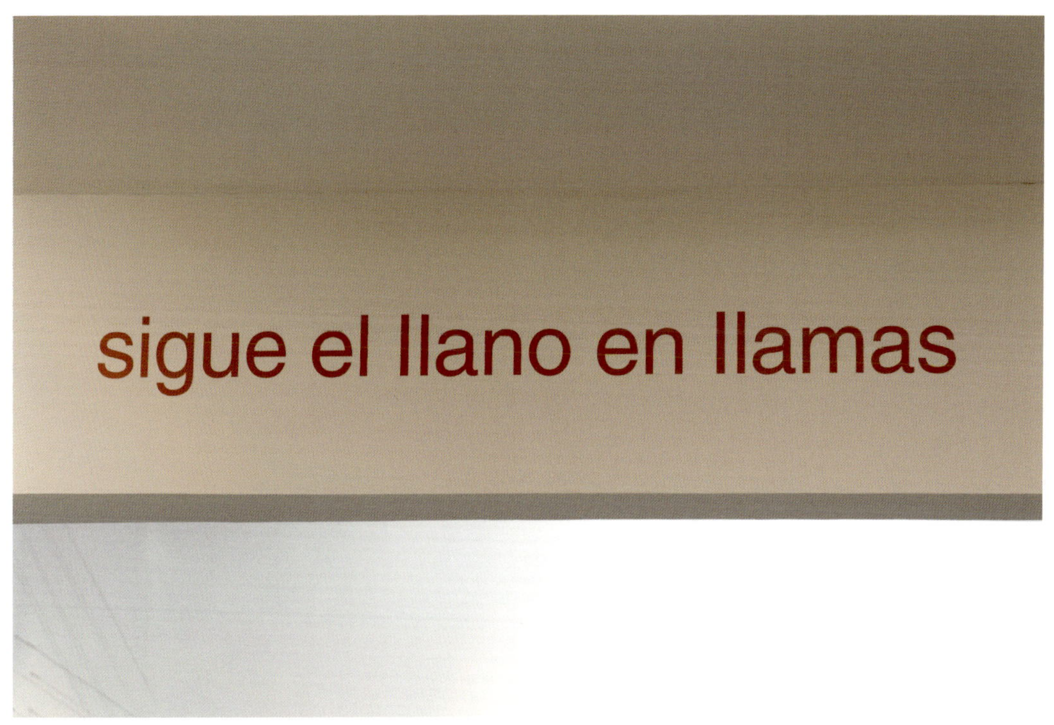

JORGE MÉNDEZ BLAKE (b. 1974, Mexico)
Sin título (Sigue el llano en llamas) / Untitled (The Plain Still Burns), 2007

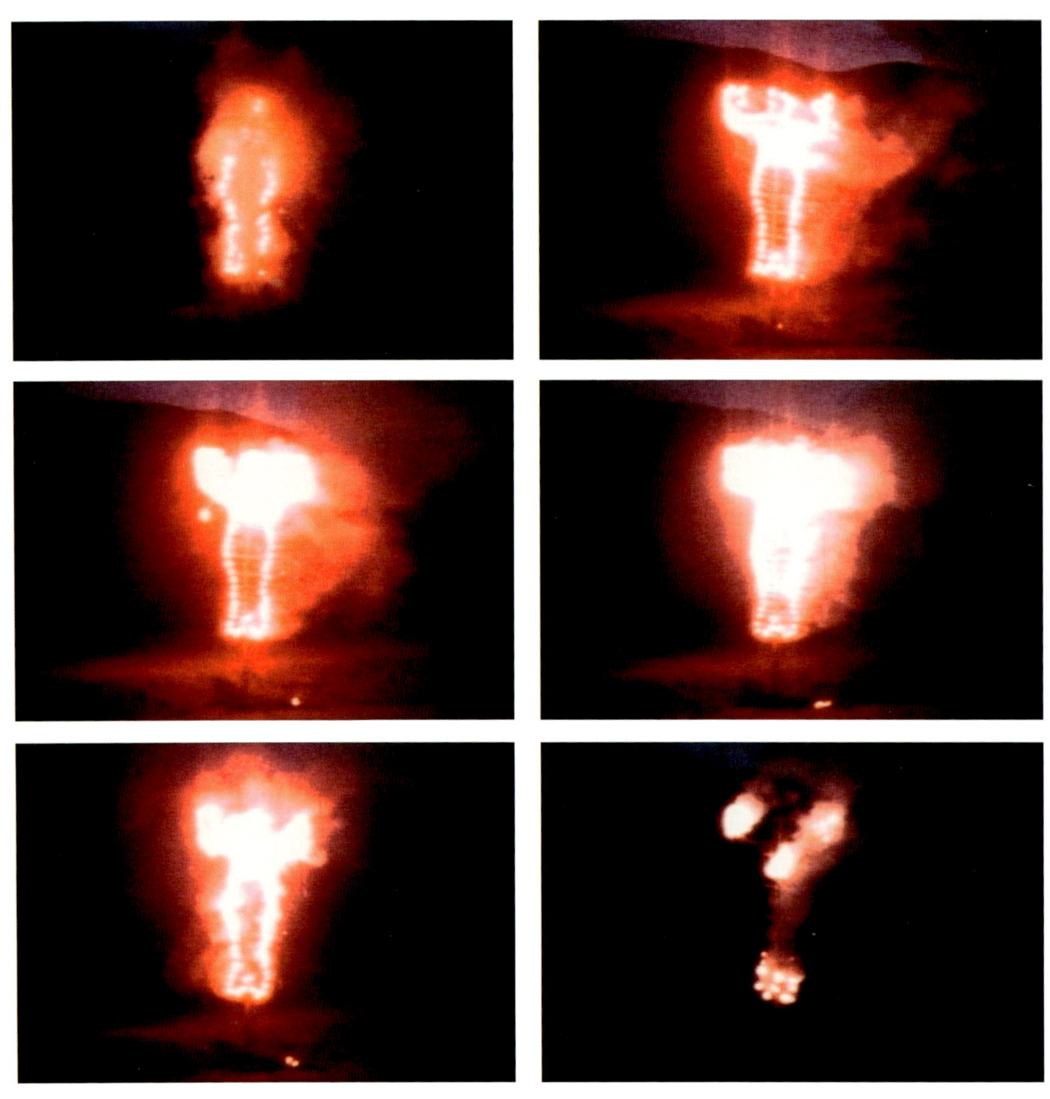

ANA MENDIETA (1948, Cuba-1985, United States)
Ánima, de la serie *Silueta de cohetes / Soul,* from the series *Firework Silhouette,* 1976

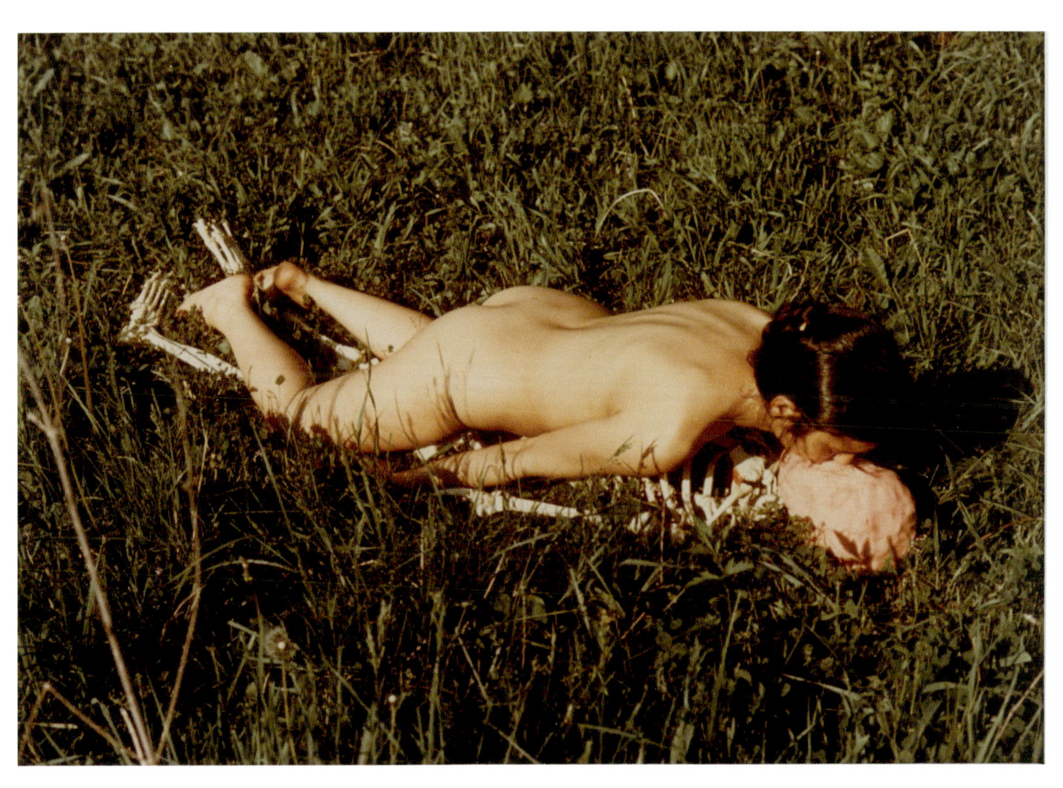

ANA MENDIETA (1948, Cuba-1985, United States)
On Giving Life / Sobre dar vida, 1975

21 de Abril de 2017 al medio dia Darwin esq. Goethe Col. Nueva Anzures México D.F.

JONATHAN MONK (b. 1969, United Kingdom)
Meeting #50 / Reunión #50, 2005-2007

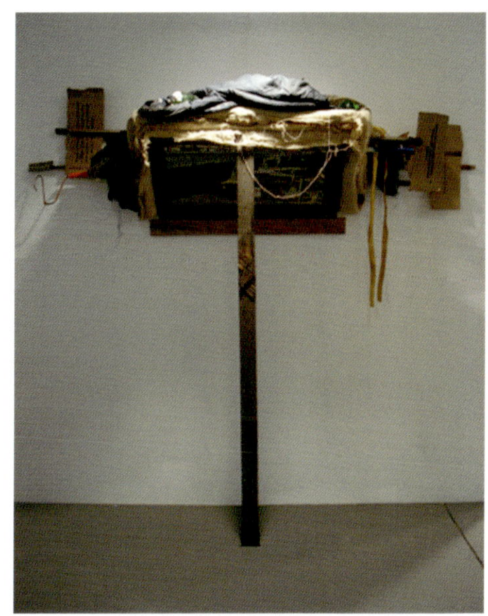

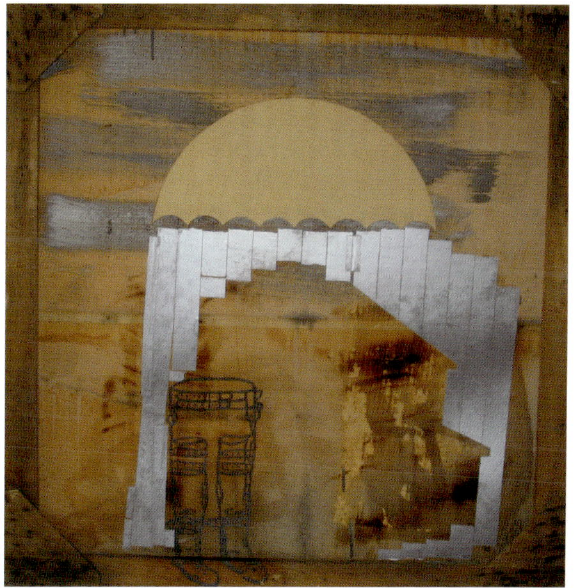

MORIS (b. 1978, Mexico)
Hermoso paisaje #1 / Beautiful Landscape #1, 2007
Impermeable / Waterproof, 2006

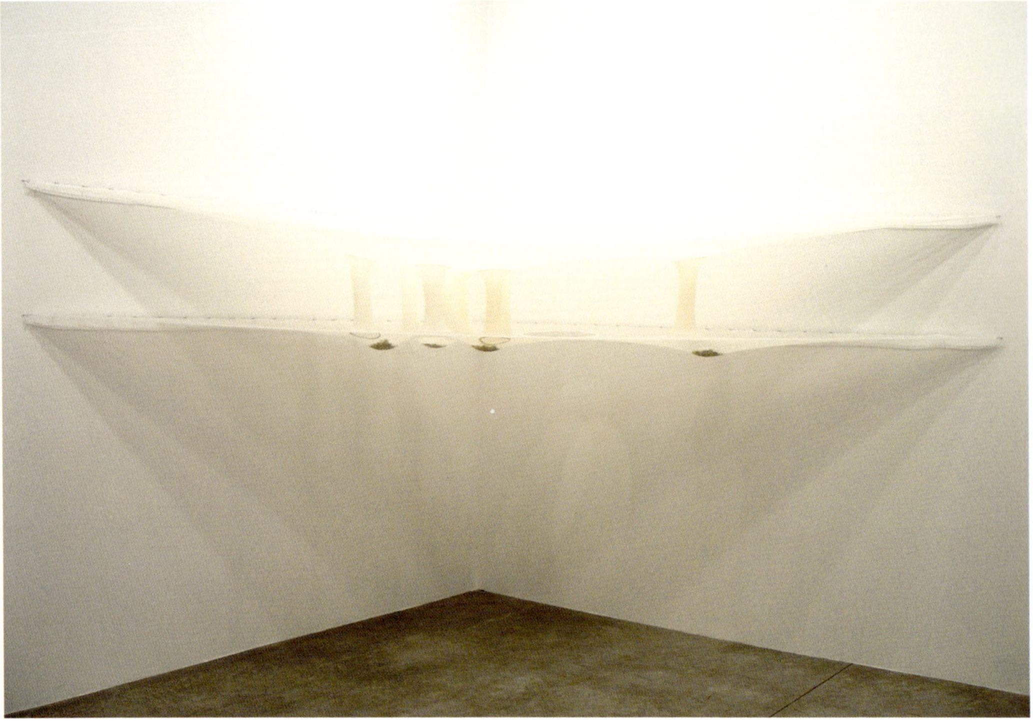

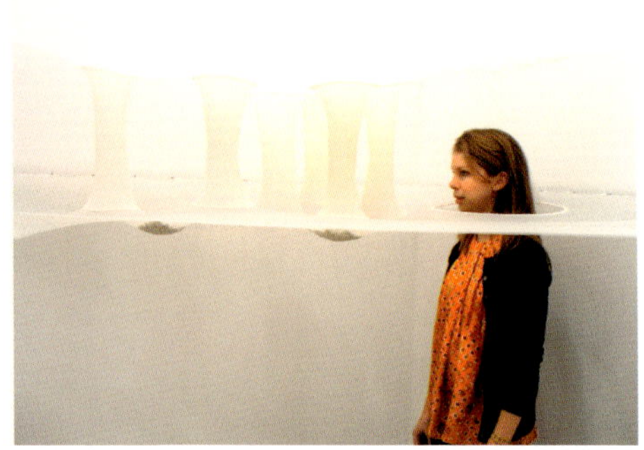

ERNESTO NETO (b. 1964, Brazil)
A Horizon of Events, Point of View / Un horizonte de eventos, punto de vista, 2006

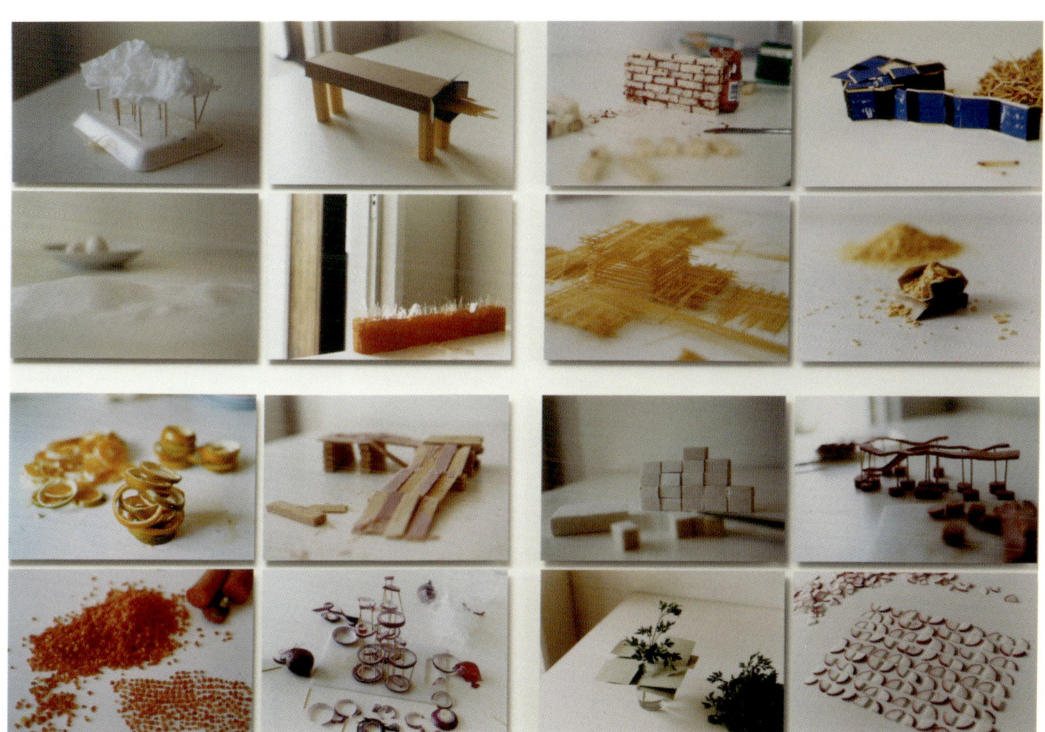

RIVANE NEUENSCHWANDER (b. 1967, Brazil)
Canteiros / Conversations and Constructions / Canteiros / Conversaciones y construcciones, 2006

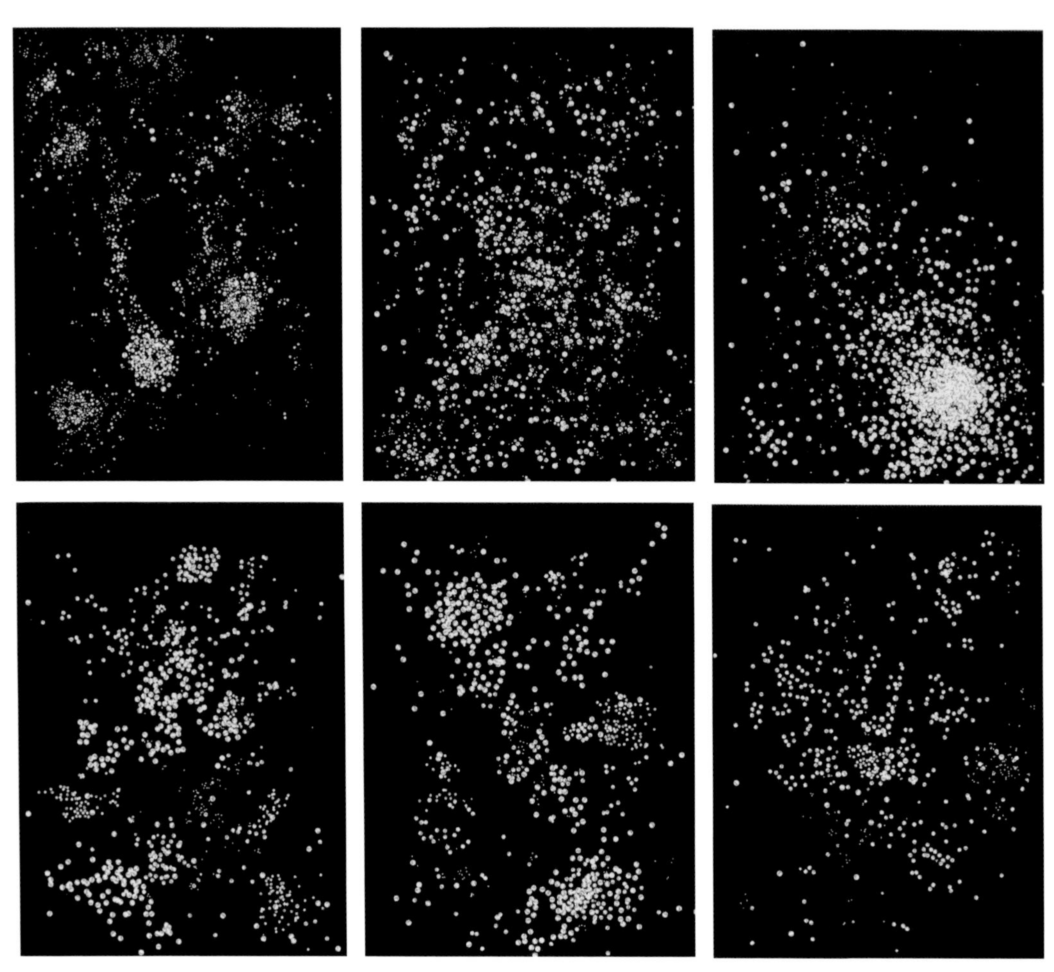

RIVANE NEUENSCHWANDER (b. 1967, Brazil)
One Thousand and One Possible Nights [N. 60] [N.63] / Mil y una posibles noches [No. 60] [No. 63], 2007

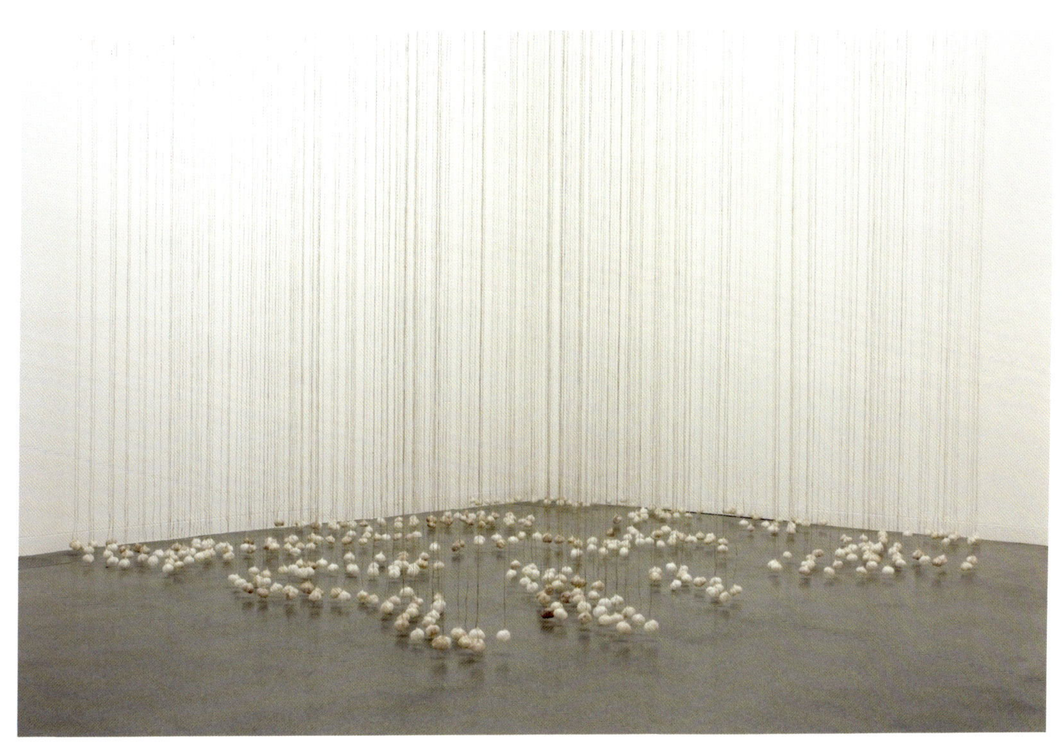

RIVANE NEUENSCHWANDER (b. 1967, Brazil)
Suspended Landscape / Paisaje suspendido, 1997

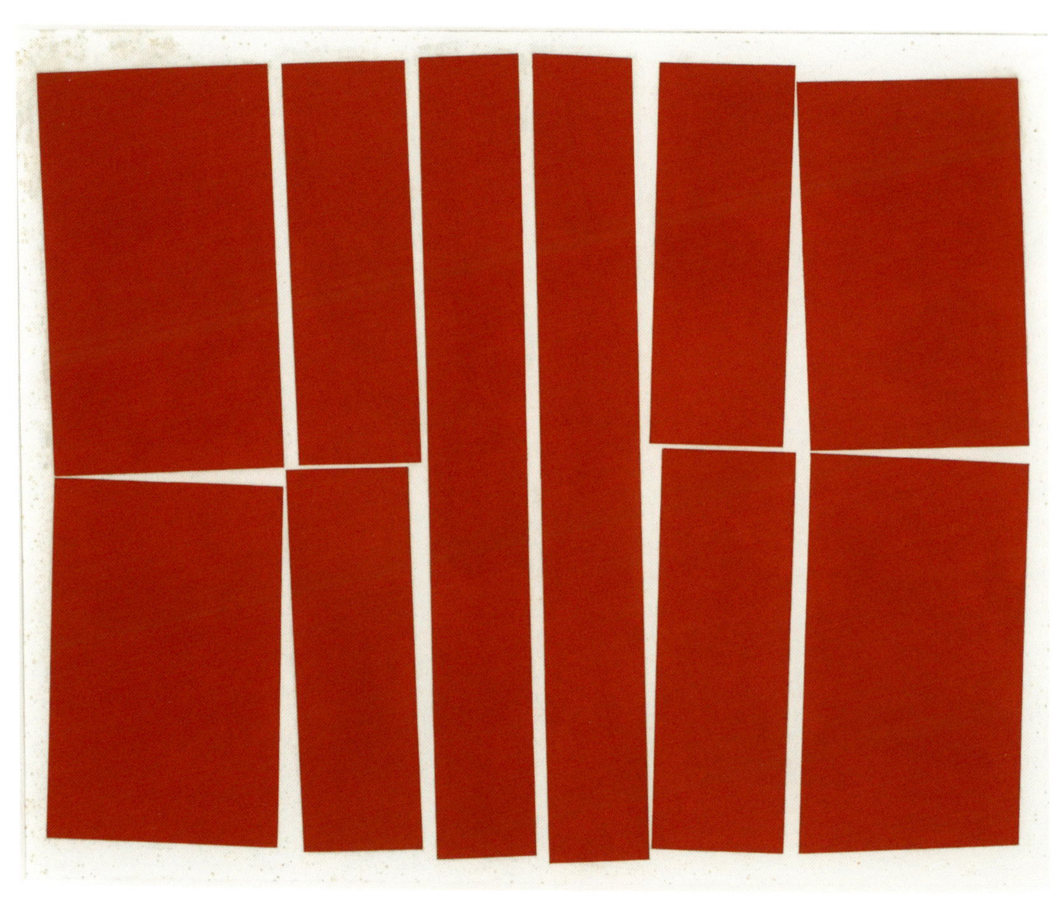

HELIO OITICICA (1937-1980, Brazil)
Metasquema 354, 1958

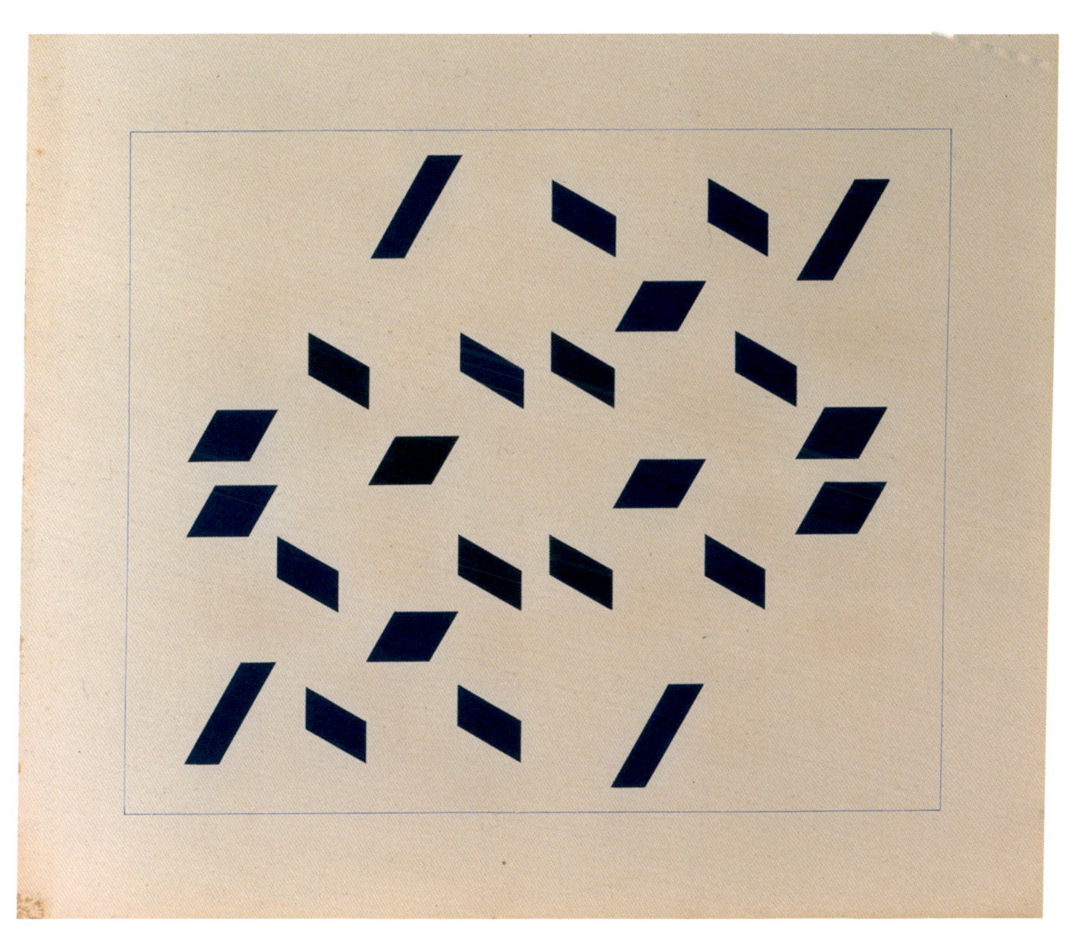

HELIO OITICICA (1937-1980, Brazil)
Metasquema 214, 1957

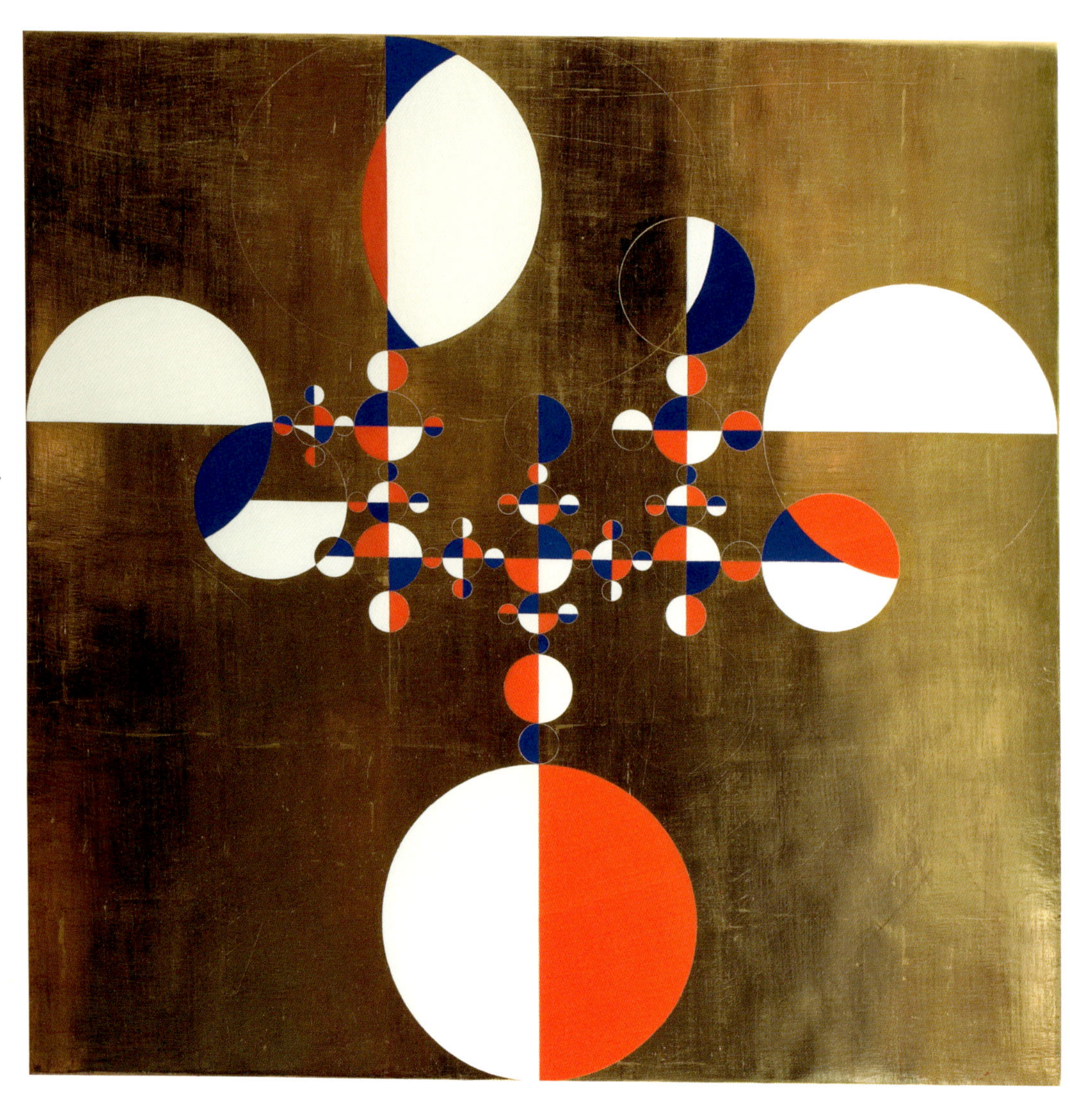

GABRIEL OROZCO (b. 1962, Mexico)
Árbol Nuevo / New Tree, 2006

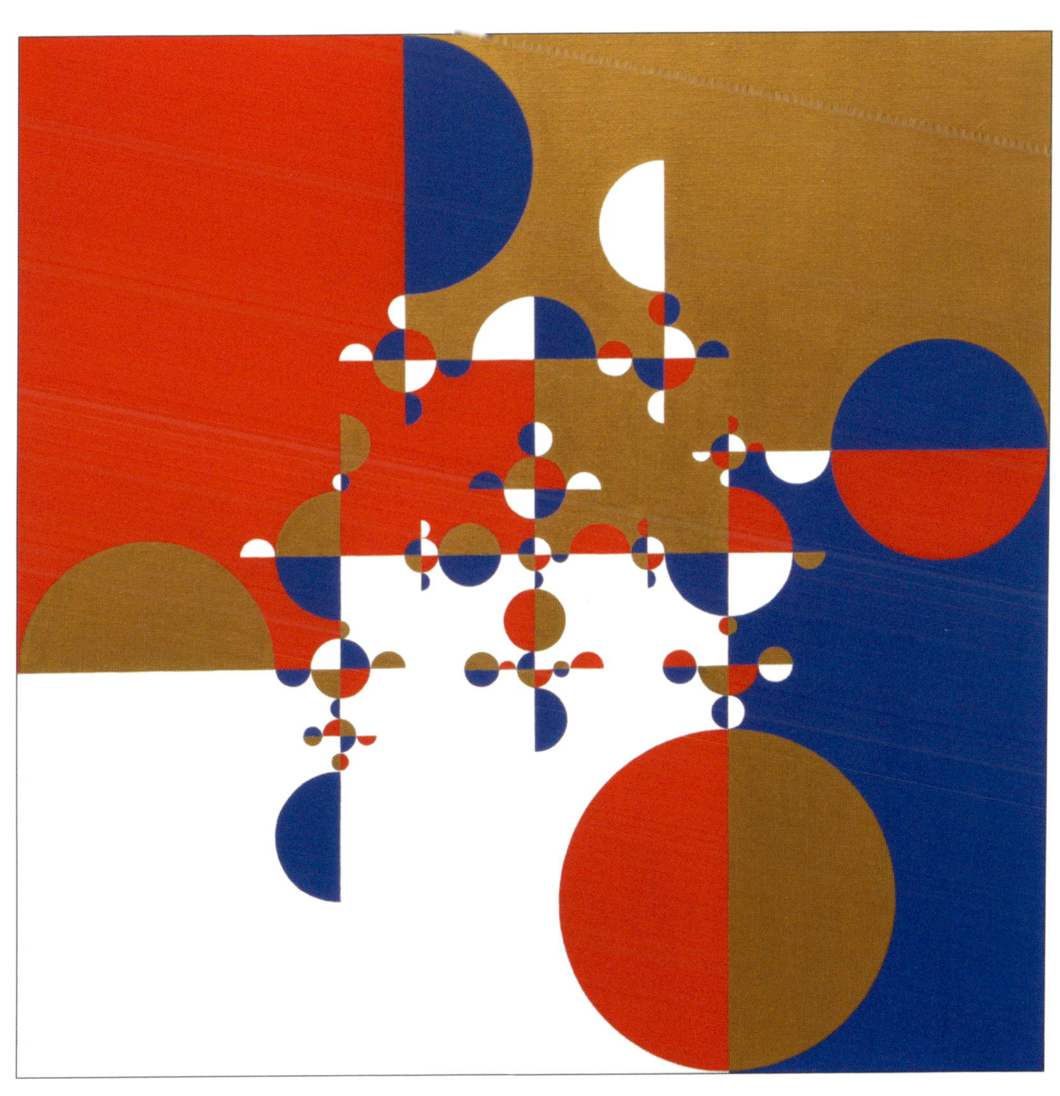

GABRIEL OROZCO (b. 1962, Mexico)
Cuadro fértil / Fertile Painting, 2004

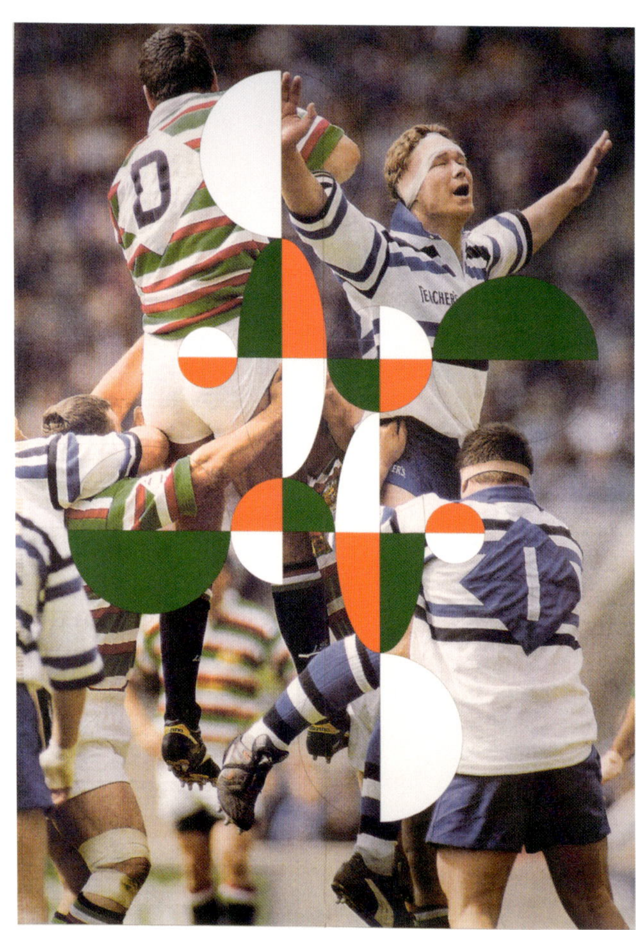

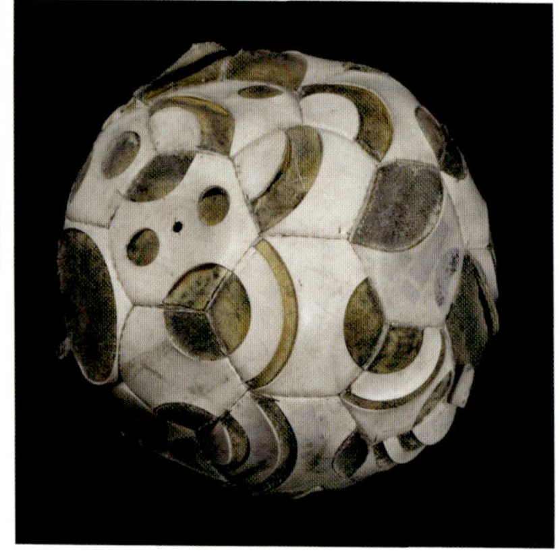

GABRIEL OROZCO (b. 1962, Mexico)
Atomists: Ascention / Atomistas: Ascensión, 1996
Soccer Ball 2 / Balón de fútbol 2, 2002

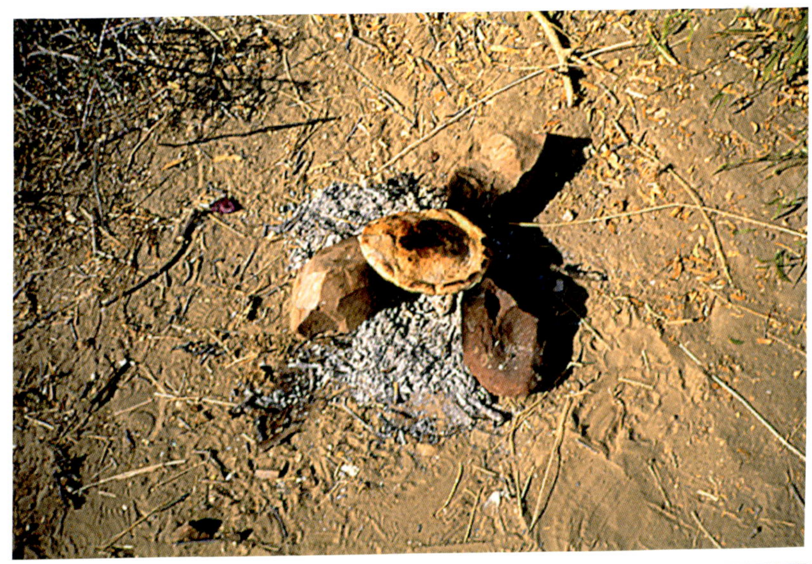

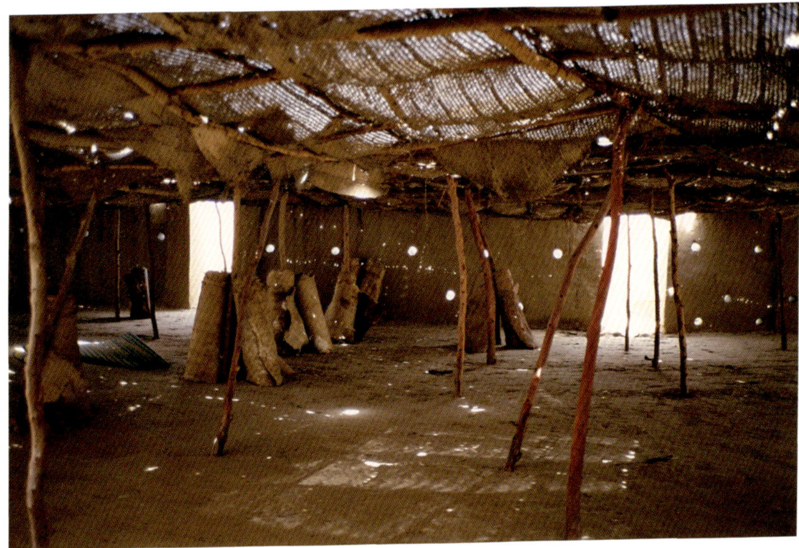

GABRIEL OROZCO (b. 1962, Mexico)
Center of the Universe / Centro del universo, 1997
Percepción total / Total Perception, 2002

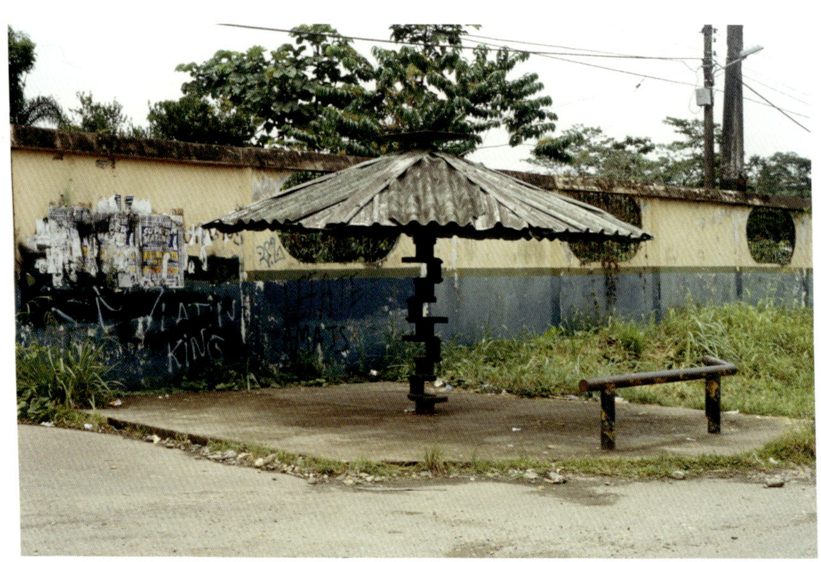

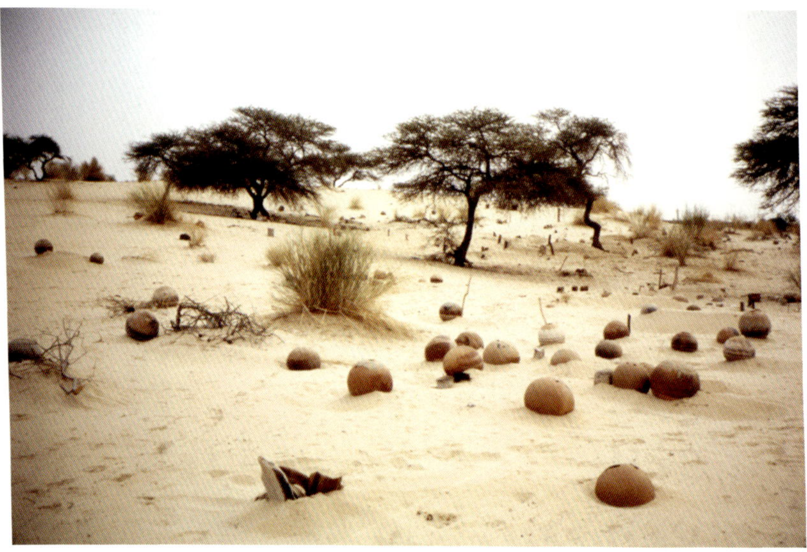

GABRIEL OROZCO (b. 1962, Mexico)
Bus Stop / Parada de autobús, 2007
Cementerio 2 / Cemetery 2, 2002

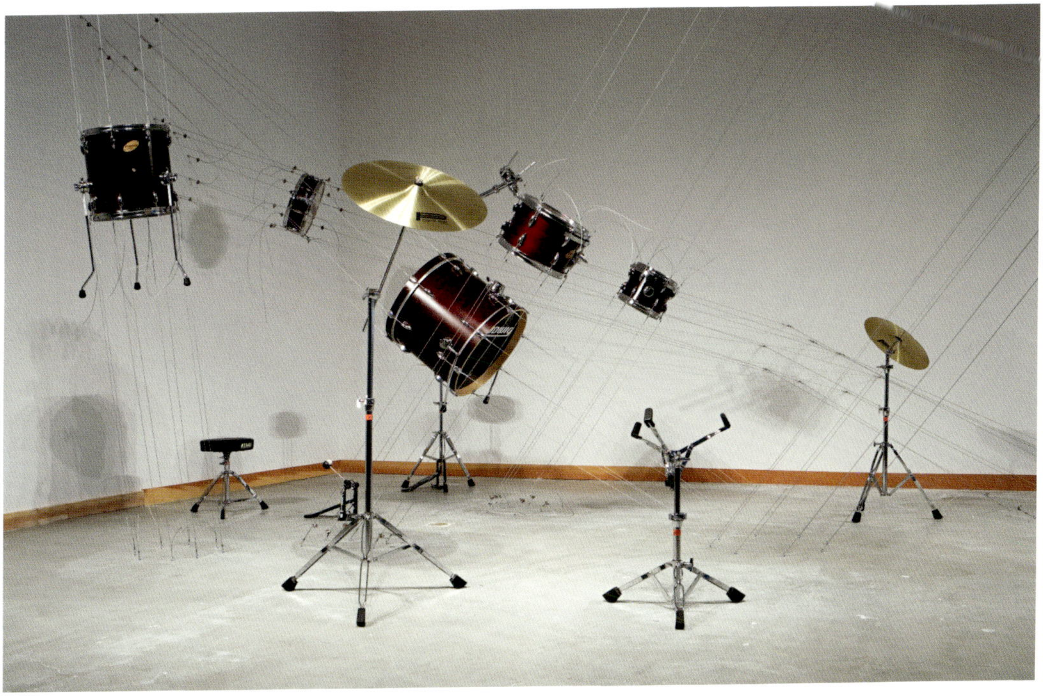

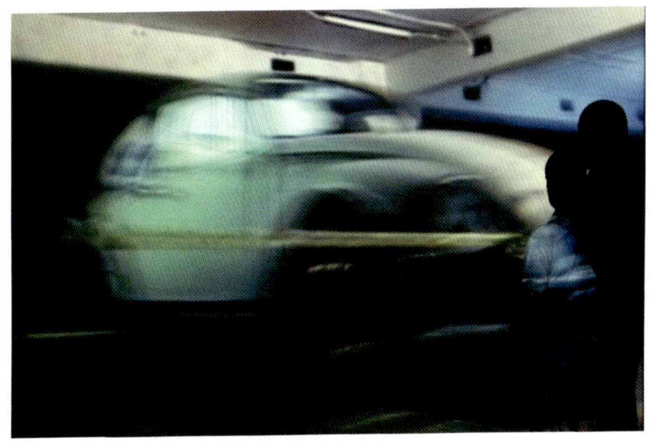

DAMIÁN ORTEGA (b. 1967, Mexico)
Geometría expandida / Expanded Geometry, 2005
Moby Dick, Mexico, 2004

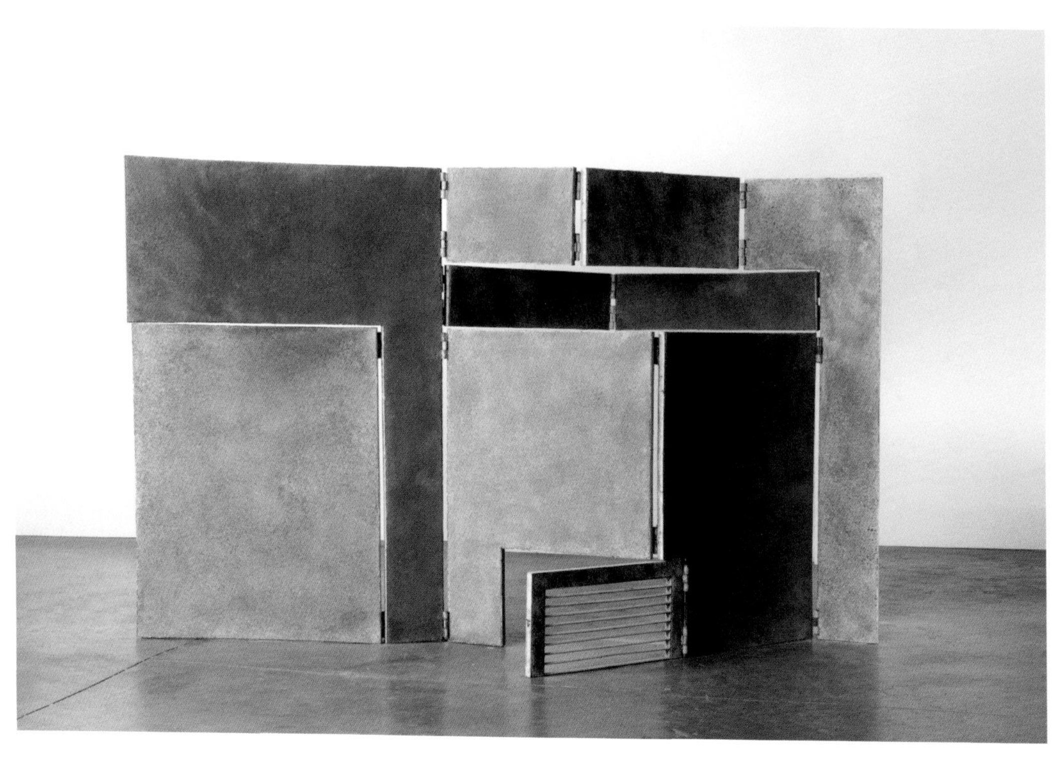

DAMIÁN ORTEGA (b. 1967, Mexico)
Biombo / Folding screen, 2004

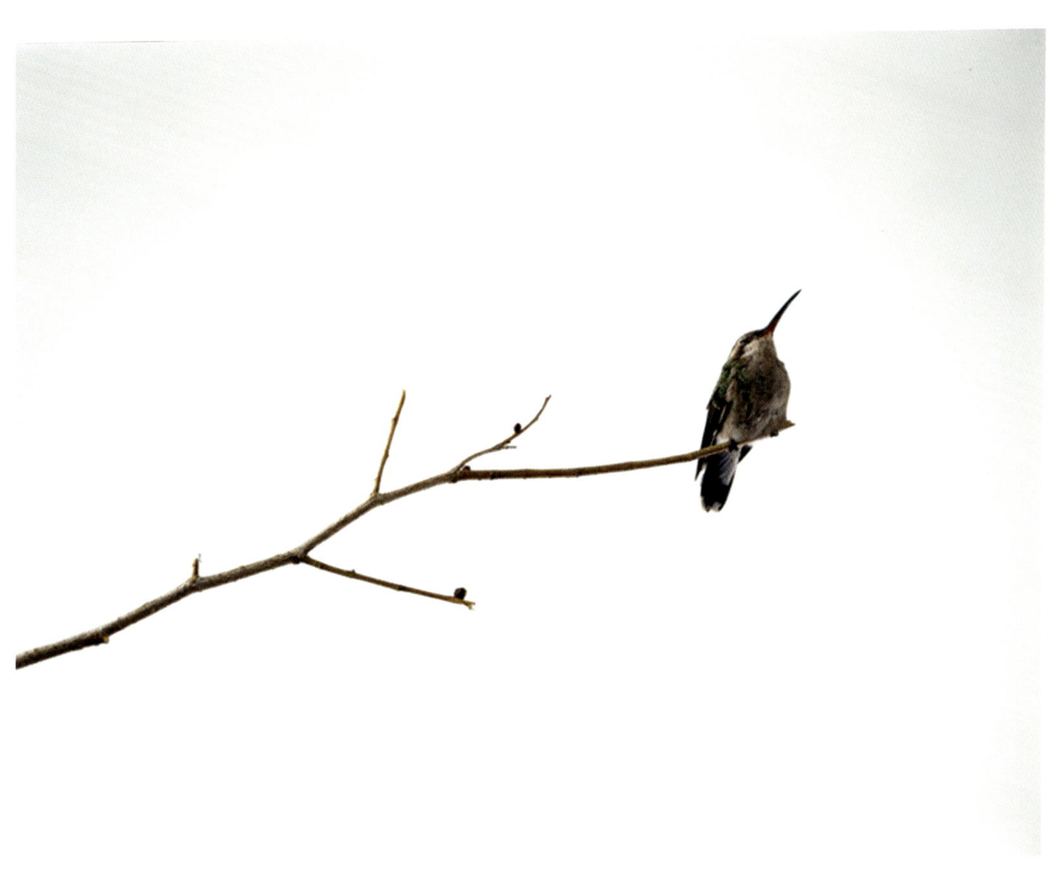

FERNANDO ORTEGA (b. 1971, Mexico)
Colibrí inducido a sueño profundo / Hummingbird Induced to a Deep Sleep, 2006

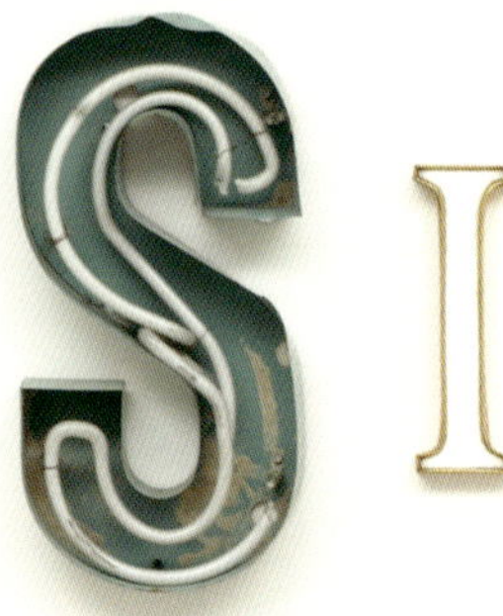

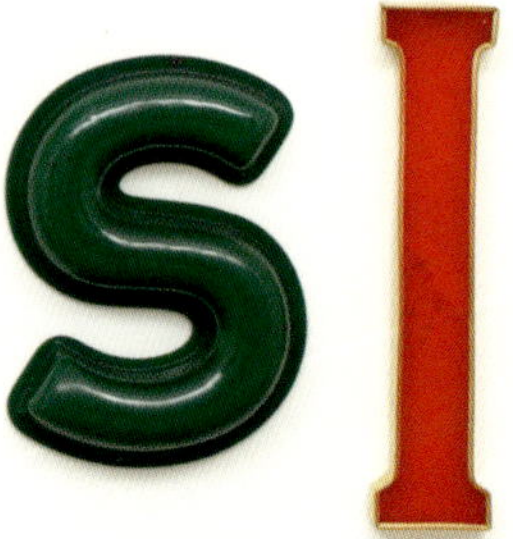

JACK PIERSON (b. 1960, United States)
Si Si Si, 1995

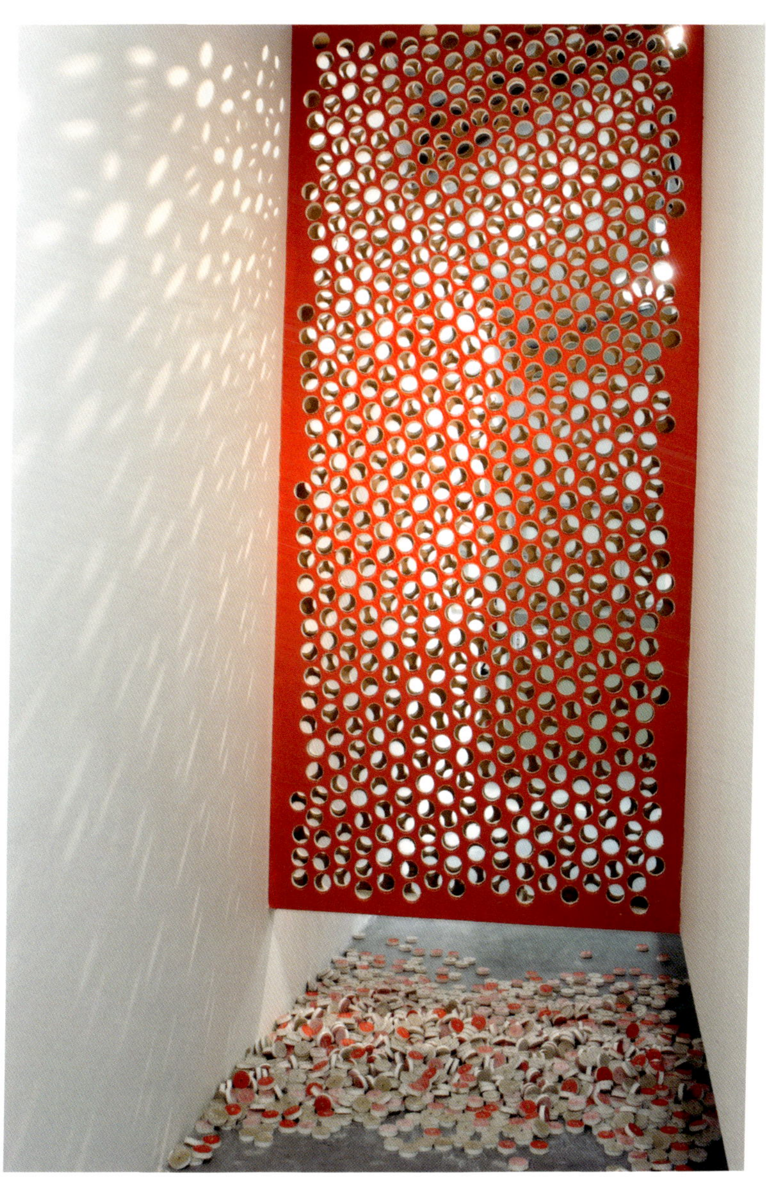

RICARDO RENDÓN (b. 1970, Mexico)
Muro falso / False Wall, 2008

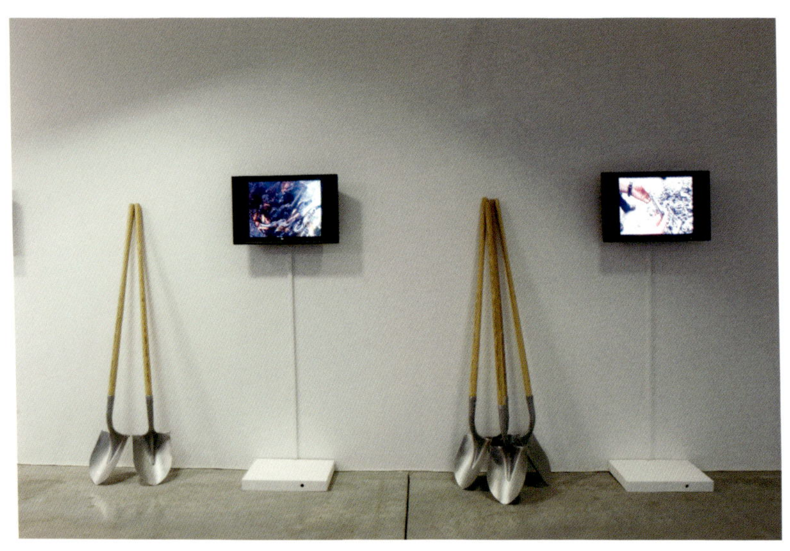

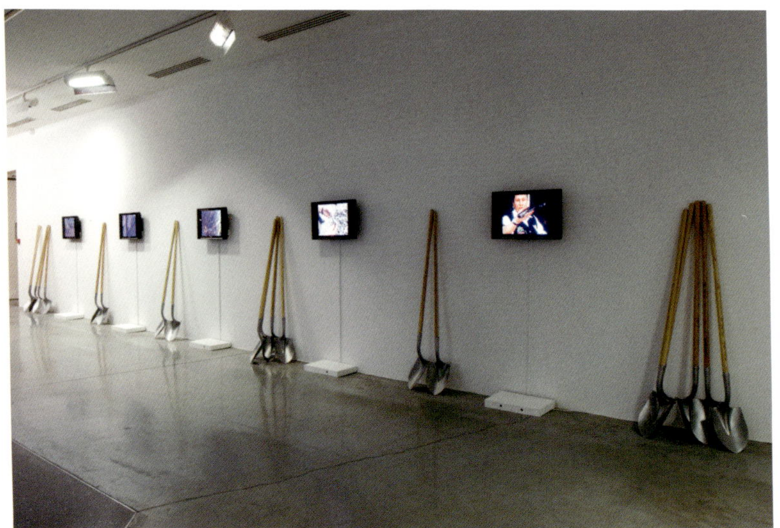

PEDRO REYES (b. 1972, Mexico)
In collaboration with Rafael Ortega (b. 1965, Mexico)
Palas por pistolas / Shovels for Guns

THOMAS RUFF (b. 1958, Germany)
Star Series: Étoile 06h 36m/ -65 / Serie estrella: Estrella 06h 36m/ -65, 1992

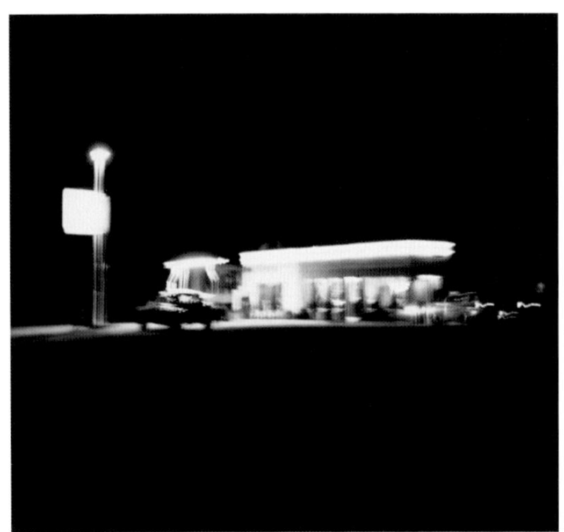

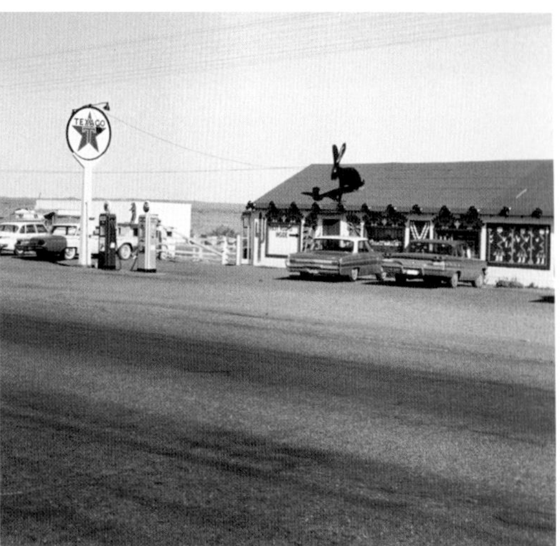

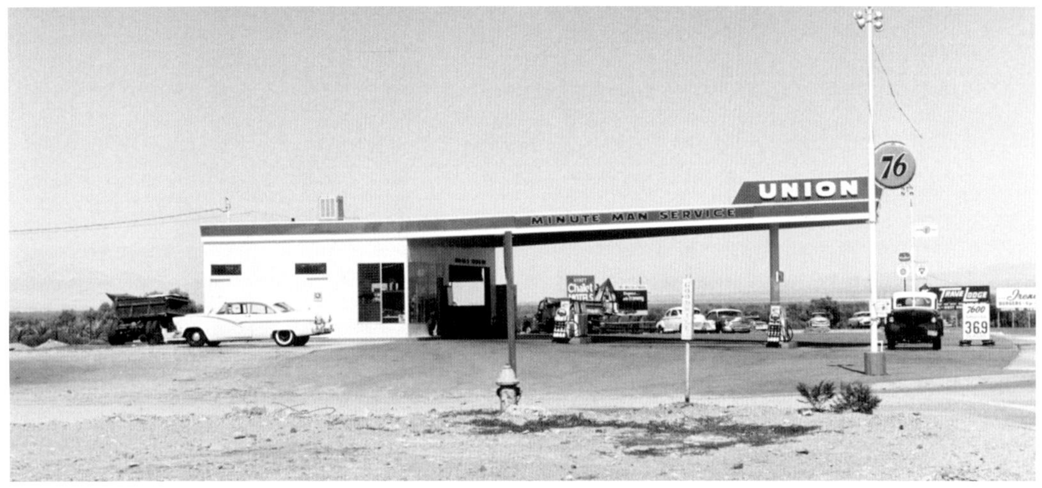

ED RUSCHA (b. 1937, United States)
Gasoline Stations (Shell, Dagot. California) #2 / Estaciones de gasolina (Shell, Dagot. California) #2, 1962-1989
Gasoline Stations (Texaco, Jackrabbit. Arizona) #4 / Estaciones de gasolina (Texaco, Jackrabbit. Arizona) #4, 1962-1989
Gasoline Stations (Union, Needles. California) #1 / Estaciones de gasolina (Union, Needles. California) #1, 1962-1989

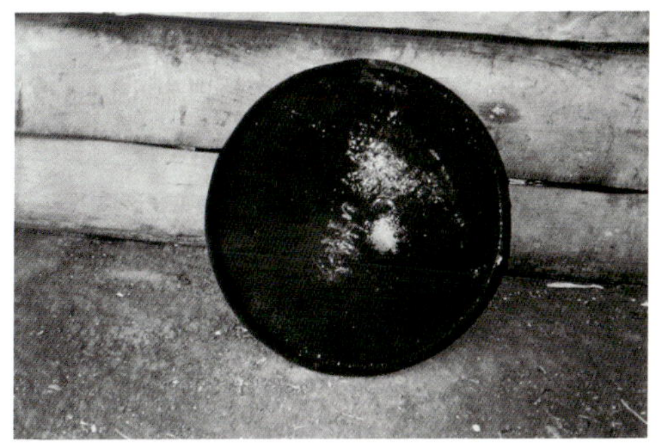

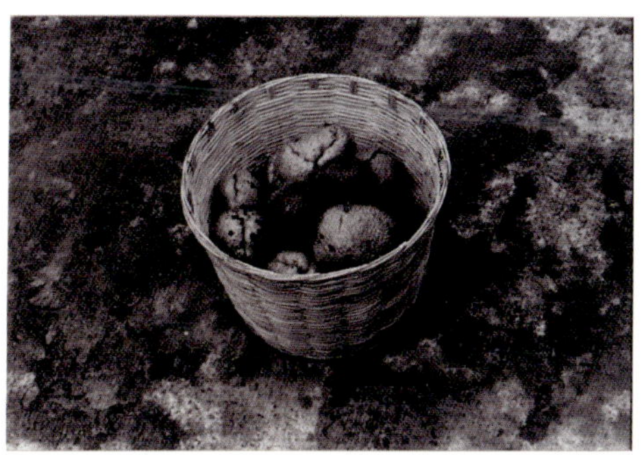

Ak'alal chich' likel lok'el ta k'ok' li semete,
mu xtun jk'eltik li slebe,
ta xch'i ta jsatik ja' la tzlok'ta li butumtike.

Mu xtun jlo'tik vach ch'umte'
k'usuk no'ox lobolal,
yu'un la vach chtal olol.

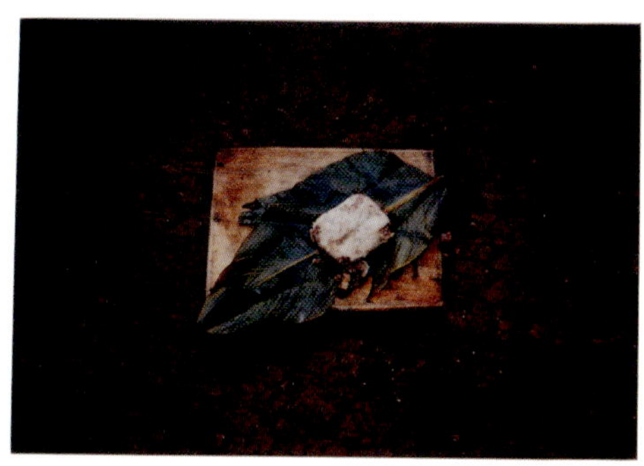

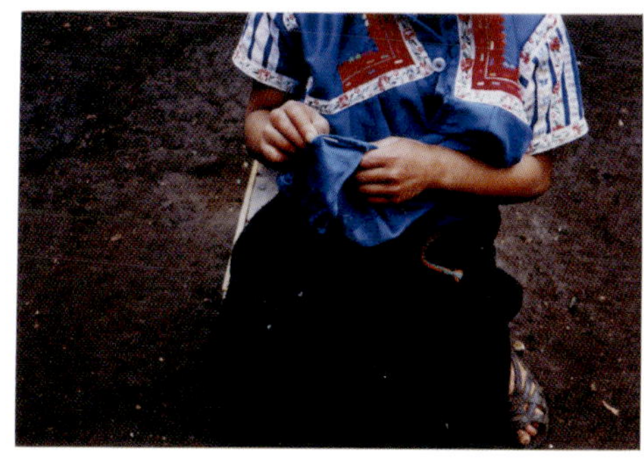

Mi oy buch'u ta slajes yil chenek'
vaj ta svaeche, yu'un ja' yik'al xlaj
ta milel, mi mo'oj ja' ta xlaj ta
milel ti xch'ulele.

Mu xtun jlapojtik jtz'is jk'u'tik,
yu'un ta la xijpas ta jkotkovil; ja'
la ti buy xijlok' xij'och ta
na'etike.

MARUCH SÁNTIZ GÓMEZ (b. 1975, Mexico)
No deben verse los brillos del comal al sacarlo del fuego /
The Hotplate Should Not be Burning when Removed from the Fire, 1994
Chayote, 1995
Tamal, 2000
Costura ropa puesta / Sew Clothes While Wearing Them, 2000

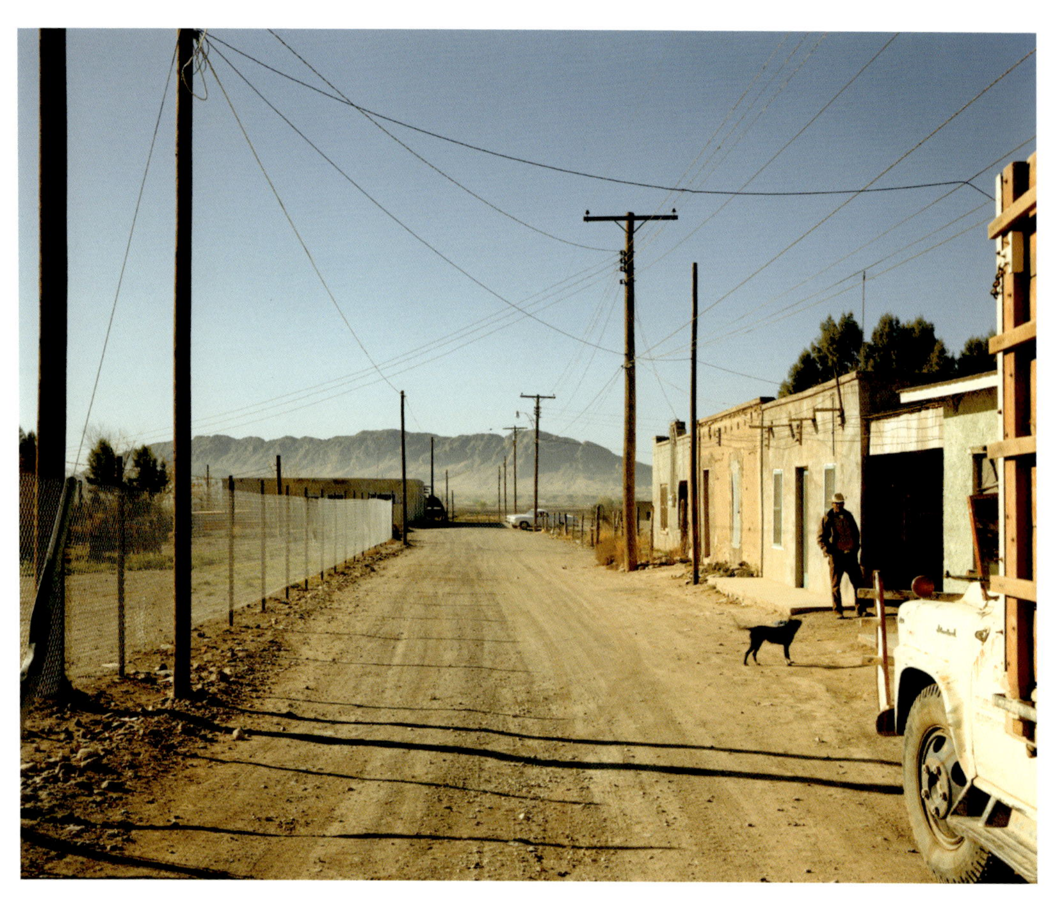

STEPHEN SHORE (b. 1947, United States)
Presidio, Texas, February 21, 1975 / Presidio, Texas, Febrero 21, 1975, 1975

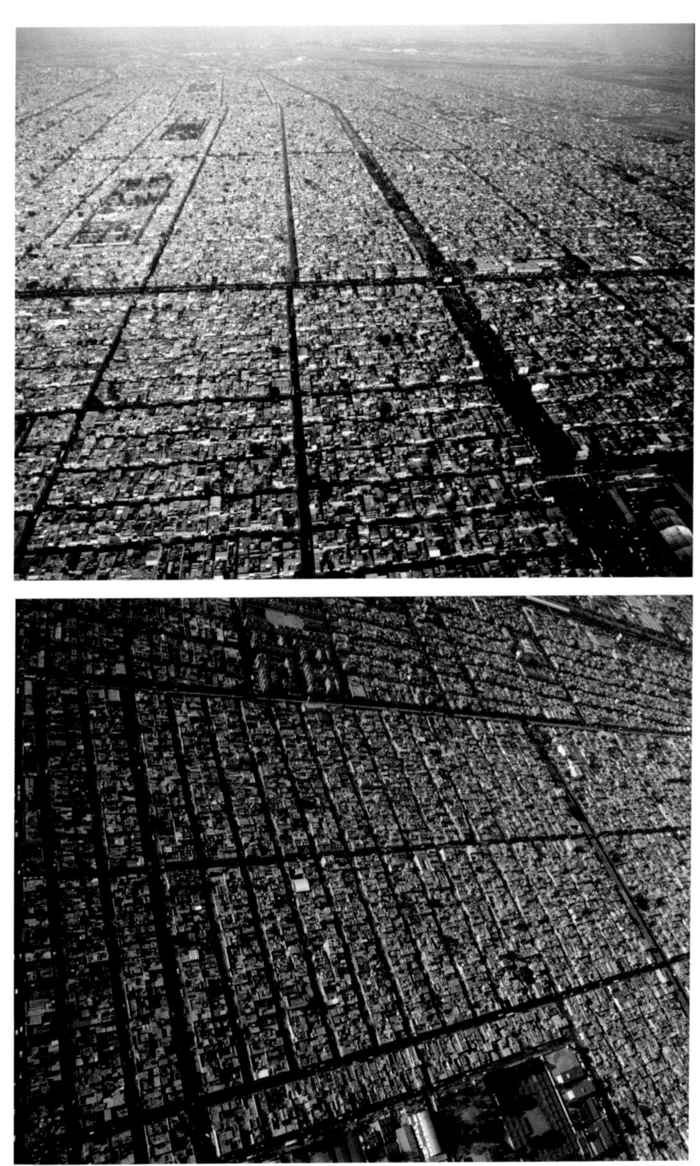

MELANIE SMITH (b. 1965, United Kingdom)
Photo for Spiral City II / Foto de ciudad espiral II, 2002
Photo for Spiral City III / Foto de ciudad espiral III, 2002

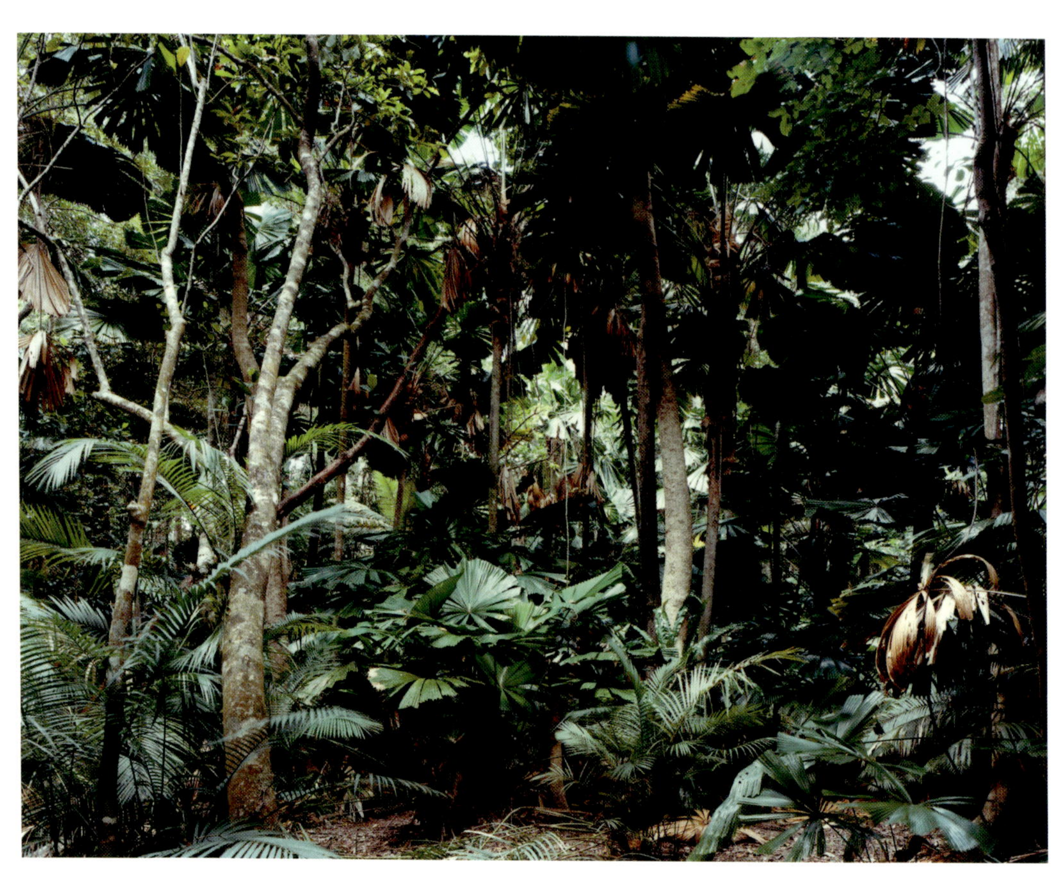

THOMAS STRUTH (b. 1954, Germany)
Paradise 2 / Paraíso 2, 1999

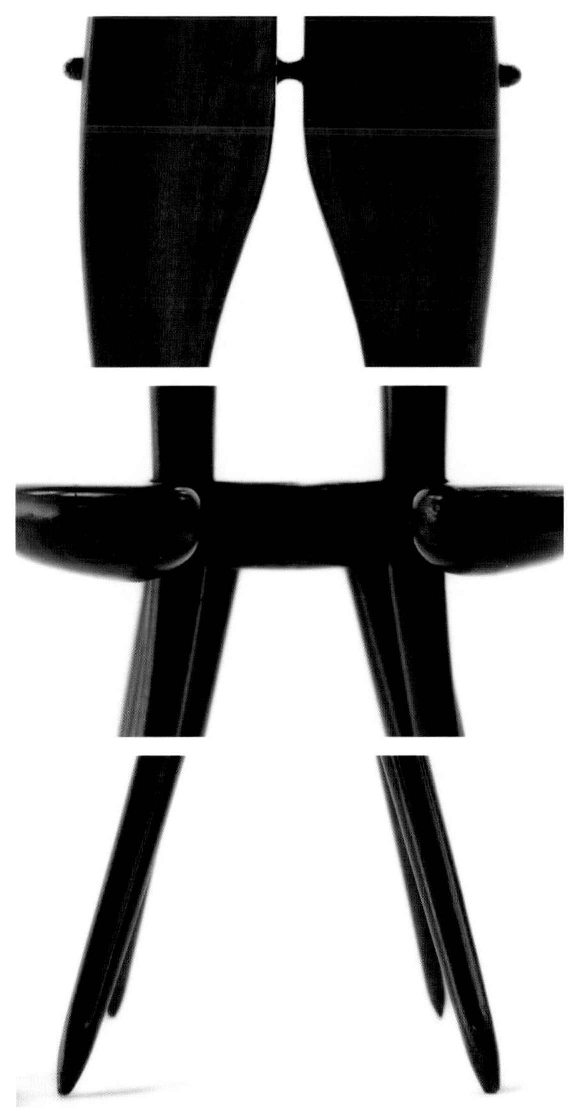

SIMON STARLING (b. 1967, United Kingdom)
Four Thousand Seven Hundred and Twenty Five (Motion Control / Molino) / Cuatromil setecientos veinticinco (Control de movimiento / Molino), 2007

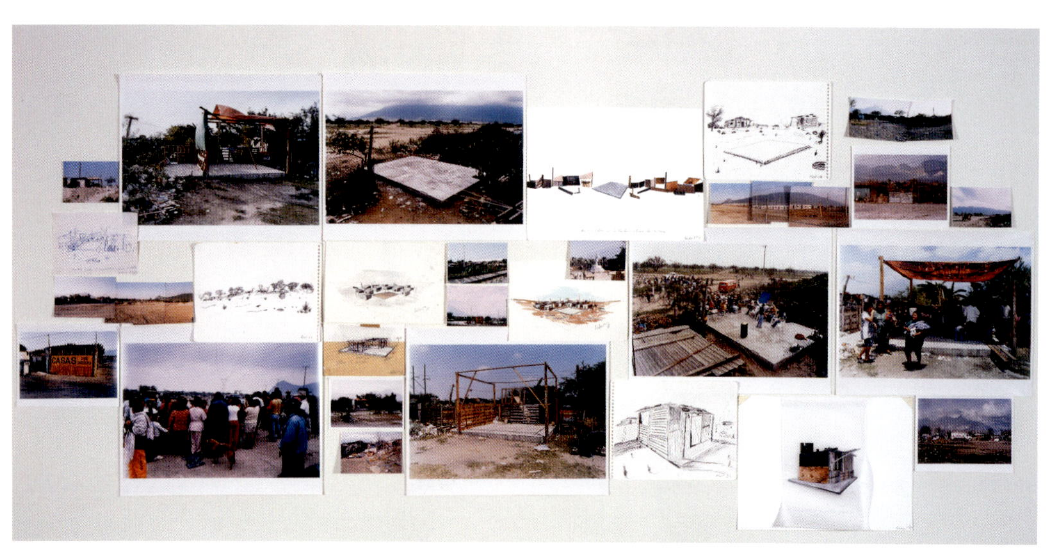

TERCERUNQUINTO (Julio Castro (b. 1975), Gabriel Cázares (b. 1976), Rolando Flores (b. 1978), Mexico)
Escultura pública en la periferia urbana de Monterrey / Public Sculpture in the Periphery of Monterrey's Urban Core, 2006

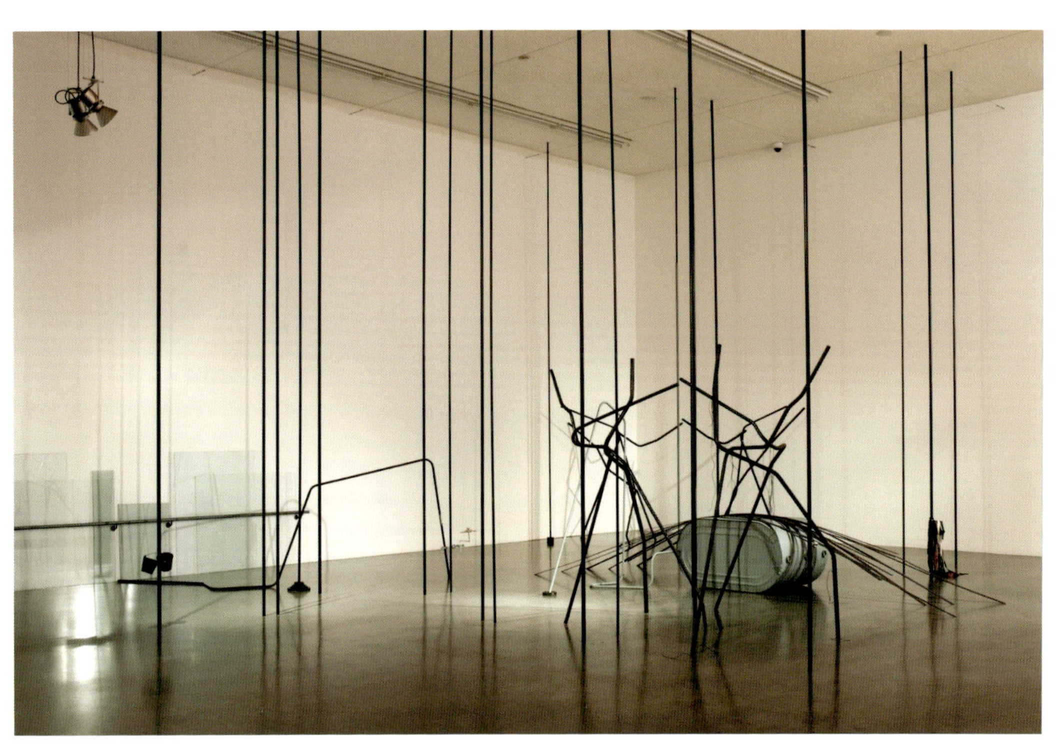

TATIANA TROUVÉ (b. 1968, France)
Sans titre / Untitled, 2008

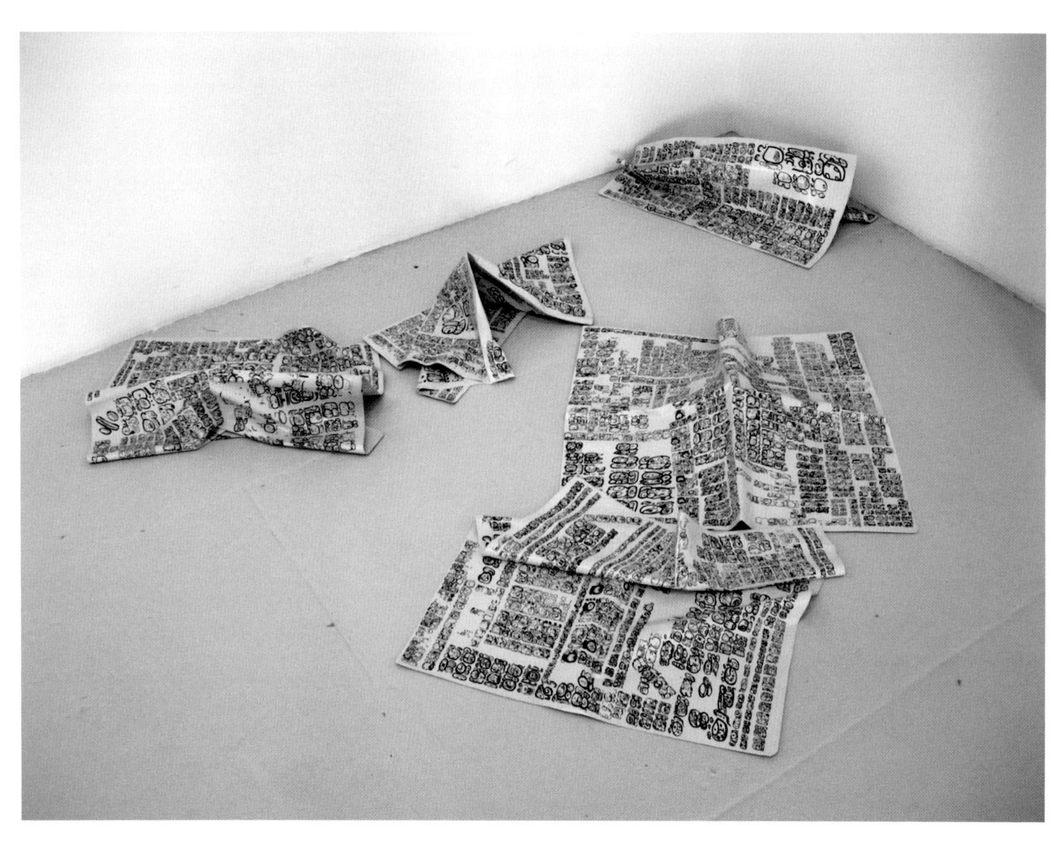

PABLO VARGAS LUGO (b. 1968, Mexico)
Bonampak News / Noticias Bonampak, 2006

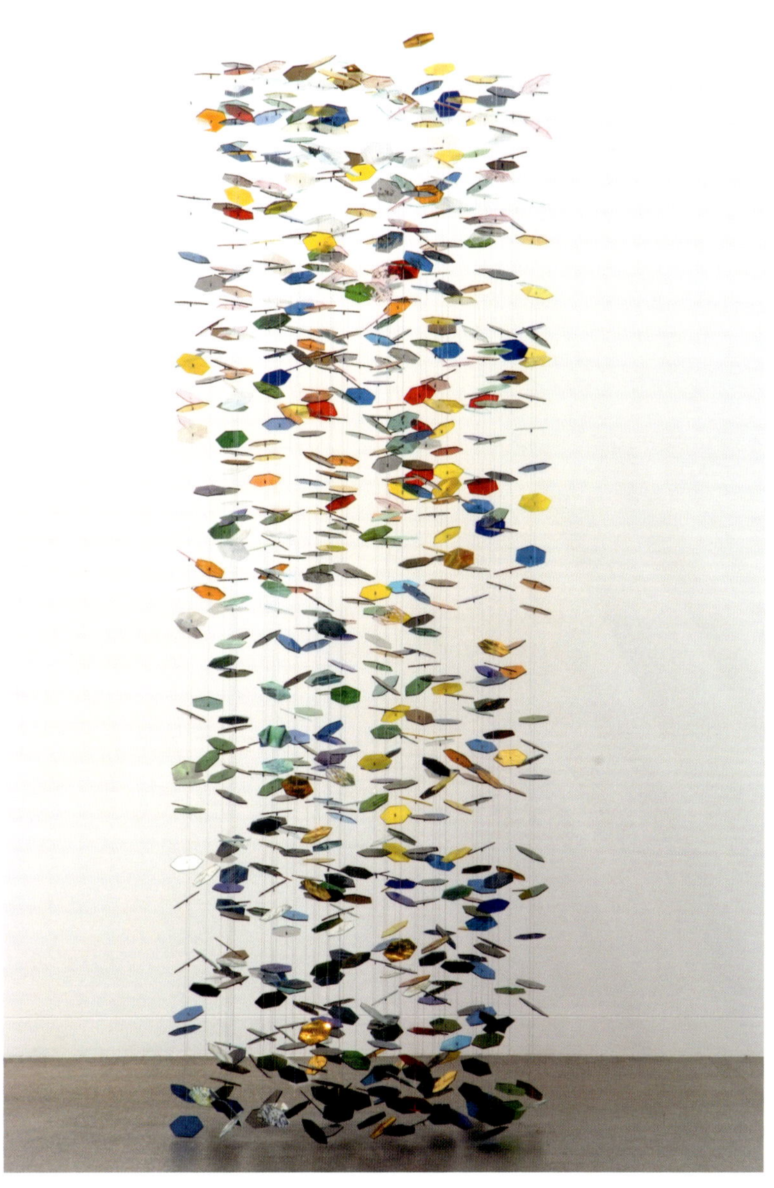

PAE WHITE (1963, United States)
Frieze Festoon / Greca adornada, 2005

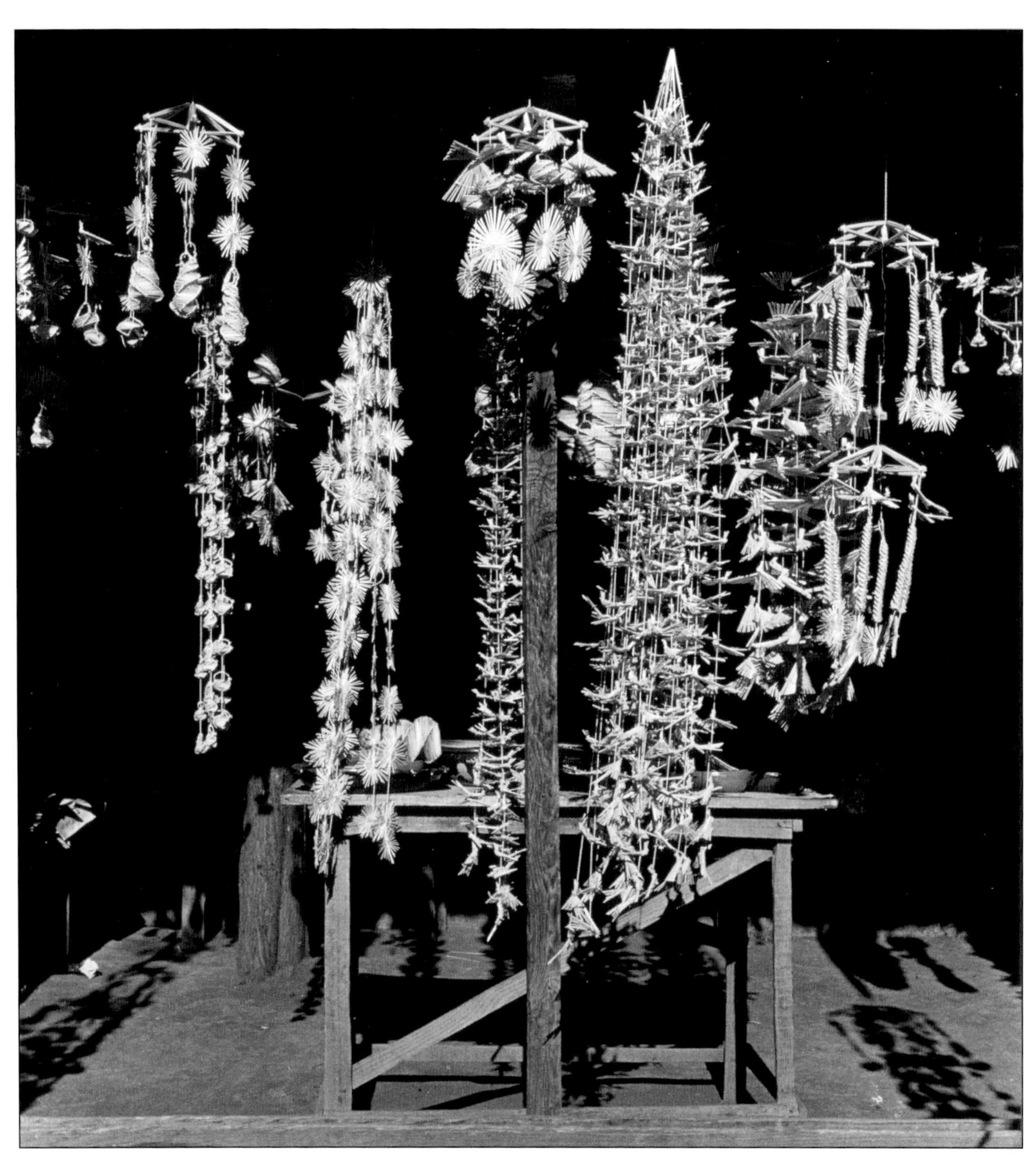

MARIANA YAMPOLSKY (1925, United States-2002, Mexico)
Adornos, Tzintzunzan, Michoacán / Ornaments, Tzintzunzan, Michoacan

MCASD CHECKLIST

FRANCIS ALŸS (b. 1959, Belgium)
Ambulantes II / Street Vendors II, 1992-2003
35mm slide projection, variable dimensions

Untitled (Cityscape) /
Sin título (paisaje urbano), 1995-1996
Painting by Francis Alÿs
oil and encaustic on canvas on wood, 4 ¼ x 6 x ½ in
Sign painting by Juan García
enamel on metal sheet, 30 ¼ x 45 x 1 in
Sign painting by Emilio Rivera
enamel on metal sheet, 48 ½ x 36 ½ x 1 in
Sign painting by Enrique Huerta
enamel on metal sheet, 24 x 31 ½ x 1 in

La ronda / The Round, 1998-2006
installation consisting of one oil and encaustic on canvas on panel painting and 25 drawings, mixed media on tracing paper, variable dimensions

In collaboration with Rafael Ortega (b. 1962 Mexico City)
Zócalo, mayo 22 1999 / Main Square, May 22 1999, 1999
video, variable dimensions

CARLOS AMORALES (b. 1970, Mexico)
The Horny Ghost 07 /
El fantasma calenturiento 07, 2007
oil on canvas, 78 ¾ x 69 in

LOTHAR BAUMGARTEN (b. 1944, Germany)
Antizipierte Gürteltiere (Anticipated Armadillos) /
Armadillos anticipados, 1969
C-Print, 22 ¼ x 25 ¼ in

Äskulap / Asclepius, 1971
C-print, 25 ½ x 33 ¼ in

Conquista Rochade / Rochade Castling, 1971
C-print, 25 ½ x 32 ½ in

MARK BRADFORD (b. 1961, United States)
Untitled / Sin título, 2007
mixed media on paper triptych, 52 ½ x 38 ¼ in, 54 ¾ x 37 in, 52 ¾ x 37 in

MIGUEL CALDERÓN (b. 1971, Mexico)
Mexico vs Brasil, 2004
Video, 90 min

MAURIZIO CATTELAN (b. 1960, Italy)
Untitled (Sitting Donkey, Trento) /
Sin título (burro sentado, Trento), 2004
taxidermied donkey, 63 x 29 x 53 in

ABRAHAM CRUZVILLEGAS (b. 1968, Mexico)
Martí, 2003
painted wood, bamboo, iron bolts and screws, variable dimensions

Progreso / Progress, 2003
brass hinges, Moroccan toothpick and weed flowers, golf tees and Campeche wax,
98 ½ x 19 ½ x 29 ½ in

Unión / Union, 2003
seeds, ceramic beads, pasta beads and pearls, variable dimensions

WILLIAM EGGLESTON (b. 1939, United States)
Untitled (Shack with Yellow Door) (from the *Los Alamos* series) */ Sin título (choza con puerta amarilla) (de la serie Los Alamos), 1965-1973*, printed 2002
dye transfer print, 16 x 20 in

KENDELL GEERS (b. 1968, South Africa)
B/Order, 2003
neon, 98 ½ x 15 ¾ x 5 ½ in

Post Pop Fuck 22, 2006
contact vinyl on wall, variable dimensions

DAN GRAHAM (b. 1942, United States)
Pseudo Tudor Style Housing, Staten Island; Kitchen Trays, Bayonne, New Jersey / Casa en estilo pseudo-Tudor, Staten Island; Charolas de cocina, Bayonne, Nueva Jersey, 1978-1966
diptych, color photographs, 34 x 24 ½ in

Two Homes Housing for Two Families and Family in Backyard / Desarrollo habitacional de dos casas para dos familias y familia en el jardín trasero, 1978-1969
diptych, color photographs, 35 x 25 ½ in

DANIEL GUZMÁN (b. 1964, Mexico)
Exilio / Exile, 2006
paint on wall, variable dimensions

ENRIQUE GUZMÁN (1952-1986, Mexico)
¡Oh! Santa bandera (serie: *Su destino secreto) / Oh Saintly Flag! (Secret Destiny* series), 1977
oil on canvas, 78 ¾ x 47 in

Postal con canica (serie: *Su destino secreto) / Postcard with marble (Its Secret Destiny* series), 1977
oil on canvas, 15 ¾ x 12 in

YISHAI JUSIDMAN (b. 1963, Mexico)
The Economist Shuffle #15 /
Juego del The Economist #15, 2007
oil and egg-tempera on wood with gilded frame, 28 ½ x 30 ½ in

The Economist Shuffle #16 /
Juego del The Economist #16, 2007
oil and egg-tempera on wood with gilded frame, 28 ½ x 30 ½ in

PHILLIP LORCA DICORCIA (b. 1953, United States)
Mexico City / Ciudad de México, 1998
Ektacolor print, 30 x 40 in

JORGE MÉNDEZ BLAKE (b. 1974, Mexico)
Sin título (Sigue el llano en llamas) /
Untitled (The Plain Still Burns), 2007
contact vinyl on wall, variable dimensions

JONATHAN MONK (b. 1969, United Kingdom)
Meeting #50 / Reunión #50, 2005-2007
contact vinyl to the wall, variable dimensions

RIVANE NEUENSCHWANDER (b. 1967, Brazil)
One Thousand and One Possible Nights [N. 60] [N.63] / Mil y una posibles noches [No. 60] [No. 63], 2007
6 collage on paper pieces, 21 x 16 in each

Suspended Landscape / Paisaje suspendido, 1997
garlic peels and vegetable fiber, variable dimensions

GABRIEL OROZCO (b. 1962, Mexico)
Árbol Nuevo / New Tree, 2006
tempera and burnished gold leaf on cedar wood panels, 19 ¾ x 19 ¾ in

Árbol simétrico / Symmetrical Tree, 2006
tempera and burnished gold leaf on cedar wood panels, 19 ½ x 19 ½ in

Bus Stop / Parada de autobús, 2007
C-print, 16 x 20 in

Center of the Universe / Centro del universo, 1997
Cibachrome print, 12 ½ x 18 ½ in

Gato en la jungla / Cat in the Jungle, 1992
Cibachrome print, 12 ½ x 18 ¾ in

DAMIÁN ORTEGA (b. 1967, Mexico)
Geometría Expandida / Expanded Geometry, 2005
drum kit and steel wire, variable dimensions

Moby Dick, Mexico, 2004
video, 9 min 42 sec

JACK PIERSON (b. 1960, United States)
Si Si Si, 1995
wall installation, variable dimensions

THOMAS RUFF (b. 1958, Germany)
Star Series: Étoile 06h 36m/ -65 /
Serie estrella: Estrella 06h 36m/ -65, 1992
negative transfer dye print, 102 ½ x 74 in

MARUCH SÁNTIZ GÓMEZ (b. 1975, Mexico)
Chayote, 1995
silver gelatin print and text in Tzotzil, 22 ½ x 18 ¾ in

Gato negro / Black Cat, 2000
color print and text in Tzotzil, 30 ¾ x 25 ½ in

No barrer la casa en la tarde /
Do Not Sweep in the Afternoon, 1994
silver gelatin print and text in Tzotzil,
22 ½ x 18 ¾ in

No deben verse los brillos del comal al sacarlo del fuego / The Hotplate Should Not be Burning when Removed from the Fire, 1994
silver gelatin and text in Tzotzil, 30 ¾ x 25 in

No sentarse en el camino /
Do Not Seat in the Middle of the Road, 1994
silver gelatin print and text in Tzotzil, 30 ¾ x 25 in

Tamal, 2000
silver gelatin print and text in Tzotzil, 30 ¾ x 25 in

Costura ropa puesta /
Sow Clothes While Wearing Them, 2000
color print and text in Tzotzil, 30 ¾ x 25 in

STEPHEN SHORE (b. 1947, United States)
Presidio, Texas, February 21, 1975 /
Presidio, Texas, febrero 21, 1975, 1975
vintage Chromogenic print, 8 x 10 in

MELANIE SMITH (b. 1965, United Kingdom)
Photo for Spiral City II / Foto de Ciudad Espiral II, 2002
silver gelatin print, 59 ¾ x 79 ¾ in

Photo for Spiral City III / Foto de Ciudad Espiral III, 2002
silver gelatin print, 50 x 59 ¾ in

Photo for Spiral City IV /Foto de Ciudad Espiral IV, 2002
silver gelatin print, 49 ¾ x 59 ¾ in

THOMAS STRUTH (b. 1954, Germany)
Paradise 2 / Paraíso 2, 1999
C-print, 69 ¼ x 91 ¾ in

TERCERUNQUINTO (Julio Castro (b. 1975), Gabriel Cázares (b. 1976), Rolando Flores (b. 1978), Mexico)
Escultura pública en la periferia urbana de Monterrey / Public Sculpture in the Periphery of Monterrey's Urban Core, 2006
C-prints, drawings and ink on paper,
variable dimensions

TATIANA TROUVÉ (b. 1968, France)
Sans titre / Untitled, 2008
bronze, iron, leather, epoxy paint, Formica, glass, cement, varnish, variable dimensions

PABLO VARGAS LUGO (b. 1968, Mexico)
Bonampak News / Noticias Bonampak, 2006
5 pieces made of fiberglass and decal prints,
variable dimensions

Grand Hotel (Fig A), 2005
lacquer on paper, 39 ¼ x 27 ¾ in

Grand Hotel (Fig D), 2005
lacquer on paper, 39 ½ x 27 ⅔ in

Grand Hotel (Fig F), 2005
lacquer on paper, 39 ¼ x 27 ¾ in

Grand Hotel (Fig B), 2005
lacquer on paper, 39 ¼ x 27 ¾ in

MOLAA CHECKLIST

EDUARDO ABAROA (b. 1968, Mexico)
BCIN (Node in a Corner) /
BCIN (Nódulo en la esquina), 2007
cotton swabs, plastic balls, wire, and white hot glue, variable dimensions

DOUG AITKEN (b. 1968, United States)
99 Cents Dreams / Sueños de 99 centavos, 2007
neon, 35 ¼ x 54 3/16 in

MANUEL ÁLVAREZ BRAVO (1902-2002, Mexico)
Niño maya de Tulum / Mayan Child from Tulum, 1942
photography, 6 ¾ x 9 7/16 in

Ventana a los magueyes / Window Looking at the Magueys, 1976
photography, 7 1/12 x 9 7/16 in

FRANCIS ALŸS (b. 1959, Belgium)
D- El jersey y la mosca / About the Sweater and the Fly, 2003
oil on canvas, diptych, 10 ¼ x 19 ½ x 1 3/16 in each panel

CARLOS AMORALES (b. 1970, Mexico)
Panorama, 2007
set of 30 collage paper drawings,
17 ¾ x 23 5/8 in each

CARL ANDRE (b. 1935, United States)
Seventh Small Steel Cardinal /
Séptimo cardinal pequeño de acero, 1975
rusted steel plate in seven parts,
1/8 x 6 1/8 x 43 ¾ in

JOHN BALDESSARI (b. 1931, United States)
Two Faces: Three Figures; One Shadow (Version #2) /
Dos rostros: tres figuras; una sombra (version #2), 1988
black and white photographs with acrylic paint on board, 48 ½ x 30 ½ in

IÑAKI BONILLAS (b. 1981, Mexico)
"Angel 01" de la serie *Martín Lunas /*
"Angel 01" from the *Martín Lunas* series, 2004
light box and color film, 19 11/16 x 19 11/16 in

"Angel 02" de la serie *Martín Lunas /*
"Angel 02" from the *Martín Lunas* series, 2004
light box and color film, 19 11/16 x 19 11/16 in

"La cabaña 03" de la serie *Martín Lunas /*
"The Cabin 03" from the *Martín Lunas* series, 2004
light box and color film, 19 11/16 x 19 11/16 in

"La cabaña 01" de la serie *Martín Lunas /*
"The Cabin 01" from the *Martín Lunas* series, 2004
light box and color film, 19 11/16 x 19 11/16 in

"La cabaña 02" de la serie *Martín Lunas /*
"The Cabin 02" from the *Martín Lunas* series, *2004*
light box and color film, 19 11/16 x 19 11/16 in

"Cuernavaca 01" de la serie *Martín Lunas /*
"Cuernavaca 01" from the *Martín Lunas* series, *2004*
light box and color film, 19 11/16 x 19 11/16 in

"Cuernavaca 02" de la serie *Martín Lunas /*
"Cuernavaca 02" from the *Martín Lunas* series, 2004
light box and color film, 19 11/16 x 19 11/16 in

"Casa Fernando" de la serie *Martín Lunas /*
"Fernando House" from the *Martín Lunas* series, 2004
Light box and color film, 19 11/16 x 19 11/16 in

SOPHIE CALLE (b. 1953, France)
Count Up to Unhappiness: Day 50 / Cuenta hacia la infelicidad: Día 50, 1984-2003
diptych, embroidered text on cloths panels,
84 ½ x 51 ¼ in

LYGIA CLARK (1920-1988, Brazil)
Bicho / Bug, 1960
aluminium model, 15 ¾ x 11 7/8 x 5 7/8 in

ABRAHAM CRUZVILLEGAS (b. 1968, Mexico)
Las Guerras Floridas II / Florid Wars II, 2003
maguey leafs, variable dimensions

JOSE DAMASCENO (b. 1970, Brazil)
Cinema Elastico / Elastic cinema, 2009
rubber and nails, variable dimensions

RINEKE DIJKSTRA (b. 1959, Netherlands)
Montemor, Portugal, May 1 A /
Montemor, Portugal, mayo 1 A, 1994
C-print, 24 3/8 x 20 ½ in

Montemor, Portugal, May 1 B /
Montemor, Portugal, mayo 1 B, 1994
C-print, 24 3/8 x 20 ½ in

Montemor, Portugal, May 1 C /
Montemor, Portugal, mayo 1 C, 1994
C-print, 24 3/8 x 20 ½ in

Montemor, Portugal, May 8 A /
Montemor, Portugal, mayo 8 A, 1994
C-print, 24 3/8 x 20 ½ in

Villafranca, Portugal, May 8 B /
Villafranca, Portugal, mayo 8 B, 1994
C-print, 24 3/8 x 20 ½ in

FISCHLI AND WEISS (b. 1952 / b. 1946, Switzerland)
Herr und Frau Birne mit ihrem neuen Hund,
Mr. & Mrs. Birne with their new dog, 1984-1986
C-print, 11 ¾ x 8 in

Über dem Abgrund / About the Abyss, 1984-1985
photograph, 9 ½ x 12 in

Untitled (Equilibrium series) /
Sin título (serie *Equilibrium*), 1986
C-print, 14 ¼ x 18 ½ in

A Day's Work / Un día de trabajo, 1986
C-print, 10 ¼ x 13 ¾ in

FLOR GARDUÑO (b. 1957, Mexico)
La Bendición. Isla del Sol. Bolivia /
The Blessing. Isla del Sol. Bolivia, 1989
silver gelatin print, 16 x 20 in

KENDELL GEERS (b. 1968 South Africa)
D/Anger, 2003
neon, 98 1/3 x 15 ¾ x 5 ½ in

Cry Wolf / Falsa Alarma, 1999
60 red emergency lights and cables,
variable dimensions

FERNANDA GOMES (b. 1960, Brazil)
Untitled / Sin título, 1999/2005
guitar string, variable dimensions

JONATHAN HERNÁNDEZ (b. 1972, Mexico)
Vulnerabilia (Water, Fire, Mass, Ruins) /
Vulnerabilia (agua, fuego, masa, ruinas), 2005
set of 4 panels newspaper cuttings on cardboard
45 1/16 x 53 ¾ in; 47 7/8 x 55 ¾ in;
48 7/8 x 55 ½ in; 47 5/8 x 56 ¾ in

GRACIELA ITURBIDE (b. 1942, Mexico)
El Señor de los pájaros. Nayarit /
Man of Birds. Nayarit, 1985
gelatin silver print, 20 x 24 in

Pájaros en el poste de luz. Carretera a Guanajuato /
Birds in the Light Post. Road to Guanajuato, 1990
gelatin silver print, 22 x 26 in

Cementerio, Juchitán Oaxaca /
Cemetery, Juchitán Oaxaca, 1988
gelatin silver print, 24 x 20 in

TERENCE KOH (b. 1977, China)
Untitled (Skeleton Paintings) /
Sin título (pinturas de esqueleto), 2006
painting/sculpture installation and
video-documentation of performance
15 mirror parts, 68 x 36 in each ;
skeleton, 5/8 x 15 1/8 x 8 1/16 in

HELEN LEVITT (b. 1913, United States)
Untitled (México, D.F.) / Sin título (México, D.F.), 1941
silver gelatin print, 9 ½ x 6 3/8 in

JORGE MACCHI (b. 1963, Argentina)
El beso / The Kiss, 2005
hammer, hemp thread and nails, 78 ¾ x 157 ½ in

MAREPE (b. 1970, Brazil)
Sanfoninha, 2006
print on paper and plexiglass box,
variable dimensions

TERESA MARGOLLES (b. 1963, Mexico)
Recados Póstumos (Cine Avenida) /
Posthumous Notes (Avenida Movie Theatre), 2006
C-print, 53 ⅛ x 74 ½ in

Recados Póstumos (Cine Metropolitan) /
Posthumous Notes (Metropolitan Movie Theatre), 2006
C-print, 53 ⅛ x 74 ½ in

GORDON MATTA-CLARK (1948-1973, United States)
Circus or the Caribbean Orange /
Circo o el Caribe naranja, 1978
Cibachrome print, 20 x 30 in

Conical Intersect / Intersección cónica, 1974
Video in 16 mm, 18 min 40 sec.

Day's End Pier 52 / Final del día en el muelle 52, 1975
Cibachrome print, 40 x 30 in

Day's End / Final del día, 1975
DVD, 23 min 10 sec.

JORGE MÉNDEZ BLAKE (b. 1974, Mexico)
!Diles que no me maten! (Editado por Rulfo) /
Tell them not to kill me! (Edited by Rulfo), 2003
audio installation

ANA MENDIETA (1948, Cuba-1985, United States)
Ánima, de la serie *Silueta de cohetes / Soul, from the series Firework Silhouette,* 1976
video, 3 min

Sweating Blood / Sudando sangre, 1973
video, 3 min

Untitled (Blood and Feathers #2) /
Sin título (sangre y plumas #2), 1974
video, 3 min 30 sec

On Giving Life / Sobre dar vida, 1975
photograph, 7 ⅞ x 10 1/16 in

MORIS (b. 1978, Mexico)
Hermoso paisaje #1 / Beautiful Landscape # 1, 2007
mixed media, variable dimensions

Impermeable / Waterproof, 2006
pencil and tape on wood, 45 ¼ x 46 ½ in

ERNESTO NETO (b. 1964, Brazil)
A Horizon of Events, Point of View /
Un horizonte de eventos, punto de vista, 2006
installation, 15 x 155 ⅛ x 61 in

RIVANE NEUENSCHWANDER (b. 1967, Brazil)
Conversations and Constructions / Canteiros /
Conversaciones y construcciones, 2006
poliptych of 16 photographs C-prints, 15 ¾ x 23 ⅝ in

HELIO OITICICA (1937-1980, Brazil)
Metasquema 354, 1958
gouache on paper, 21 ⅜ x 18 ¼ in

Metasquema 214, 1957
gouache on paper, 16 ¾ x 19 ½ in

GABRIEL OROZCO (b. 1962, Mexico)
Atomists: Ascention / Atomistas: Ascensión, 1996
2 part computer generated print, 77 ½ x 27 ½ in

Cementerio 2 / Cemetery 2, 2002
C-print, 34 ½ x 46 in

Center of the Universe / Centro del universo, 1997
Cibachrome, 12 7/16 x 18 ⅝ in

Cuadro fértil / Fertile Painting, 2004
acrilyc on canvas, 31 ½ x 31 ½ in

Percepción total / Total Perception, 2002
C-print, 33 ¾ x 46 ¾ in

Soccer Ball 2 / Balón de fútbol 2, 2002
cut out soccer ball, 11 15/16 in diameter

Multiple Pourings (2) / Vertidos múltiples (2), 2003
polyurethane foam sphere, 19 in diameter

DAMIÁN ORTEGA (b. 1967, Mexico)
Biombo / Folding screen, 2004
metal, concrete, plaster, 63 x 118 ⅛ x 2 ¾ in

FERNANDO ORTEGA (b. 1971, Mexico)
Colibrí inducido a sueño profundo /
Hummingbird Induced to a Deep Sleep, 2006
video, 1 hr 1 min 37 sec

RICARDO RENDÓN (b. 1970, Mexico)
Muro falso / False Wall, 2008
intervened drywall

PEDRO REYES (b. 1972, Mexico)
In collaboration with Rafael Ortega (b.1965, Mexico)
Palas por pistolas / Shovels for Guns
1527 shovels manufactured with recycled metal from 1527 fire-arms voluntarily donated by citizens of Culiacán, Sinaloa, Mexico and to be used for planting 1527 trees.
1527 shovels numbered from 0001 to 1500 and 27 shovels from A to Z.

ED RUSCHA (b. 1937, United States)
Gasoline Stations (Dixie, Upton. Arizona) #6 / Estaciones de gasolina (Dixie, Upton. Arinzona) #6, 1962-1989
gelatin silver print, 20 ¼ x 23 ⅝ in

Gasoline Stations (Fina, Groom. Texas) #10 / Estaciones de gasolina (Fina, Groom. Texas) #10, 1962-1989
gelatin silver print, 20 ¼ x 23 ⅝ in

Gasoline Stations (Flying, Kingman. Arizona) #5 / Estaciones de gasolina (Flying, Kingman. Arizona) #5, 1962-1989
gelatin silver print, 20 ¼ x 23 ⅝ in

Gasoline Stations (Knox, Lex. Oklahoma City) #9 / Estaciones de gasolina (Knox, Lex. Oklahoma City) #9, 1962-1989
gelatin silver print, 20 ¼ x 23 ⅝ in

Gasoline Stations (Phillips 66, Flagstaff. Arizona) #3 / Estaciones de gasolina (Phillips 66, Flagstaff. Arizona) #3, 1962-1989
gelatin silver print, 20 ¼ x 23 ⅝ in

Gasoline Stations (Shell, Dagot. California) #2 / Estaciones de gasolina (Shell, Dagot. California) #2, 1962-1989
gelatin silver print, 20 ¼ x 23 ⅝ in

Gasoline Stations (Texaco, Jackrabbit. Arizona) #4 / Estaciones de gasolina (Texaco, Jackrabbit. Arizona) #4, 1962-1989
gelatin silver print, 20 ¼ x 23 ⅝ in

Gasoline Stations (Union, Needles. California) #1 / Estaciones de gasolina (Union, Needles. California) #1, 1962-1989
gelatin silver print, 20 ¼ x 23 ⅝ in

SIMON STARLING (b. 1967, United Kingdom)
Four Thousand Seven Hundred and Twenty Five (Motion Control / Molino) / Cuatromil setecientos veinticinco (Control de movimiento / Molino), 2007
35 mm film, 3 min 9 sec

PAE WHITE (1963, United States)
Frieze Festoon / Greca adornada, 2005
installation, variable dimensions

MARIANA YAMPOLSKY
(1925, United States-2002, Mexico)
Adornos, Tzintzunzan, Michoacán / Ornaments, Tzintzunzan, Michoacan
silver gelatin print, 16 x 20 in

ARTIST BIOGRAPHIES

EDUARDO ABAROA

Eduardo Abaroa was born in Mexico City in 1968. Abaroa is an artist, professor and writer. He studied art at Escuela Nacional de Artes Plásticas at UNAM and holds a MFA from California Institute of the Arts. He was a co-founder of the influential Temistocles 44, an artist-run space in Mexico City (1993-1995) and is currently course director at SOMA in Mexico.

Abaroa works by appropriating daily materials and symbols and transforming them into aesthetic objects. The result of this process is a redefinition of the meaning of the objects. Some of his works deal with the idea of the movable monument; in other cases he builds non-functional objects that become part of a functional context; his work tries to subvert fixed ideological systems and ideal models.

In 1999 he started using cotton swabs for his installations. BCIN, the most ambitious piece in this series of works, is an acronym for "the Body Cavity Inspection Network." Resembling a structure that is similar to the design of exchange networks in computer science, biology or sociology the artist states that the piece is a type of generalized surveillance that could penetrate everything, including the human body.

As a writer, Abaroa has been an art reviewer for Reforma newspaper, and has written for other important publications including *Curare, Casper, Moho, D.F.* and *Codigo 06140*. The artist has exhibited his work at significant institutions such as MUAC (2010), Sala de Arte Público Siqueiros (2006) and Museo de Arte Carrillo Gil (1999) in Mexico; MOCA in Los Angeles (2007), Guggenheim Museum in New York (2005) and Museo Nacional

DOUG AITKEN

Doug Aitken was born in Redondo Beach, California in 1968. He studied at the Art Center College of Design in Pasadena. His practice is distinguished by his exploration of new technologies and the way in which he uses images and sound in his video installations, conveying a peculiar temporality in relation to narrative.

The subject matter of his work relates to the existence of the post-modern human being with media, pop culture and notions of time and industrialization. Aitken's scenes do not follow conventional narrative forms. In them, the beginning and the end of the story are not important and instead the images seen by the audience are always happening at the present moment; they are fragments of a reality that generate different stories and stimulate the imagination. In his most recent pieces he has started working with sculpture, using neon structures to create sentences and forms that convey messages about dreams and ideals that are familiar in the context of today´s culture.

By leaving the interpretation of his works open, the artist makes them more visceral and experimental. His art plays with the experience of the senses as dreams do, and in his video installations the spectator is immersed in an environment designed for the senses, which produces altered states of perception not based in linear time.

In 1999 he was awarded the International Prize at the 48th Venice Biennial for his video *Electric Earth* and in 2000 his work was part of the Whitney Biennial. His latest show at the New York MoMA was titled *Sleepwalkers* (2007). He has also shown his works in solo exhibitions at the Aspen Art Museum (2006), the Musée d'Art Moderne de la Ville de Paris (2005), the Aldrich Museum (2004) and the Kunsthalle Zurich (2003).

MANUEL ÁLVAREZ BRAVO

Manuel Álvarez Bravo was born in Mexico City in 1902. He attended the Escuela Nacional de Bellas Artes (National School of Fine Arts) in 1918 to study art and painting. However, his grandfather—who was a photographer—had already introduced little Manuel to the medium that would become his profession, along with film. During the 1920s and 30s, Álvarez Bravo met Hugo Brehme, Edward Weston, Paul Strand, Henri Cartier-Bresson and André Breton. Although all of them would be important in the development of Álvarez's career, it was also influenced by the cultural and intellectual effervescence of post-revolutionary Mexico. In that context, he became a close friend of Tina Modotti and Diego Rivera and worked in films with Luis Buñuel, Sergei M. Eisenstein and John Ford.

During the 1930s he took photographs of the Mexican mural painters and collaborated with *Mexican Folkways* magazine. He was also interested in portraying the city and country life of his country and its traditions. His work shows a great capacity to assimilate international trends and it documents modest scenes, isolated details and portraits of everyday life in a my sterious and surrealist tone.

The pieces shown here, *Espejo negro* (Black Mirror) (1947), *Niño maya de Tulum* (Mayan Boy from Tulum) (1942) and *Ventana con magueyes* (Window with Magueys) (1976) explore the nude, and the physiognomies, architecture and natural landscapes of his native country.

He was one of the founding members of the Museo de la Fotografía en México (*Museum of Photography in Mexico)* (1980), the first of its kind in the country. His photographs have been shown at the Museum of Modern Art, New York (1997), the J. Paul Getty Museum, in Los Angeles (2001), the Walker Art Center in Minneapolis (2002) and the Museo de Arte Moderno in Mexico

City (2004). He was awarded the Premio Nacional de las Artes (México, 1975), an official medal from the Ordre des Arts et Lettres Français (France, 1981), the Víctor Hasselblad Prize (Sweden, 1984) and the Master of Photography of the ICP (USA, 1987). His work and trajectory certainly make Álvarez Bravo part of the history of photography and one of the greatest Mexican artists of the twentieth century. He died in 2002.

FRANCIS ALŸS

Francis Alÿs was born in Antwerp, Belgium in 1959. He studied Architecture and Urban Planning and has been living in Mexico City since the 1980s. His works include videos, performances, photographs, drawings and paintings.

Most of Alÿs's artworks deal with urban life. Centered on the dialogues that happen within specific settings, his pieces emphasize the constant communication between the elements that come together to shape a particular context. Alÿs works from the perspective of an inmigrant who is able to capture details that go unnoticed by the locals. His artworks use the intangible to illustrate the ordinary, making the automatic behavior and dynamics of city dwellers become visible, a topic to be discussed and reflected upon by the audience.

Walking through cities has become a trademark of this artist's practice. It is during these walks—reminiscent of the *derivé* as it was conceived by the French Situationists—that he observes and accumulates the objects and anecdotes which are used to chronicle the life of the cities he works in. In his practice, Alÿs does not try to denounce social or political situations. Instead, he merely portrays ordinary characters like the street vendor who carries the tools of his trade, or the line of people taking shelter from the sun under the shadow of the flagpole in Mexico City's main square, the Zócalo.

Alÿs is the subject of the major retrospective *Francis Alÿs: a Story of Deception*, organized by the Tate Modern with WIELS Centre of Contemporary Art, Brussels and The Museum of Modern Art, New York (2010). His work has been widely collected and internationally exhibited at the Melbourne International Biennial (1999), the Havana Biennial (1994) and several times at the Venice Biennial, among others. In 2007 the UCLA Hammer Museum presented the first retrospective of his work in the United States. His work has also been shown in different international museums such as the Antiguo Colegio de San Ildefonso, Mexico, D*iez cuadras alrededor del estudio* (2006), the MALBA, Argentina, *A Story of Deception, Patagonia 2003-2006* (2006), the Israel Museum, Israel, *Sometimes Doing Something Poetic Can Become Something Political and Sometimes Doing Something Political Can Become Something Poetic* (2005) and the Kunstmuseum Wolfsburg, Germany, *Walking Distance from the Studio* (2004).

CARLOS AMORALES

Carlos Amorales was born in 1970. He is remarkable amongst a new generation of Mexican artists. Amorales' varied artworks reflect a peculiar vision of the world, and in them the viewer is immersed in fantastic settings that arouse ambiguity, anxiety and fear. Questions that afflict human existence are always present in his work, which is continuously populated by an eclectic wildlife. Amorales' early works were performances in which he explored identity issues confronting individual consciousness and the eternal conflict between what we are and what we represent. That series of work, inspired by Mexican pop culture, was based on *lucha libre*, a local form of wrestling. The most important piece was *Amorales vs. Amorales*, performed at the Tate Modern in London, where two wrestlers wearing masks based on the artist's features fought each other as though in a mirror, representing the confrontation of the individual with himself.

Amorales works in several media including performance art, video, animation, installation, drawing and music. Throughout his career the artist has gathered a collection of icons and images that he collectively named the "Liquid Archive." He constantly uses images from this archive in various artworks and they acquire fresh meanings and connotations. The main colors used in Amorales' drawings and videos are red, black and white. In his latest pieces he uses high-impact design images that trigger a series of associations in the audience, which are meant to activate the collective unconscious.

Amorales studied at the Gerrit Rietveld Academie in Ámsterdam between 1992 and 1995, and in 1996 he continued his studies at the Rijksakademie van Beeldende Kunsten, of the same city. His mid-career retrospective, *Vivir por fuera de la casa de uno*, was organized by the Museo Amparo, Puebla (2010). His work has been shown at the Philadelphia Museum of Art (2008), Irish Museum of Art (2008), Museo de Arte Latinoamericano, Buenos Aires (2006), Museo de Ciencias y Arte, Mexico City (2006), Museum Boijmans van Beunigen (2003), and at the San Francisco MoMA (2003). He was also part of the Dutch pavilion at the 50th Venice Biennial (2003).

CARL ANDRE

Carl Andre is an American artist who was born in Quincy, Massachusetts in 1935. His sculptural installations possess a minimalist approach following linear and gridded formats. He uses basic building materials (i.e. bricks, stones and tiles) and arranges them in symmetrical compositions without any binding material.

Andre studied art at the Phillips Academy in Andover and formed acquaintances with several artists that would influence his art such as Hollis Frampton, Constantin Brâncuşi and Frank Stella. He, along with the rest of the men in his family, had experience with blue collar labor, such as building or metal working trades.

Although several elements of architecture are present in his installation (i.e. building materials, symmetry and mathematical principles) what is absent are the very factors that join the elements together (the binding material). This fact qualifies these installations as aesthetic instead of functional. It is not the artist's aim to connect the units to one another to create a building structure, but rather to arrange them. Thus, he is establishing both a synecdochical relationship between each unit to the whole, as well as its relationship to the exhibition space that it inhabits.

Several retrospective shows of Andre's work have taken place at the Solomon R. Guggenheim Museum, New York (1970), the Whitechapel Art Gallery, London (1978), Dallas Museum of Fine Arts (1979), the Stedelijk Van Abbemuseum, Eidehoven (1987), the Haus Lange und Haus Esters, Krefeld (1996), the Musée Cantini, Marseilles (1997) and The Cinati Foundation in Marfa (2010).

JOHN BALDESSARI

John Baldessari was born in National City, California in 1932. He has been defined as a conceptual artist since the late 1950s, when he was "born again" after burning all of his previous work as a painter. A constant aspect of his work is his eclecticism and his ability to challenge expectations. Throughout five decades of continuous work, Baldessari has reinvented himself by using different media such as painting, photography, sculpture, collage and installation. Teaching has also been a very important part of his career. He taught several generations of artists as a professor at the California Institute for the Arts, and more recently was part of the *The Rolex Mentor and Protégé Arts Initiative* (2007). In this program an established artist mentors a younger one for a period of one year.

The pieces *Figure (Green) with Side of Beef/Two Figures (Gray) with Food (1990)* and *Two Faces: Three Figures; One Shadow* (1988) are perfect examples of how Baldessari has worked with appropriation of images and photography. Pre-existing images (photographs in this case) have been manipulated by the artist by covering them or cutting from them specific forms or strategically placed dots. In doing so, a figure that is cut out is seen as a mere outline, whether it is filled in with acrylic paint or left empty. Both of the pieces presented here create an uncanny feeling by concealing the faces of the characters. For instance, in *Figure (Green)*... we cannot see the couple standing before the food. We do not know who they are or why they are there. Baldessari uses fragmentation, cutting and appropriation to create new images from old ones, compelling the audience to question where these pictures (or people) are coming from, and what are they trying to tell us.

Baldessari's practice has gone through several stages; he has worked on abstract painting, appropriation and manipulation of found photographs, as well as T.V. and film stills, sculpture and exhibition design. A constant in his artistic production has been the combination of texts, appropriated photos and images from T.V. and film. He has shown his work extensively around the world, and some of his latest exhibitions include: *John Baldessari: Pure Beauty* at LACMA, Los Angeles (2010), *John Baldessari: From Life* at the Musée d'art Contemporain, Nimes, France, and *John Baldessari: Life's Balance,* (Works 1984-2004) at the Museum Moderner Kunst Stiftung Ludwig Wien, in Vienna, Austria, both in 2005. In 2006 he had solo exhibitions at the Marian Goodman Gallery in París and New York, and in 2008 his work was part of the Whitney Biennial.

LOTHAR BAUMGARTEN

Lothar Baumgarten was born in Rheinsberg, Germany in 1944. He works in a broad range of media, including photography, slide projections, sculpture, drawing and installation. Baumgarten utilizes objects and written words to explore geography and history in relation to exchange, colonization and migration processes. The son of an anthropologist and a student of Joseph Beuys, Baumgarten is familiar with the works of Claude Lévi-Strauss. In his works, he questions the representation of "the other" in the West, often by analyzing ethnographic museums and their models and methods.

Baumgarten, who works in the space between art and anthropology, often focuses on representations of South-American myths, tropical wildlife and jungle landscapes as a way to point to the cultural implications in representations of nature. This can be seen in his works *Antizipierte Gürteltiere* (1969), *Äskulap* (1971) and *Conquista Rochade* (1971), in which animals and tropical scenes are presented under titles that reference Western European culture, such as Greek mythology: Asclepius, the god of medicine, is represented by two serpents intertwined around a branch. The juxtaposition of the scene with the title leads to unexpected associations.

Another example is the traveling exhibition entitled *Carbon*, in which Baumgarten presented photographs along railway lines in the United States to document the decay of bridges, structures, traffic lights and locomotives. In this work, the names of the stations often reference the Native Americans that first inhabited the land, and represent the encounter and the clash of ancient cultures with progress. The native tongues are juxtaposed with the unstoppable European penetration. Some of his works have been designed for specific contexts. America *(Invention)* (1993) was made for the Rotunda of The Solomon R. Guggenheim Museum. In this piece he imprinted the name of Native American peoples on the interior curves of Frank Lloyd Wright's famous ramp.

Lothar Baumgarten has had numerous exhibitions. His most recent solo exhibitions are *Kunsthaus Bregenz*, Bregenz, Austria (2009) and *Autofocus Retina*, Museu d'Art Contemporani de Barcelona (MACBA) (2008). His group shows include *Universal Archive: The Condition of the Document and the Modern Photographic Utopia,* Museu Colecçao Berardo, Lisbon, Portugal (2009), among many others. He has participated in Documenta four times, and won the Golden Lion of the 41st Venice Biennial (1984) and the Lichtwark Prize in Hamburg (1996).

MARK BRADFORD

Mark Bradford was born in Los Angeles, California in 1961 and lives and works in that city. He received a BFA (1995) and MFA (1997) from the California Institute of the Arts in Valencia where he was a student of Daniel Joseph Martínez, who influenced his approach to identity politics.

Bradford is best known for his "paintings" made out of recycled, scavenged materials taken from the billboards and broadsheets posted as advertisement in the streets. Bradford reapplies these raw materials and their references to underground economies and migrant communities on to large and middle-scale canvases, which are then carefully reworked into abstract works whose forms often recall urban maps, populated streets and networks diagrams. Memories of their source remain however, making them artifacts of a specific time in the city—and particularly of the artist's own African American community of South Central Los Angeles, where he has lived since childhood.

Mark Bradford has received many awards, including the Bucksbaum Award (2006); the Louis Comfort Tiffany Foundation Award (2003) and the Joan Mitchell Foundation Award (2002). He has been included in major exhibitions at the Institute of Contemporary Art Boston (2010); Los Angeles County Museum of Art (2006); Whitney Museum of American Art, New York (2003); REDCAT, Los Angeles (2004) and Studio Museum in Harlem, New York (2001). He has participated in the XXVII São Paulo Bienal (2006); the Whitney Biennial (2006) and *inSite: Art Practices in the Public Domain*, San Diego, California and Tijuana, Mexico (2005).

IÑAKI BONILLAS

Iñaki Bonillas was born in Mexico City in 1981. He works primarily with photography. His work is both a reflection on the physical and mechanical act of taking pictures, and the way in which those pictures are organized. Therefore, the archive is as important for him as the production of the object to be classified. In his early works, Bonillas's interest in photography as a technique did not involve an interest in the represented subject, but rather the formal features such as how light and time were represented in the image. In doing so he dealt with the way in which we perceive the "back" of things, making an analogy between the image and its negative. His works are always built in relationship to the archive and its seriality and lately he has started working with given sets of images and photographs that belong to his personal and family environment.

Bonillas is not particularly interested in the visual qualities of an isolated photograph, but rather in photography as a techique. Therefore, his artworks are often presented as installations or sound art pieces, where he uses technical procedures to research, question and document representation itself, emphasizing the qualities that might go unnoticed at first sight.

The series *Martín-Lunas* was made using a family photo album he inherited from his grandfather, J. R. Plaza. The series is composed of images in which the face of Martín Luna has been obliterated by being covered with a black spot. The album inherited from his grandfather has been a source of inspiration for Bonillas, who interprets it in different ways every time he works with it, finding material for his projects.

Bonillas' work has been shown at the Middelheimmuseum (2008), the Casa del Lago Juan José Arreola (2006), the Prague Biennial (2005), the Venice Biennial (2003), the San Diego Museum of Art (2002) and the Museo de Arte Carrillo Gil (2000).

MIGUEL CALDERÓN

Miguel Calderón was born in Mexico City in 1972. He received a Masters of Arts at the San Francisco Art Institute (1994). Calderon's practice is characterized by the adoption of pop culture and mass media aesthetics and languages. Even if he transgresses the traditional imagery and approach of Mexican art, he also uses some symbols and behaviors unique to contemporary Mexican society—and does so ironically, with a sharp sense of humor.

Calderón has been catalogued as the *enfant terrible* of Mexican contemporary art for challenging the aesthetics of conceptual art and making clever satires of middle-class aspirations. During the 1990s, the economic and political situation in Mexico underwent major changes, which brought about a socio-political crisis that

Calderón has portrayed from a scathing and critical perspective. This practice involves recycling commonplace icons and situations in contemporary society while allowing the audience to feel part of the artwork.

In 2004 Calderón was invited to represent Mexico at the Sao Paulo Biennial with the piece *México vs Brasil*. In this video, sport fanatism is used as a strategy to deconstruct nationalist symbols. Through careful editing, Calderón created an imaginary soccer match where Mexico beats Brazil with a final score of 17-0, a utopian aim for any Mexican soccer fan.

Calderon's artwork has been widely exhibited, including: *Las implicaciones de la imagen, Colección Isabel y Agustín Coppel* at the MUCA, Mexico City (2008); *Playback* at the Musée d'Art Moderne de la Ville de Paris, Paris (2007); *Emotive and Ironic-2 Mexicans* at the Speed Art Museum, Louisville (2006); *Ultra Baroque: Aspects of Post-Latin American Art* at the Walker Art Center, Minneapolis (2002) and *Joven Entusiasta* at the Museo Tamayo de Arte Contemporáneo, Mexico City (1999). His works were also shown at the Sao Paulo Biennial (2004) and at the Yokohama International Triennale of Contemporary Art (2005).

SOPHIE CALLE
Sophie Calle, born in Paris, France in 1953, is a conceptual artist who primarily works with photography, installation, performance and writing. Fascinated by human vulnerability as well as issues of identity and intimacy, her early work involved revealing different aspects of strangers' lives. The artist is especially interested in presenting the limit between our public lives and our private selves.

The suffering from a break up is the subject of the piece *Count up to Unhappiness: Day 50*. In 1984 Calle was awarded a grant to go to Japan. The start of that trip marked the beginning of a 92 day countdown to the end of a love relationship she was having. The artist defines the break up as the unhappiest moment of her life. On the 92nd day of her trip the artist was supposed to meet with her lover in New Delhi, instead she received a phone call from him to end their relationship. On the left side of the work Calle embroidered the text that refers to the conversation she had with her lover together with a photograph of the phone she used to talk to him. For the right side of the piece the artist asked people to describe their worst day of their lives and she embroidered their response together with a photograph to illustrate it. The artist stated that these stories made her pain manageable.

Calle has individually exhibited her work at Palais de Tokyo in Paris (2010), Museum of Modern Art in Salvador de Bahia, Brazil (2009), 52nd Venice Biennale in Italy (2007), Centre Georges Pompidou in Paris, France (2003), Museum Ludwig in Budapest, Hungary (2001), the Tate Gallery in London (1998) and Fundación La Caixa in Madrid, Spain (1996). Her work has been part of group exhibitions in institutions such as the San Francisco Museum of Modern Art (2010) and Solomon R. Guggenheim Museum in New York (2010), among many others.

MAURIZIO CATTELAN
Maurizio Cattelan was born in Padua, Italy in 1960. Using different media such as sculpture, performance and installation, Cattelan plays with ethical limits with a peculiar irony and cynicism, giving new meaning to situations that denounce the absurdity of human existence in the contemporary world. Utilizing role-playing and exploiting the potential of a staged theatrical simulation, Cattelan sets forth a range of characters whose perplexing actions often push the audience's tolerance to its limits.

The characters in Cattelan's works adopt opposing roles from the ones they usually have in their ordinary lives, often pushing them to coexist in contradictory landscapes and to generate their own context. Cattelan often works with taxidermied animals which adopt human behavior such as suicidal squirrels to mice comfortably sitting in beach chairs. The sculpture *Untitled (Sitting donkey, Trento)* (2004) is, as the title suggests, a donkey sitting in a pensive pose—a postmodern melancholic thinker at odds with the world.

Cattelan's work has been widely exhibited and collected. Solo shows include Kunsthaus Bregenz, Bregenz, Germany (2008), Tate Modern, London (2007), Museum fur Modern Kunst, Frankfurt am Rhein (2007). He has participated in group exhibitions around the globe, such as *Mapping the Studio: Artists from the François Pinault Collection,* Punta della Dogana, Venice (2009), *Las Implicaciones de la Imagen, Colección Isabel y Agustín Coppel* at the MUCA, Mexico City (2008); in Now, at the Mussee d'Art Moderne de la Ville de Paris (2004); at MOCA Los Angeles (2003); in *Felix*, at the MCA Chicago (2003-2001) and in *Forum*, at the Centre Georges Pompidiu (2000). His work has also been part of some important biennials such as the IV Berlin Biennial for Contemporary Art (2006), The Whitney Museum of American Art Biennial (2004) and the 49th and 50th Venice Biennial (2001) (2003).

LYGIA CLARK
Lygia Clark was born in Brazil (1920) where she died in 1988. The work by this artist defies categories. Clark made paintings, sculptures, performances, objects and also worked as a researcher, a theoretician and a therapist. Along with Hélio Oiticica and Lygia Pape, Clark was part of Neo-Concretism. At the beginning

of her career her work was influenced by Neo-plasticism and Russian Constructivism, although later Clark abandoned abstract geometry and centered her explorations on the idea of the audience as an active participant in the works. In 1967 she created her work Sensorial Masks, which were meant to be worn over the head. These masks include eyeglasses, earplugs, scented pockets and mirrors, offering an unusual experience for the senses.

In 1960 she started working on her series of metal structures called *Bichos* [Bugs], sculptures made of hinged plates of metal that could be manipulated by the audience. Thus, the shape and the meaning of the piece could be changed by this interaction and its configuration became open and unpredictable. The piece shown in this exhibition is part of this series.

Her work has been shown four times at the Sao Paulo Biennial. She was part of *Documenta X* (1997) and *XII* (2007), as well as the 34th Venice Biennial (1968), where she presented the installation The House is a Body. Since the early 1990s Clark has received increasing international recognition and today her work is key to understanding the participatory dimension in contemporary art. The Fundación Antoni Tàpies held a solo show of the artist in 1997, and recently she has been part of the traveling exhibition *Tropicalia: a Revolution in Brazilian Culture* (2005).

ABRAHAM CRUZVILLEGAS

Abraham Cruzvillegas was born in Mexico City in 1968. His work explores two different aspects of sculpture. On the one hand, he works with appropriated *ready-made* objects; on the other, he redefines the manual work and crafts used in traditional folk techniques by putting them in the context of Mexican contemporary art today. His appropriation of objects and new ways of using old techniques as a contemporary artistic practice have become the central axis of Cruzvillegas' inquiries, who assumes the cultural condition of an artist who works *from and in* Mexico City. His work tries to assimilate the permanence of certain work methods which are increasingly obsolete, the mechanisms of survival employed by craftspeople, as well as utilizing craft as a symbol. In other words, Cruzvillegas brings attention to the different social and economic classes aligned with labor economies who still subsist in Mexico today.

Between 1995 and 1997 Cruzvillegas visited several indigenous communities in the state of Michoacán "with the intention of learning the craft techniques that have traditionally constituted the means of sustenance for the Purépecha population," he explained. This preconceived plan marked the intellectual position of the artist in relation to what he has established as a series of opposites: the individual identity confronting mass identity; manual labor versus industrial labor and fine arts versus crafts.

In 2003 he started working on a series of pieces that point to the paradox of Mexican modernity which exists in a space between a pre-industrial period of handcrafts and post-industrial culture. In this series he juxtaposes the names of the streets of the neighborhood where he grew up—*Unión, Progreso, Sindicalismo, Ciencias, Ingenieros, Constitución*—with his choice of materials to represent them. Progreso (2003), for example, is made of brass hinges, Moroccan toothpick, weed flowers, golf tees and Campeche wax, which are put together to create an abstract, highly evocative sculpture.

Cruzvillegas has exhibited widely, including *The Exhibition Formerly Known as Passengers*, Wattis Institute, San Francisco (2009), *Autoconstrucción: The Soundtrack* at The Centre for Contemporary Arts, CCA Glasgow (2008); *Las implicaciones de la imagen.* Colección Isabel y Agustín Coppel at the Museo de Ciencias y Artes, Mexico City (2008); *Los dos amigos. Dr. Lakra & Abraham Cruzvillegas* at the Museo de Arte Contemporáneo de Oaxaca, Mexico (2005); *Abraham Cruzvillegas* at the Museo de Arte Contemporáneo de Monterrey, Mexico (2004). His work was part of the 50th Venice Biennial (2003) and of the Sao Paulo Biennial (2002). In 2008 he was awarded a Smithsonian Institute Artist Research Fellowship and in 2009 the Capp Street Residency en Wattis Institute for Contemporary Arts, San Francisco, California.

JOSE DAMASCENO

Jose Damasceno was born in Rio de Janeiro, Brazil in 1968 where he continues to live and work. He studied architecture at Santa Úrsula University and shows a playful and participatory approach to sculpture. He primarily derives his ideas from those developed during the 1950s and 1960s in Brazil by neo-concrete artists such as Lygia Clark, Amilcar de Castro, Lygia Pape or Helio Oiticia. A second generation of artists working with sculpture and installation in Brazil in the 1970s including Cildo Meireles and Waltercio Caldas are also seminal for the artist.

Damasceno often manipulates unorthodox materials such as telephone books, chess pieces or blackboard erasers, to create works that develop meticulous repetitions related to systems and improvisation. Ideas of order and chaos are also the subject of his works of art as well as the duality of organic forms versus geometric and mathematical shapes. Through his artistic manipulation of architectural spaces, Damasceno generates specific dialogues with the surrounding areas creating displacement and unexpected events that cause awareness of issues related to scale, proportion and perception.

Damasceno has individually showed his work at Museo Nacional Centro de Arte Reina Sofía in Madrid, Spain (2008), 52nd Venice

Biennale in Italy (2007) and Museo de Arte Moderno in Rio de Janeiro, Brazil (2001), among others. His work has been part of group exhibitions at Centre Pompidou in Paris, France (2008), Museu de Arte Moderna de Bahia in Salvador de Bahia, Brazil (2007), New Museum of Contemporary Art in New York (2003) and Museo de Arte Contemporáneo in Mexico City (2000). Damasceno is part of the permanent collection of MACBA, Barcelona, Spain, Daros Latinoamerica in Zurich, Switzerland, Museo de Arte Moderno in Sao Paulo, Brazil and CIFO in Miami.

RINEKE DIJKSTRA

Rineke Dijkstra was born in Sittart, in the south of Holland, in 1959. She studied at the Gerrit Rietveld Academie of Amsterdam from 1981 to 1986, where she specialized in photography. Ever since she was a student, Dijkstra worked for newspapers, taking pictures of young people in nightclubs. From that moment on, she was interested in depicting people who are undergoing some sort of change, when their attitudes and personalities vary in a meaningful way. With time, capturing these changes became the main feature of her portraits.

The work by Dijkstra became known worldwide with the series *Beaches* made between 1992 and 1996 in the United States and Eastern Europe. In these photographs, we see children and teenagers in classical portrait poses (seen from the front, with a very simple backdrop such as the seashore). The images are also singular because they reflect a very significant moment for them, the moment when they become adults. Another important example of her work is the series of portraits of boys and girls as they enter the military service, during their exercises and when they leave. In these before-and-after portraits the artist reflects on how these young people, to some extent, abandon their individual identity when they become part of a collective group.

The series of bullfighters was created in 1994, just after she made the portraits of women who had just given birth to their first babies. Dijkstra traveled to Portugal where she took pictures of *forcados* just after they had been in a bullfight. In many of these images we can see the expression of satisfaction and tiredness in the faces of her subjects, who appear covered in blood and mud. It is obvious that they have gone through an experience where they have risked their lives, but also that this experience is a source of pride. Like the tired and satisfied mothers of a first-born baby that appear in the pictures she did during the same period, the *forcados* look satisfied and exhausted after risking their lives. In both these portraits the artist shows male and female archetypes, portraying these men and women in a critical and transforming instant of their lives.

Dijkstra has shown her work in solo exhibitions in Europe, the United States and Israel: in 2001, the Art Institute of Chicago showed *FOCUS: Rieneke Dijkstra*, in 2005 La Caixa in Barcelona showed *Rieneke Dijkstra-Portraits*, in 2006 she had a retrospective at the Rudolfinum in Prague called Rieneke Dijkstra, Portraits (Retrospective). In 2008 her work was part of the group show: *Street & Studio: An Urban History of Photography* at the Tate Modern in London.

WILLIAM EGGLESTON

William Eggleston was born in Memphis, Tennessee. He started his career in 1937 photographing the Southern United States. From the mid 1970s on he turned to color photography to capture ordinary people, unlike other photographers of that time, who used black and white to distinguish their pictures from fashion and advertising photography. Studying Eggleston's work in color photography is fundamental to the understanding of twentieth-century art photography.

From Elvis Presley's mansion to the Smokey Mountains in the Appalachians, his photographs witness the history of his native country. Eggleston also made several trips abroad, photographing in Europe, Africa, Asia and Latin America and has collaborated on several films with directors such as Gus Van Sant. His photography has also been associated with the music industry because of his portraits of celebrities like David Byrne and his collaborations with *Rolling Stone* Magazine.

The 1976 solo show *Eggleston's Guide*, at New York's Museum of Modern Art, defined Eggleston as a seminal color photographer spanning the fields of street photography to contemporary art photography. In 2002 his *Los Alamos* series—a group of pictures taken between 1964 and 1973—started touring important museums in Europe and the United States. The photograph *Untitled (Shack with yellow door)* included in this exhibition is part of that series. It portrays one of the typical shacks in this region of Texas in lively yellow, orange and green hues.

William Eggleston is the recipient of a 1974 grant from the Guggenheim. In 1975 and 1978 he got other grants from the National Endowment for the Arts. In 1998 he received the Hasselblad Award and in 1996 the Getty Images Lifetime Achievement Award. His work has been shown in museums around the world, the most recent exhibition was the traveling retrospective *William Eggleston Democratic Camera,* 1961-2008, Whitney Museum of Art, New York (2008).

FISCHLI AND WEISS

Since 1979 Peter Fischli (b. 1952) and David Weiss (n. 1946) have been collaborating together to create a very diverse body of work that includes film and photography, art books, sculptures and multi-media installations. They are among the best known contemporary artists from Switzerland. In their work Fischli/Weiss combine, rearrange or manipulate their daily experiences into something new and unexpected. The base of their artistic vision is the use of everyday objects that they transform into surprisingly lifelike quality items. The childlike spirit of their productions, as well as the humor and irony they use, encourage the viewer to perceive reality with a new fresh perspective. The best known work of art by Fischli/Weiss is probably the video *The Way Things Go* (1987) in which an improbable chain of events makes objects fly, crash and explode across the studio.

Fischli/Weiss have exhibited their work in solo exhibitions at Museo Nacional Centro de Arte Reina Sofia, Madrid, Spain (2009), Tate Modern, London (2006), Museo Tamayo, Mexico (2005), Walker Art Center, Minneapolis (2004), White Cube, London (1998), Museum of Modern Art, San Francisco (1997), Centre George Pompidou, Paris (1992) and IVAM, Valencia, Spain (1990), among others.

FLOR GARDUÑO

Flor Garduño was born in Mexico City in 1957. When she was very young her family moved outside of the city. Between 1976 and 1978, she studied at the San Carlos Academy (with Hungarian photographer Kati Horna) and before she finished her studies she started working in the photo lab of Manuel Álvarez Bravo, one of the most important artists of twentieth century Mexican photography. In 1981 and 1982, she worked on a project for the *Secretaría de Educación Pública* (Department of Public Education) coordinated by photographer Mariana Yampolsky. Her job was to travel to different states in Mexico, portraying the ethnic groups who lived there and their way of life. That experience shaped her way of seeing and understanding portraiture, creating the style that has made her a well-known artist.

Several books on her work have been published outside of Mexico. In *Flor/Inner Light*, published in 2002, the artist presents images of women who are only illuminated by natural light. These women all of them Garduño's friends often decided their own poses and the objects they wanted to be portrayed with. In this series, Garduño shows her interest in the female body and its resemblance to a flower, hence the Spanish title of the book. In 2005, she published *Silent Natures*. This book includes a series of photographs taken between 1988 and 2003 where we see fruits, animals, and photos of paintings in works that emphasize composition and shape.

The Blessing, from 1990, is part of *Witnesses of Time* the 1992 publication and traveling show which contains a series of pictures of indigenous peoples in Mexico, Guatemala, Ecuador, Peru and Bolivia; of their religious rituals and their everyday life. In *The Blessing* we see the hands of a man who seems some sort of religious authority while he soaks a flower in a small cup with holy water in it. The image, simple and delicate, shows several characteristic features of the work by Garduño: the indigenous world, the contrast of defined tones and textures in her pictures and nature as subject matter. All of these elements are combined in her work, evoking a previous time that, nonetheless, is still present in our society.

The work of Flor Garduño has been shown around the world. Some of her most important solo and group exhibitions are: *Flor* (2006) at the Scottsdale Museum of Contemporary Art in Scottsdale, Arizona, *Flor* at the Mois de la Photographie (2006) in Paris, France and *Testemunhos Do Tempo* (Witnesses of time) shown at the Portuguese Center for Photography and at ARCO 2008 in Madrid, Spain.

KENDELL GEERS

Kendell Geers was born in May 1968 in South Africa, a fictitious date notoriously corresponding to the political world movements of May 1968 in Paris as well the date of Marcel Duchamp's death. Geers, who now lives in Brussels and London, has been making artworks with a strong political and conceptual content since the end of the 1980s. His provocative art questions politics, as well as racial and religious stereotypes, from the perspective of the art world. With the use of very few elements, his pieces often convey strong and hostile messages in a subtly poetic way.

Geers' 2007 exhibition entitled *Kannibale*, at the Yvon Lambert Gallery in Paris is a good example of his approach. The show was based on the *Antropophagic Manifest*, written by Brazilian poet Oswald de Andrade in 1928. In that context, cannibalism is a metaphor for the incorporation of values and cultures that are "not ours, foreign to us." The title was also a tribute to *Cannibale*, a Dadaist magazine published by Francis Picabia in1921, where the term was related to the way in which men "eat" each other during wars. Constantly keeping a point of tension and a confrontation between the works and the audience, Geers appropriated these cultural and ideological notions of cannibalism to deal with issues related to politics, abuse of power, economical exploitation and domination over foreign cultures. In the 2007 exhibition he showed a replica of the Nike of Samothrace—the iconic winged Greek sculpture that has been displayed at the Louvre since 1884—totally painted over with the word FUCK. With this work, Geers clearly exemplifies the "cannibalization" of artworks by different cultures and societies.

The neon sculptures *B/ORDER* and *D/ANGER* (2003) speak of the ambiguity of the "border/order" and "danger/anger." These neon signs seem to have a short circuit that makes the first letter go on and off intermittently, pointing at the cause and the effect of their meaning while obscuring the relationship. Even as the artworks confront the viewer with notions of power, submission, and domination, they also involve the sharp sense of humor displayed in many works by Geers.

In 2008, the first large retrospective of this artist's work called *Irrespektiv* was held at the BALTIC Contemporary Art Center in Gateshead, England. The show traveled to the Musée Art Contemporain in Lyon, France in September 2008 and to the Museo di Arte Moderna e Contemporanea in Trento, Italy in February 2009.

FERNANDA GOMES

Fernanda Gomes was born in Rio de Janeiro, Brazil in 1960. Her artistic investigation involves the scavenging of ordinary "things" and exhibiting them in installations and assemblages. She creates an intimate relationship between these seemingly insignificant objects and integrates them into the exhibition space. Her objective is for the viewers to discover and pay attention to these subtle interventions and to rediscover the significance of such ordinary "things."

Her installations are commonly considered as site-specific; she collects seemingly insignificant things in and around the surrounding area where the exhibition is to take place. The exhibition space itself is integral to the installation because the artist is concerned with the way the works of art engage with their surroundings. In this way, Gomes makes a direct correlation between the project and the site by bringing in the discarded things and preserving them in the artistic process.

An exhibition that took place at the Baumgartner Gallery in New York (2006) featured objects, such as clear packaging tape, wire and thin threads that were placed in such a way as to impose a physical barrier between the viewer. Once these objects were discovered, the awareness of the subtleties of surface required the viewer to pay attention to the trace that the objects left behind in the space.

She has participated in the Venice Biennial, 2003; the Sydney Biennial, 1998; the International Istanbul Biennial, 1995 and the São Paulo Biennale, 1994. Her work has been featured in solo exhibitions at Matadero, Madrid (2008), the Museu de Arte Contemporânea de Serralves, Porto (2006), Patio Herreriano, Museo de Arte Contemporáneo Español in Valladolid (2005) and the Museu de Arte da Pampulha, Belo Horizonte (2004). The artist lives and works in Rio de Janeiro, Brazil.

DAN GRAHAM

American artist Dan Graham was born in Urbana, Illinois in 1942. During the 1960s and 70s he was a pioneer of installation, performance and video art. At that time he also ran an art gallery in New York, where artists such as Robert Smithson, Dan Flavin and Donald Judd had their first exhibitions. He has used a wide range of media to produce experimental works. For instance, *Schema* (1966) is a set of instructions for a magazine article that changes from publication to publication, as the content of the article is merely a descriptive calculation of its published components (verbs, nouns, type of paper and so on).

Throughout his career, Graham has had a special interest in the relation between art and architecture. One example is the project *Two-Way Mirror* (1991), a glass structure designed as a small scale urban park on the rooftop of a building in Chelsea, New York, made in collaboration with architects Mojdeh Bartaloo and Clifton Balch. His interest in architecture has led him to present pieces in all kinds of public spaces, including art biennial pavilions such as Sao Paulo or Venice, where the audience is confronted with notions of transparency and reflection, the public and the private and the development of surveillance systems in open and enclosed spaces.

Between 2004 and 2006 he presented the installation *Don't Trust Anyone Over Thirty (Entertainment by Dan Graham and other Collaborators)*. This project is an ironic reflection on the hippie slogan, using a mini rock opera with puppets, people and video screenings to project the vision of those who lived that moment and have grown to realize how youth seduces society, and that idealist movements might still be corrupted.

In 1966, a series of images by Graham called *Homes for America* was published in *Arts Magazine*. This series was an answer to the notion of the grid in the writings of artists such as Sol LeWitt and Donald Judd. They related urban development with conceptual art. *Homes for America* is a series of pictures showing houses in New Jersey, where Graham grew up. The images capture the architecture of American suburbs and, in some cases, the families that lived inside, for example *Two Homes, Housing for Two Families and Family in Backyard* (1978/1969). This series is a photo and image essay on the changes of color and style in domestic architecture.

Graham has shown his work individually and in group exhibitions in important galleries and museums around the world. Some of his latest solo shows are *Dan Graham: Beyond*, Museum of Contemporary Art, Los Angeles, Whitney Museum of American Art, New York; Walker Art Center, Minneapolis (2009); *Dan Graham*,

Museo d'Arte Contemporaena, Turin, Italy (2006); *Dan Graham. Retrospective* at the Chiba Museum of Art in Chiba, Japan (2004) and the traveling exhibition *Dan Graham Works: 1965-2000* shown at the Museu Serralves, Porto, Portugal; the Arc/Musée d'Art Moderne de la Ville de Paris, Paris, France; the Kröller-Müller Museum, Otterlo, Netherlands and at the Dusselforf Kunsthalle, Germany (2001-02).

DANIEL GUZMÁN

Daniel Guzmán was born in 1964 in Mexico City, where he lives. Guzmán works in a variety of mediums and explores male identity, rock culture and self-portraiture as vehicle of persistent longing. His formal strategies often include appropriation of 1970s and 1980s pop icons—personal heroes and unreachable images from the past that allow the artist to engage in role-playing and projection.

Guzmán is best known for his drawing to which he takes a variety of approaches that include the appropriation of the visual language of Mexican pulp fiction, graffiti and the design styles of informal economies such the underground, pirated music and film industry. But his work is also layered with high art references, particularly to the prints and drawing of Mexican muralist José Clemente Orozco, which are often twisted on their heads or conflated with figures to create imagined, highly poetic narratives.

Exilio (Exile) (2006) is a simple black and white graphic image drawn from a well-known portrait of John Lennon, which is doubled and elongated, as if seen through a psychedelic haze or a fun-house mirror. Loaded with contradictory emotions like nostalgia and irreverence, the piece expresses a direct engagement with the recent history of visual and musical history that persists through the generation that came of age in the 1970s. Daniel Guzmán has participated in solo and group exhibitions, including *Double Album: Daniel Guzmán and Steven Shearer* at the New Museum, New York, USA, MUCA CU, Mexico City (2008); *Golpe De Suerte* at Museo de las Artes, Guadalajara, Mexico (2000); *El horizonte del topo* at BOZ AR, Brussels (2009); *Where do we go from here* at Colección Jumex and Bass Museum of Art, Miami (2009).

ENRIQUE GUZMÁN

Enrique Guzmán was born in Guadalajara, Mexico in 1952. He lived a complex and tragic life which was reflected in his works and ended with his suicide at age 33. The main sources of inspiration in Guzmán's paintings were his memories of things that actually happened or of ideas and imaginary events that only existed in his inner world.

In 1971 he moved to Mexico City to study at the Escuela Nacional de Pintura y Escultura "La Esmeralda," but he abandoned his studies shortly after. Even without formal training, by 1972 he was already a professional artist who took the Mexican art scene by surprise. Mexican contemporary art was undergoing a transformation and that time is known collectively as the "Ruptura" or period of "Rupture." The artists in this group had moved away from Mexican Modernist painting and Muralism into abstract art. Instead, Guzmán worked with figurative paintings influenced by Surrealism and recovered the use of national icons in a game that oscillated between kitsch and sarcasm. In the painting *Oh Santa Bandera (Oh Holy Flag)* (1977), for example, we see the Mexican flag, but instead of the coat of arms at its center there lies an open mouth that seems to be shouting or laughing.

His work is a milestone in the history of twentieth-century Mexican Art. His work was the subject of a retrospective entitled *Enrique Guzmán. Su destino secreto (Enrique Guzmán: His Secret Fate)*, which was presented at the Museo de Arte Contemporaneo, Monterrey, and at the Museo de Arte Moderno, Mexico City (1999). It has been exhibited in important group historical surveys such as *Eco - Arte Contemporaneo Mexicano* at the Museo Nacional Reina Sofia, 2005 and *La Era de la Discrepancia Arte y Cultura Visual en Mexico 1968-1997* at the MUCA, 2007.

JONATHAN HERNÁNDEZ

Jonathan Hernández was born in Mexico City in 1972. The artist uses the Mexican context to establish a dialogue between the audience and reality combining ironic and humorous compositions that show the shortcomings, vices and realities of the Mexican people. From an analytic point of view, we could say that the books, collages, objects and videos by Jonathan Hernández freeze time, resembling snapshots that constitute a personal-social, individual -collective record. All of his pieces—his research and subject matter—are works in progress, a function of recorded time, of the possibility of displacement. Jonathan locates himself on the other side, on the other side of the border, virtually self-displaced; hence his early identification with the figure of the tourist—the consumer of representations. This de-centered intellectual position is the one that allows him to create what he calls "another social and mental space."

Perhaps the peculiar craftsmanship and the imperfection that accompanies the objects manufactured by him are nothing but another intellectual construction of time, as if he stubbornly aged whatever is contemporary. Hernández has positioned himself in what we would define as a skeptical intellectual position. Hence, the interference of humor in his constructions comes as a response to the quest for demolishing any notion of certitude, and not from a nostalgic vision of the close past, or a criticism of modernity—even if that criticism is also included in his works. His practice revolves around observing and recording—from a different perspective—the construction of thought as it is shaped by the media, as if they were able to restructure the notion of time.

Vulnerabilia (Water, Fire, Mass, Ruins) (2005) is a work-in-progress made of newspaper cuttings that gather a "visual essay" that addresses social, political, and cultural concerns. Although the artist is still working on this piece, he has also used it as the source for other works, such as the *Ronwrong* collages and the series *Estados vaciosos.*

Among his most important exhibitions are: Pospreterito at Sala de Arte Público Siqueiros (2006), *Tráfago*, organized by Kurimanzutto in Mexico City (2004) and *Bon Voyage*, in Centro de Arte Contemporáneo de Málaga, Spain (2003). He has also participated in exhibitons such as: *En Algún lugar alguién está viajando furiosamente hacia ti*, La Casa Encendida, Madrid; *Come Closer*, Künstlerhaus Bethanien, Berlin and FarSites: *Urban Crisis & Domestic Symptoms in Recent Contemporary Art*, San Diego Museum of Art.

GRACIELA ITURBIDE

Graciela Iturbide was born in Mexico City in 1942. Her photographic work is well-known for its portrayal of the culture, traditions, rituals and every day life of Mexico. In 1962, Graciela Iturbide began studying at the Centro Universitario de Estudios Cinematograficos. In 1970, she met Manuel Álvarez Bravo and soon became his student and assistant. This experience was fundamental in her choice to pursue photography as a career. Her images are composed of particular realities and ordinary characters. In her photographs, each scene tells a little story inspired by her trips and the curiosity she feels for "otherness."

Throughout her career she has collaborated with different artists, and her work has been praised throughout the world. Her photographs often depict scenes that evoke nostalgia and tell stories related to the Mexican culture. Death is also a frequent subject matter in her works. The artist lost her 6 year old daughter in the early 1970s and her photographs convey this experience by affirming the relation between life and death.

She has also been interested in taking photographs of some of Mexico's native communities, such as the Zapotecas from Juchitán or the Seris from Sonora. In this documentary-style work she combines social elements with the natural environment. In *Cementerio, Juchitán, Oaxaca* [Cemetery, Juchitán, Oaxaca](1988), Iturbide portrays a Zapoteca woman picking twigs. The photograph shows a melancholic and quiet atmosphere, and it turns reality into something that—to the eyes of the audience—appears as dream-like scene.

Her works have been in exhibitions throughout the world, some of her major solo shows are: *The Goat ́s Dance,* The J. Paul Getty Museum, Los Angeles (2007), *Ojos para volar*, Centro de la Imagen, Mexico City (2007); *Pájaros / Naturata*, Centro Fotográfico Manuel Alvarez Bravo, Oaxaca, (2005); *Naturata*, Museo de Bellas Artes, Río de Janeiro (2005) and *Graciela Iturbide: Images of the Spirit*, Milwaukee Art Museum, Milwaukee (2003). Her most important retrospective show, Graciela Iturbide: Images of the Spirit was exhibited for the first time at the Philadelphia Art Museum in 1997 and then traveled to several cities in the United States and France until 2003. The exhibition *Juchitán pueblo de nube* traveled through the United Kingdom, Argentina and Japan between 1987-1988. She has received several awards, including the W. Eugene Smith Memorial Foundation Award in 1987. In 2007 she received the Legacy Award from the Smithsonian Latino Center and she also received an Honorary Degree in Photography from the Museum of Contemporary Photography at Columbia College, Chicago.

YISHAI JUSIDMAN

Yishai Jusidman was born in Mexico City in 1963 and lives and works in Los Angeles, California. He is known for his conceptual approach to representational painting, which often seeks to implicate the viewer in the representational systems delimited by the picture frame and the tradition of painting.

The Economist Shuffle #15 and *The Economist Shuffle # 16* (2007) are good examples of his recent work. The images are taken from small journalistic photographs from the *The World this Week* section of The Economist magazine. Jusidman fixates on small images that he intuitively feels can become "good paintings," an imaginative move that relies on the artist's deep understanding of the conventions of the genre. Thus enlarged into oil and egg-tempera on wood panels, these images acquire the gravitas of Dutch landscape and are granted the potential drama of history painting.

Solo museum shows include *mutatis mutandis/Working Painters* at S.M.A.K., Ghent, Belgium (2002); MEIAC, Badajoz, Spain (2002) and MARCO, Monterrey, Mexico (2003); *Sumo/en-treat-ment* at Museo Carrillo Gil, Mexico City, (1999) and *Pictorial Investigations*, a traveling show organized by Otis College of Art and Design (1996-98). Jusidman's work was featured at Harald Szeemann's *Platform of Humankind* in the 2001 Venice Biennale; *Eco: Contemporary Art from Mexico*, Reina Sofía, Madrid, (2005) and Ultrabaroque,

Aspects of post-Latin American Art, which traveled from Museum of Contemporary Art San Diego to, SFMOMA, Walker Art Center, MAM Miami, (2000-03). His survey show took place at Museo de Arte Moderno, Mexico City, (2009).

TERENCE KOH

Terence Koh was born in Beijing, China, in 1977, and grew up in Toronto. He lives and works in New York, Berlin and Beijing. His work often consists of site or situation specific performances that generate sculptures, installations and videos. Many of his pieces are monochromatic and in them he uses white, black, red or golden hues. Although his practice does not belong to a specific movement and the final outcome of his working process often involves multiple elements, his work is heavily influenced by minimalism and abstraction.

Duality is important for Koh: emptiness and excess, classicism and kitsch, birth and rebirth. His piece *Skeleton Painting* is a clear example. *Skeleton Painting* is the outcome of a 2006 performance, where Koh—naked—danced with a skeleton covered in white paint, sweat and other bodily fluids, while he held a lit candle in his hands. He danced in front of several mirrors in a darkened space and the mirrors were splashed with white paint and left covered with white strokes. For Koh, the skeleton symbolizes his "Other," and the painting—as the outcome of the dance—the splitting up of his being.

Terence Koh has shown his work in solo exhibitions at the Whitney Museum of Art (2007), the Kunsthalle Zurich (2006) and the Museo de Arte Contemporáneo de Castilla y León (2008). His most relevant group exhibitions are *USA Today* at the Royal Academy in London (2006) and *The Zabludowicz Collection: When We Build, Let Us Think That We Build Forever*, at the BALTIC Centre for Contemporary Art, Gateshead, UK (2008).

HELEN LEVITT

Helen Levitt was born in 1914, in Brooklyn, New York. At 18, after becoming the assistant for a portrait photographer, she pursued a long and productive career in photography. Levitt is one of the most important photographers of the twentieth century. She had a very peculiar style and unlike most of her colleagues she was interested in the life of common people in the streets (especially children). She also was a pioneer of American experimental cinema and one of the first photographers to use and experiment with color in her pictures.

After a period in which she took documentary photographs of the intense social activity of the time (like the Great Depression or the communist movement in the United States), Levitt became deeply influenced by Henri Cartier-Bresson's idea of the decisive moment. Beginning in the 1930s she worked portraying the common people of the poor areas in New York, with a brief period in Mexico City in 1941, where she took the photograph on view (*Untitled, Mexico, D.F.*). Here children of the street are shown in their everyday life with her delicate and poetic way of looking at them.

Levitt's work has been shown around the world, and has recently been presented in diverse retrospectives such as: *Helen Levitt*, Centre National de la Photographie, Paris, France, 2001 and *Helen Levitt: New York Streets*, 1938 to 1990s, Henri Cartier-Bresson Foundation, Paris, France, 2007. In 2008 she won the 6th International Price of Photography Spectrum, given by the Foundation of Lower Saxony, in Hannover, Germany. She died in New York City in 2009.

PHILIP-LORCA DICORCIA

Philip-Lorca diCorcia was born in Connecticut in 1951. The work by Lorca diCorcia represents a kind of photography that wanders between fiction and reality, since the characters portrayed in his images often seem like actors who position themselves on a stage under the orders of a director. The photographs by Lorca diCorcia have a careful film-like illumination. In them, light seems to point at gestures that highlight certain aspects of the portrayed characters or scenes.

The subjects in diCorcia's most important works are often characters who live on the fringes of society: in his series *Hustlers*—made between 1990 and 1992—he used the money of a National Endowment for the Arts grant to hire young men and take them to the places he had chosen for the photo sessions. Each image has the name of the man, his age, his place of origin and the amount he charged for posing. Sometimes the boys seem relaxed, but at others they adopt awkward poses. In *Heads* (1999-2001), another well-known series, diCorcia set some stroboscopic lamps in New York's Times Square and made pictures of unaware passers-by. Even if the photos seem staged because of the lighting and the expressions in the faces of his subjects, they are just snapshots that capture a specific person in a given moment. Emphasized by the drastic close-ups and the theatrical illumination, the coldness of people in large cities is even clearer in these pictures.

The piece *Mexico City,* 1998 is part of his *Streetwork* series made in cities through Europe, the Americas and Asia between 1996 and 1998. In each city, Lorca diCorcia placed lamps in places where the passerby could not notice that a photograph was being taken. The photographer made the shot operating the shutter and a light attached to the camera from afar. The images that come from this process have a detailed and strong illumination as often happens in his work. This photograph—as all the others in this series—shows a group of people in a Mexico City street. The effect makes the photograph look like a film-still; and the poses of the subjects seem contrived as if they were carefully staged by performers: a woman who worries, a man selling sweets who laughs, a child who is eating something and a man who touches his side as he walks self-absorbed.

The work by diCorcia has been shown all around the world including the following solo exhibitions: *Philip-Lorca diCorcia*, Los Angeles County Museum of Art, Los Angeles (2008) and The Institute of Contemporary Art, Boston (2007). He has also participated in numerous group exhibitions such as *Tears of Eros*, Museo Thyssen-Bornemisza, Madrid (2009-10), *Familiar Feelings: On the Boston Group*, Centro Galego de Arte Contemporánea, Santiago de Compostela (2009) and *Mapping the City*, Stedelijk Museum Amsterdam.

JORGE MACCHI

Jorge Macchi was born in Buenos Aires in 1963. He is a contemporary artist who works in a variety of media including collage, photography, installations and video. He works primarily with found objects and establishes paradoxical relationships that drive the viewer to make associations and discoveries between the different objects in question.

His artistic investigations involve the mapping of certain found objects. As he establishes a pattern, he extrapolates from them and translates them in order to explore the ideas of fate, accident, chance, coincidence and violence. He creates these paradoxical works of art and experiments, but does so in a purposeful manner, as to defy what would happen in reality. He does so in a contrived environment where he controls the variables.

The juxtaposition of found objects with opposing characteristics tends to emphasize the extreme differences between them. In *Untitled* (pillow and glass), the idea of a pillow, which immediately evokes the characteristic of softness is covered in a sheet of fractured glass. In *Still Song*, he takes a stationary disco ball and marks the surrounding walls with slashes of where the light would originally be reflected. Thus, he transforms these passive objects into volatile ones.

Macchi has had a long standing artistic collaboration with the composer Eduardo Rudnitzky and different aspects from the music world have also been part of his work. In *Nocturne: variation on Nocturne I by Erik Satie*, Macchi substitutes the music notes on the sheets of music with nails that stab the sheets to the walls. The replacement of a symbol that serves as the visual aide in the physical act of playing music with something potentially violent, abruptly changes the perception of the object.
In 2000 he was awarded the Banco de la Nación Argentina Prize and in 2001 he received the Guggenheim Memorial Foundation Fellowship. His work has been featured in the Venice Biennal (2005); the São Paulo Biennal (2004) and the Istanbul Biennal (2003). He has exhibited his work in solo exhibitions at Centro Galego de Arte Contemporaneo in Santiago de Compostela (2008) and the Blanton Museum of Art in Austin (2007), among others.

MAREPE

Marepe was born in Santo Antonio de Jesús, Bahía, Brazil, in 1970. He is internationally known as Marepe, an acronym for Marcos Reis Peixoto. His professional education includes studies in visual arts and agronomy and his artistic vocabulary is nourished by household customs, labor, agriculture, commerce, family and popular celebrations. His father owned a hardware store; the artist often uses objects that come from this kind of store in his work.

Marepe has taken Marcel Duchamp's idea of the *readymade* to create the *nécessaire*, an art object inspired by everyday needs. His installations frequently use accumulations of objects such as slingshots, balloons, buckets, cotton candy, umbrellas and chachaça (distilled liquor). In the installation entitled *Sanfoninha* (2006) the artist showed a pile of papers with the notes for a botany exam on different kinds of leaves. The circle closes when one becomes aware that the paper on which the notes were written comes from trees.

Other installations by Marepe have dealt with issues such as improvised commercial spaces and the poetics of survival. In them, he generates architectural environments that can be modified by the spectators and that provide—in a reduced space—all that is needed to have a cozy home.

The work by Marepe has been shown at the São Paulo Biennial (2002), the Venice Biennial (2003) and the Sydney Biennial (2004). He has also participated in group shows such as When lives become form at Yerba Buena Center for the Arts in San Francisco (2010), *Neohoodoo: Art for a Forgotten Faith* at P.S.1 MOMA, New York (2009), The Thread Unraveled (2001) at the Museo del Barrio in Nueva York, and *Braaaasiiiil* (2008) at the Museo Nacional Centro de Arte Reina Sofía in Madrid.

TERESA MARGOLLES

Teresa Margolles was born in 1963 in Culiacán/Sinaloa. She studied Art at the Dirección de Fomento a la Cultura Regional del Estado de Sinaloa (DIFOCUR) and Forensic Medicine and Communications at UNAM. In 1990 Margolles founded the group SEMEFO – 'Servicio Médico Forense' together with Arturo Ángulo Gallardo, Juan Luis García Zavaleta and Carlos López Orozco. At first the group was active mainly as a rock band and an underground performance group, then it moved into the art scene.

Margolles continued working on her own developing social and conceptual artistic strategies based on the use of bodily substances and images of corpses. Her study of death as her primary subject is related to her concern on researching issues of economic and political disparities, social exploitation and the way violence characterizes the cultural and philosophical landscape of today. Margolles is interested in using the cadaver as a reflection of today's culture and the morgue as an evaluation of the society.

The photographic series *Recados Póstumos* (2006) is based on Margolles' research during her residency at Instituto Cabañas in Guadalajara, México, a city in which the number of deaths by suicide is extremely high (400 deaths per year). The artist used the letters and notes left by the people that committed suicide and placed some of the sentences on the marquees of abandoned movie theatres throughout the city. The artist presents these works as a study of death and a social pattern in a profoundly Catholic community.

Teresa Margolles' work has been exhibited individually in numerous institutions and biennials, including the 53rd Venice Biennale, Italy (2009), and the Liverpool Biennial, United Kingdom (2006), Museo Experimental El Eco, Mexico (2007), Centre d'Art Contemporain de Bretigny, France (2005), Art Palace, Spain (2002); as well as at numerous group exhibition at significant institutions including Museo Carrillo Gil, Mexico, the Guggenheim Museum, U.S.; and the Herzliya Museum of Contemporary Art, Israel.

GORDON MATTA-CLARK

Gordon Matta-Clark was born in 1943 in New York City. He studied Architecture at Cornell University in Ithaca, New York and Literature at the Sorbonne in Paris. His most important body of work was made between 1969 and 1978, the year he died in New York. Matta-Clark was one of the most innovative artists of his period. Although he worked in a variety of media, he is best known for his development of what he called "anarchitecture"—a practice by which he cut and removed sections of abandoned buildings, bringing them back to life before they were definitively destroyed.

Matta-Clark, who worked with sculpture, drawing, performance, film and photography, even experimented with the possibilities of cooking when he fried Polaroid pictures with gold-leaf in oil. His first large-scale "anarchitecture" work was *Splitting*, from 1974. In it, Matta-Clark cut out a two-inch strip from the middle of a house in Englewood, New Jersey, removed the upper corners of the building and then dug the earth from under one of its sides. When the middle part of the house and the excavated earth were removed, one of its sides slightly tilted. This piece gave the artist international fame and led him to make a series of high-impact cuts in buildings in America and Europe. Before he died he had solo shows at the Museo de Bellas Artes in Chile (1971) and at the Musée d'Art Moderne de la Ville de Paris (1974). In 2007 the retrospective exhibition *Gordon Matta-Clark: You are the measure* was shown at the Whitney Museum of American Art in New York, the Museum of Contemporary Art in Los Angeles, California and the Museum of Contemporary Art of Chicago.

JORGE MÉNDEZ BLAKE

Jorge Méndez Blake was born in Guadalajara, Mexico in 1974 and studied architecture at the Instituto Tecnológico de Estudios Superiores de Occidente (ITESO) of Guadalajara. In his installations, videos and sound art pieces Méndez Blake explores the relations between classical literature, art and contemporary culture.

In *The Artist Can Write*, Méndez Blake's first solo show in New York at the Intar Gallery (2002), the artist wrote the names of the authors who had been awarded the Nobel Prize for Literature and left some pieces of chalk lying on the floor so the audience could pick them up and write on the walls. On another wall he wrote the name Shakespeare, but misspelled it as *Shaekspeare*. With these two installations, Méndez Blake questions notions of knowledge and our understanding of important characters in world culture. Another of his solo exhibitions, *Fiction is the Beginning of Exile*—shown at the OMR Gallery in Mexico City in 2006—the artist explores possible interpretations of what happened to Sherlock Holmes when he went missing before his last adventure. The videos, models, paintings, drawings, sculptures and photographs in this exhibition recreate and interpret this story that was never written by Conan Doyle.

In the works *Diles que no me maten (Tell them Not to Kill me)* (2004) and *Sin título (Sigue el llano en llamas) (Untitled (The Plain Still Burns))* (2007), Méndez Blake works with the collection of short stories *El llano en llamas (The Burning Plane)* by Mexican author Juan Rulfo published in 1953. In *Diles que no me maten,* Méndez Blake edited a recording of Rulfo's voice reading this story and used repetition and silence to generate a time that seems to have stopped in the tension of this plea. In *Sin título (Sigue el llano en llamas)*, the artist manipulated the title of the short story collection by Rulfo to indicate—in a humorous way—that Mexico has not changed since Rulfo wrote his stories in the 1950s.

Solo exhibitions by Méndez Blake include *The Red Library,* Meessen De Clercq, Brussels (Belgium), *La Marquesa salio a las cinco*, Museo Tamayo, Mexcio D.F., *All the Poetry Books*, Museum of Latin American Art, Long Beach, (Fall 2010); *The Castle*, Museo de Arte Moderno, Ciudad de México (Mexico) (2008); *El tesoro de Isla Negra* at the Sala de Arte Público Siqueiros, Mexico City (2005) and *Los personajes intervienen con la arquitectura,* Casa Encendida, Madrid, Spain (2005). Some of his major group shows include Stardust, at the Val-de-Marne Museum of Contemporary Art, Paris and at Vento-Sul, 4th Exhibition of Latin American Visual Art of the Instituto Paraenense de Arte, Curitiva, Brasil (2007).

ANA MENDIETA

Ana Mendieta was born in Havana, Cuba in 1948 and died in New York in 1985. Mendieta's practice was concerned with notions of cultural displacement and the processes through which female identity is shaped. She addressed these issues through super 8 films, videos, performances, drawings, sculptures and prints. Her works often documented or involved the artist's body, which was the main instrument used by Mendieta in her exploration of gender and cultural identity.

Mendieta's first performance pieces are from the early 1970s. Although at first she worked by transforming her body through different cosmetic procedures, her interest in the social connotations of the female body soon lead her to change to create different kind of works. In 1973 she invited her colleagues to her apartment in Iowa where they became the audience of a performance in which Mendieta staged her own rape. In *Rape Scene* the artist appeared naked from the waist down, tied-up and covered in blood. By doing so she forced the audience to become the viewer of this violent event. During this phase of her career, the artist based her works on the notion of the audience as a witness, and therefore, the presence of photo and/or video cameras that recorded both her performance and the reactions of the audience was a fundamental part of her pieces. At the time, Medieta's main concern involved violence and crime against women as a constitutive component of modern society.

In this process the artist also started exploring the constitutive condition of the female body, independently of society. During this period the artist became increasingly interested in nature, mythology, rituals associated to femininity, and the relation of the body with death considered as the only thing that may bring forth new life. In this context and in a quest for exploring her own condition as a cultural outcast—as someone who had been exiled—, she focused on notions of origin in cultural terms. In this period, the body only appears in her works as traces left by its presence—the silhouettes—and the audience is no longer present in her performances; leaving only the artist in her quest for identity and photography and video as the only records of her process. In her quest for her heritage she also incorporated references to Afro-Cuban religions in her works.

The work Anima, Silueta de cohetes (Fireworks Piece) (1976)—from the Silhouettes series—is a result of the introspection and exploration process that lead Mendieta to a "return to the earth" and to work with the natural materials from the places where her performances were made. All of the pieces in this series were made in the State of Oaxaca, Mexico. While they are akin to the concerns of Land Art or Body Art, in these pieces the artist used rituals of origin that ended by defining her queries into identity processes.

Some of the most important solo shows of Mendieta's work are: *TRACES- Body and Idea in Contemporary Art* at the National Museum of Modern Art, Tokyo (2005); *Ana Mendieta: Earth Body Sculpture and Performance 1972-85* at the Miami Art Museum (2005) and at the Hirshhorn Museum and Sculpture Garden (2004); Ana Mendieta- Earth Body at the Whitney Museum of Art (2004); *Ana Mendieta* at the Museo Tamayo Arte Contemporáneo, Mexico City (1999) and *Ana Mendieta* at the MoCA, Los Angeles (1998).

JONATHAN MONK

Jonathan Monk was born in Leicester, United Kingdom in 1969. He lives and works in Berlin. He studied at the Glasgow School of Arts, and from the moment when he graduated in 1991, he became one of the most important representatives of his generation along with Douglas Gordon and David Shrigley. In his pieces, Monk reinterprets ideas and projects coming from the conceptual art of the 1960s and 1970s, or from artists he admires such as Ed Ruscha, Keith Arnatt or Robert Barry. These appropriations are often humorous and playful, and establish a game between fact and fiction through a variety of media that ranges from painting, sculpture and photography to installation and performance art, or film and sound.

The work *Meeting 50* (2005-2007) is part of a series called *Meeting Pieces*. This series is made of works through which the artist establishes a future relationship with whoever buys each of them. Each piece has three components: an invitation, an a ppointment, and a document that registers the moment when the piece was bought and the appointment was made. In this case the meeting is scheduled for April 21, 2017 at the corner of Goethe Street and Darwin Street in Mexico City. In these works, Monk works with uncertainty, since the situation might or might not happen but he also addresses the idea of the artwork as potential encounter between the artist and an audience.

In 2008, the exhibition *Jonathan Monk, Classified Football Results* was shown at Tramway, Glasgow; at the Palais de Tokyo and the Musée d'Art Moderne in Paris and at the Jan Mot Gallery in Brussels. His work has been part of several important group shows in Europe, the United States and Israel.

MORIS
Moris (a.k.a. Israel Meza Moreno) was born in Mexico City in 1978. He holds a BFA from the National School of Painting, Sculpture and Graphic Arts La Esmeralda in Mexico City.

Moris creates works of art from street objects which are either exchanges or purchases from homeless people. He utilizes various strategies including appropriation of knowledge, as well as of raw materials to configure a visual spectrum comprised of drawing, collage and installation with the aim to stage dialectic relationships between contradicting realities from everyday life in Mexico. The artist uses anti-aesthetic concepts derived from neo-conceptual and povera art to produce functional art pieces that comment on social issues of inequality. In some cases Moris manipulates the objects in order to return them and contribute to improving the homeless living way; one of his better known actions consisted of "borrowing" a mattress that a homeless person was using as a shelter and manipulating it in order to return it to him converted into a sleeping bag. He has also gathered strips of wood to create a precarious refuge that ended up turned into a home for the homeless. To produce his pieces, the Mexican artist always uses objects found in the neighborhoods—such as pieces of metal, cardboard or used bottles.

Moris has exhibited his work at MOCA in Los Angeles (2010), Museo Experimental El Eco (2008) and MUAC (2008) in Mexico, The Bass Museum (2009) and CIFO (2008) in Miami and the 9th Havana Biennale (2006) in Cuba. He is the recipient of the CIFO Grants and Commissions Programs Awards (2008) and the SIVAM Visual Arts Acquisition Prize in Mexico (2005).

ERNESTO NETO
Ernesto Neto was born in Rio de Janeiro, Brazil in 1964. His exploration of the body and the organic nature of things is integral to his aim of establishing a connection between his abstract installations and his viewership. His abstract installations tend to dominate the exhibition space and create an enveloping experience that encourages the public to use their senses and interact with the work.

To create his amorphous sculptures, he uses stretchable fabrics and stuffs them with lightweight styrofoam pellets, or in some instances, spices. By choosing a material that is not fixed and rigid, he is capable of creating sculptures that can take on a variety of shapes and forms that can be displayed in a number of ways, whether it be by laying them on the floor or dangling them from the ceiling.

By creating this organic, albeit artificial environment, the viewer is invited to explore the landscape of the body within. The interaction subconsciously works on another level to reveal the sensuality and tension that we experience as we form a voyeuristic connection with the sculptures. As our bodies interact with the installation, we commune with both the exterior and interior of the forms through our visual, tactile and olfactory senses.

In *Anthropodino*, an installation that was housed at the Park Avenue Armory, he built on his previous work by creating an over encompassing experience of venturing forth inside the maternal womb. A cavernous tent made of translucent Lycra fabric and wooden bones created an extension of the hall. Fabric tubes filled with spices stretched down from the canopy for viewers to smell. He transformed the exhibition space by implementing an organic architecture that guided the visitor into and through the womb.

In 2006 Neto was awarded Chevalier de L'Ordre des Arts et des Lettres of France. He has participated in the Venice Biennale (2001), the Liverpool Biennial (1999) and the São Paulo Biennial (1998). Neto's installations have been featured in Cincinnati Contemporary Art Center (2010), MOMA in New York (2010), MACRO in Rome (2008) and Museum of Contemporary Art San Diego (2007).

RIVANE NEUENSCHWANDER
Brazilian artist Rivane Neuenschwander was born in 1967 in Belo Horizonte, where she lives and works today. Neuenschwander, who has defined her work as "ephemeral materialism," mostly works with the natural world, making pieces that fully engage the senses. Her artworks are made for all the senses and not just sight. The artist has created sculptures and installations using unusual natural materials such as pepper, saffron, garlic, water, tomatoes, dry flowers and olive oil.

Neuenschwander's installations often require that the audience become an active part of the piece. In *Suspended Landscape* (1997) Neuenschwander utilizes hundreds of garlic skins hanging by thin threads from the roof. This work evokes the fragility of existence. The audience may walk through the installation, penetrating this light and delicate space. In *Quarries / Conversations and Constructions* (2006), we see 16 constructions made from organic materials. The artist uses orange peels, saffron, onions, eggs and salt to form little architectures which remind us of actual buildings such as the Modern Art Museum of Sao Paolo by Oscar Niemeyer. By using food as a material and as a metaphor the artist sets forth the possibilities of communication between the materials and the audience. In O*ne Thousand and One Possible Nights* (2006), Neuenschwander cut out fragments from the well-known Arabic book One Thousand and One Nights and pasted the pieces on 38 black cardboard sheets. This number may be a reference to the duration of the exhibition where this piece was first shown in New York in 2006, but may also address the necessity to narrate and describe art repeatedly in order to understand it, changing its meaning every time this happens.

Rivane Neuenschwander has had many solo shows, the most recent being the traveling retrospective *Rivane Neuenschwander: A Day Like Any Other* shown at the New Museum, New York, NY, the Mildred Lane Kemper Art Museum, St. Louis, MO, the Scottsdale Museum of Contemporary Art, Scottsdale, AZ, the Miami Art Museum, Miami, FL and the Irish Museum of Modern Art, Dublin, Ireland (2010). Among her numerous group exhibitions are *Shot in the dark*, The Walker Art Center, Minneapolis (2010-2011) and *Dominó Caníbal*, Contemporary Art Project (PAC) - Sala Verónicas, Murcia (2010).

HÉLIO OITICICA

Hélio Oiticica was born in Rio de Janeiro, Brazil in 1937 and died in the same city in 1980. He studied at the school of the Modern Art Museum of Rio de Janeiro. He is one of the fundamental artists in the the Brazilian avant-garde and influential in shaping the transition from Modern to Contemporary art in Latin America. Oiticica started to gradually create more abstract art that demanded the participation of the audience. For him, art was a tool to create new spaces within the aesthetic, questioning the ways in which art had been perceived up to that point.

In 1995 he joined the Grupo Frente, an artistic movement based on the ideas of Concrete Art. In 1959 Ferreira Gullar founded the Neo-Concrete movement along with Lygia Clark, Franz Weissman and Amílcar de Castro. Oiticica would join this group later on. This movement redefined the concepts of Concrete Art by adopting a critical position in relationship to the rationalist thought represented by it. Neo-concrete art was partially inspired by the phenomenology of the French philosopher Maurice Merleau-Ponty and it tried to make the aesthetic experience richer by having the audience participate directly in the artwork.

In his first pieces, Oiticica used geometric shapes to explore properties of painting such as color, medium and the ficticious space created by the different planes on the painting. The artist created a unique and precise abstract language by distorting the linear rationale of the surface and forming gaps between colored geometric figures. The *Metasquemas* [Metaschemes] are a clear example of these ideas. Later on, Oiticica used this working process again, but incorporated the audience in a participative aesthetic experience.

Some of his more important exhibitions are: *Hélio Oiticica Quase-Cinemas*, New Museum of Contemporary Art, New York (2002); *Tropicalia: A Revolution in Brazilian Culture,* MCA, Chicago; *Hélio Oiticica: Cor, Imagem, Poética, Centro de Arte Hélio Oiticica*, Río de Janeiro (2003); *Cosmococa Programa in Progress*, in collaboration with Neville D'Almeida, MALBA, Buenos Aires (2005) and Hélio Oiticica, The Body of Color, MFAH in Houston and Tate Gallery in London (2006-2007). The Tate Modern Gallery in London dedicated an important show to him in 2006, *Helio Oiticica: The Body of Colour.*

GABRIEL OROZCO

Gabriel Orozco was born in Jalapa, Veracruz, Mexico in 1962. When he finished his art studies at the Escuela Nacional de Artes Plásticas of the UNAM (1981-1984), he moved to Madrid where he studied at the Círculo de Bellas Artes (1986-1987). Although Orozco developed his career outside his native country, he did not loose his Mexican roots and influences. He lives and works in Paris, New York and Mexico.

Orozco makes minimum interventions or works with objects he finds during his walks and trips. These simple but culturally significant objects acquire a new meaning when they are photographed or transformed into sculptures by the artist. Orozco has a wide artistic vocabulary that involves changes of scale, play, everyday life accidents and crafts; he uses materials that range from graphite or traditional clay to polyurethane foam.

Although Orozco's work might seem extremely simple, that is not the case. His work involves notions taken from mathematics, geometry and philosophy. His series of paintings that use colored-circles divided in two or in four are good examples of his techniques; their sizes and colors are defined according to precise rules based on the movements of the horse in the game of chess.

In this exhibition, several pieces that are included portray his artistic vocabulary and variety of techniques. As an example of diverse techniques there are photographs such as *Bus Stop* and *Center of the Universe,* paintings like *Fertil Square*, reutilized objects in *Soccer Ball* and polyurethane foam in *Multiple Pourings.*

His works have been shown in museums all over the world, in several group and solo exhibitions such as the Venice Biennial (1993 and 2005), where he also participated as a guest curator in 2003; he was also part of *Documenta X* (1997) and *XI* (2002). In 2009 a solo exhibition of his work was presented at MOMA New York. This exhibition will be traveling to Centre Pompidou in Paris and Tate Modern in London. In 2007, there was an important retrospective of his work at the Palacio de Bellas Artes in Mexico City. In that same year he was also awarded the *Blue Orange Prize* and he had an exhibition at the Ludwig Museum in Cologne.

DAMIÁN ORTEGA

Damián Ortega was born in Mexico City in 1967. His work, which revolves around the found object as a constructive system with its physical, urban and cultural connotations altered by a critical position, owes much to his origins as a political cartoonist. For Ortega, transformation is the main principle behind his work, addressed through a process of deconstruction of objects or situations that defines a spatial relationship. He uses fragmentation and its processes to move away from the primary representation of things, towards a new representation. This deconstructive phase is mediated by economy and politics, the accident and balance, by solidity and stability, distribution of energy and time and desire.

Cosmic Thing (2003) is the first part of *The Beetle Trilogy*, a series of three pieces featuring a Volkswagen Beetle. This austere economy sedan is a symbol of modernity that arrived to Mexico City during the 1960s and soon became a focus of street culture, and promoted the development of informal spare-parts businesses. Taking these connotations into account, Ortega used a "Beetle" or "*bocho*" (as it is called in Mexico) which was separated into parts and presented disaggregated in space. In *Cosmic Thing* the tension between the separate components of the car also defines the relation between its parts. The sculpture generates a new spatial configuration through reorganizing the car components physically, but also conceptually.

Moby Dick is the second part of this trilogy, and was performed in 2004 in Mexico City and restaged in Los Angeles in 2005. With this work, Ortega devoted a whole music performance to a Beetle. The work included a rock trio with the drum kit as their central visual element; the stage was marked by a series of circles demarcating a playing field; and the Beetle was tied as if held down by strong ropes. As the action started, the tuning of the instruments became a cathartic cover of Led Zeppelin's *Moby Dick*, while Ortega and some of his bandmates battle the Beetle, as if wanting to tame it. The tension generated by the futile attempts to overpower the car—that overlap a wish to liberate but also control the desired object—also lead to a transformation of the space where the performance was staged. The piece *Expanded Geometry* is a result of these actions. The work formally follows the disaggregated structure of *Cosmic Thing* and involves tension between the parts to the whole, but also suggests an anti-homage to John Bonham's famous drum solo, where despair and creation generate a transformation which involves the confrontation between ideas and an object.

Ortega has exhibited internationally including solo exhibitions at the Institute of Contemporary Art, Boston (2009), the Centre Pompidou, Paris (2008), the Ikon Gallery, Birmingham (2007) the Gallery at REDCAT and the Museum of Contemporary Art, Los Angeles (2005), Tate Modern, London (2005), Museu da Arte Pampulha, Belo Horizonte, Brazil (2005), Kunsthalle Basel (2004) and Institute of Contemporary Art, Philadelphia (2002). Group exhibitions include the São Paulo Biennial (2006), Made in Mexico, Institute of Contemporary Art, Boston (2003) and the 50th Venice Biennale (2003).

FERNANDO ORTEGA

Fernando Ortega was born in Mexico City in 1971. His work creates a fine line that separates the intangible from the perceptible as a point of departure. His pieces often deal with sound, which he uses as a metaphor for that which may not be visually perceived. Hence, his artworks establish a dialogue between sound and image. While visual references to sound are often found in every day life, Ortega also works in the opposite direction and uses sound to give meaning to images that are otherwise impossible to understand. In this way, he manages to create associations that would go unnoticed outside the context of the artwork.

Ortega belongs to the generation of Mexican artists inspired by Conceptual Art. His main influence is John Cage, who worked with the relation between sound and image during the 1960s and 1970s. Another important feature in Cage's work is the incorporation of "chance" in his compositions, which is also one of the features of Ortega's work.

In the 50th Venice Biennial he showed the piece *Untitled (Fly Electrocutor)*, 2003, a device used to electrocute insects that was connected to the energy system of the space, making it fail every time an insect got caught in the trap.

In *Deep Sleep induced to a Hummingbird*, 2006, Ortega recorded a sleeping hummingbird artificially put to sleep. The hummingbird is known for always being in movement, therefore seeing it stand still is almost impossible. In that sense the piece portrays a situation that would normally be impossible to witness.

Some of his most important exhibitions are: *Fernando Ortega* at the MUCA (Museo Universitario de Ciencias y Artes), Mexico City (2008); *Levitación suspendida*, at the Museo de Arte Carrillo Gil, Mexico City (2008); *Recital de piano. Un proyecto de Fernando Ortega* at the Casa del Lago Juan José Arreola / Radio UNAM, Mexico City (2008); *Winter Falls* at the Bonner Kunstverein, Bonn (2005) and *Intervención Sonora*, at the Centro de la Imagen, ciudad de México (2000). His work was also shown at the 27th Sao Paulo Biennial (2006) and at the 50th Venice Biennial (2003).

JACK PIERSON

Jack Pierson was born in Plymouth, Massachusetts in 1960 and studied at the Massachusetts College of Art in Boston. While his artistic practice includes photography, drawing, collage and installation, he is best known for his neon-letter sculptures. Pierson collects these letters, which have lost their original purpose, from garbage dumps. They acquire a new meaning when they become part of one of his works.

Pierson's artworks use visual and literary references to speak of lost love, sexuality and hope with a fascinatingly withered sensual charm. In Pierson's words, his works "show the disaster inherent in the quest for glamour." His neon signs are easily recognizable as they remind us of something we see every day: neon letters as found in any street of any large city. Even if they are a reference to familiar sights, each individual viewer may imagine a unique story when looking at them. This is the case of the work in this show, where the words "yes, yes, yes" appear in green, white and red, the colors of the Mexican flag.

His works have been exhibited in museums in Europe, Asia and America since the mid 1990s. Some of the museums that have presented solo shows of Pierson's work are: the Irish Museum of Modern Art in Dublin, Ireland (2008), the Centre de Art Santa Mónica in Barcelona, Spain (2006) and the Museum of Contemporary Art in Miami, USA (2002).

RICARDO RENDÓN

Ricardo Rendón was born in1970 in Mexico City where he lives and works. He holds a degree in arts from the *Escuela Nacional de Pintura, Escultura y Grabado* (2004). Currently he is a professor at that institution. Rendón makes site-specific works in sculpture, video and multimedia art.

In his installations, Ricardo Rendón modifies existing architectural spaces with works related to the work of traditional trades such as the carpenter, the mason, the electrician or the leather goods manufacturer. Rendón is interested in the transformation of the materials he uses, such as wood and chipboard. For the artist, changes in the outer world reflect changes within oneself.

His work establishes a formal, symbolic and aesthetic relationship with the specific sites. In *Muro falso* [Fake Wall] (2008), the piece he created for this exhibition, an intervention unexpectedly discovered by the audience, the artist creates a division of the space by perforating a sheet of chipboard with a buzz saw. The residue and dust generated by this operation remain on the floor as part of the piece to highlight the working process. Rendón's installation does not only relate to the exhibition space because it is anchored to the hanging structures made for the show, it also relates to the building through the use of the Museum's distinctive color.

Some of Rendón's most important solo exhibitions are: *Inmerso foro sonoro* (2003) at the Museo Rufino Tamayo and *Zona de construcción* (2008) at the Museo Experimental El Eco, both in Mexico City. Amongst his group shows are: *Declaraciones* at the Museo Nacional Centro de Arte Reina Sofía, Madrid (2005); *Come Closer* at the Künstlerhaus Bethanien, Berlin and the Isola Art Center, Milan(2005); and *Fragmentación* at the Theo Notaras Multicultural Centre, Canberra and the JakArt@ International Art Festival, Jakarta (2008).

PEDRO REYES

Pedro Reyes was born in Mexico City in 1972. He studied architecture at the Universidad Iberoamericana in Mexico City, and his work has been developed around the actual or potential relationships between an individual or a group of individuals and art objects. His installations, videos, sculptures and architectural projects are aimed to make the art object have a useful purpose both for people and the world that surrounds them.

From 1996 to 2001, Reyes directed *La Torre de los Vientos* [The Tower of Winds], a walk-in sculpture by Uruguayan artist Gonzalo Fonseca, which was built for the 1968 Olympic Games in Mexico City. He invited several artists to present site-specific installations inside it. In 2002, he presented *Psycho-Horticulture* in this space. For this piece, the artist filled the multi-leveled inner space of the sculpture with several plant species creating a small and domestic version of the Gardens of Babylon. While the plants where in the space, Reyes conducted a seminar on horticulture. In 2004, he presented *Floating Pyramid* in In-Site a biennial and bi-national exhibition on the Mexico-USA border. This piece was a 5 x 5 x 4 wood and polystyrene pyramid which was placed in the sea. Shortly after the object had been cast into the ocean, people swam to it and used it as a place to rest or to chat with others. Reyes has shown his work in solo and group shows in Mexico, the United States and Europe. Some of his most important exhibitions are *47 Undertakers*, Bass Museum of Art, 2008, *Pedro Reyes,* Aspen Art Museum, Aspen, Colorado, 2006, *Pedro Reyes*, The Americas Society, New York, 2006, *Elephant Cemetery*, Artists Space, New York, 2007, Art Basel Projects, 2008 and Mash-Up, Contemporary Art Museum, University of South Florida, Tampa, Florida, also in 2008.

Pedro Reyes is one of the artists who have received a commission to create an artwork for the Botanical Garden of Culiacán, the capital city of Sinaloa, Mexico. In 2007 the government of the State of Sinaloa launched a campaign to encourage the population to turn in their firearms, which would then be destroyed by the government. Reyes used this situation to make the work *Palas x Pistolas* [Shovels for Guns]. In five videos (created by Rafael Ortega) we see the different steps that were followed to turn the guns (objects that represent violence and death) into shovels (objects that are used to create and build). This piece includes the TV commercials advertising the government's campaign to collect the weapons, the destruction of the guns, the melting process of the metal, the manufacturing of the shovels, and finally a group of children planting a tree with one of the shovels. These shovels will be donated to museums and other institutions around the world, on condition that the shovel is used to plant a tree.

THOMAS RUFF

Thomas Ruff was born in Zell am Harmersbach, Germany, and lives and works in Düsseldorf. He is among the most important international photographers to emerge in the last fifteen years, and one of the most enigmatic and prolific of Bernd and Hilla Becher's former students, a group that includes Andreas Gursky, Thomas Struth, Candida Höfer, and Axel Hutte.

Best known for his conceptual and serialized approach to photography, Ruff's work addresses the ubiquity of the medium through appropriation of archival photographs, the use of evident digital printing methods, as well as image reproduction in the Internet. At the beginning of his career, his initial interest was the interiors of German living quarters, with typical features of the 1950s to 1970s, which were reproduced in a dead-pan fashion in order to express the social psychology at work in post-World War II German culture. This series was followed in the 1980s by an investigation into photographic portraiture which focused on over-scaling the printing of images to monumentalize the figure—playing with the limits of focus and scale.

Ruff has consistently investigated a variety of photographic means and styles, from using night-vision cameras, to the appropriation of images. The work *Star Series: Étoile 06h 36m/ -65* (1992) is part of a well known series known as *Sterne* (Star) started from the appropriation of archived images shot by the European Southern Observatory. Ruff reproduces and enlarges specific details of those prints, including scratches and deterioration from the original document. The resulting image is literal and poetic at the same time, addressing the material limitations of the medium while expressing its potential to delimit the untouchable. Thomas Ruff has participated in numerous group and solo exhibitions, the most recent are *Look at me. Faces and Gazes in Art 1969-2009*, Museo Cantonale d'Arte, Lugano (2010); *Thomas Ruff* at Schwarzwald. Landschaft, Museum für Neue Kunst, Freiburg/Breisgau, Germany; Oberflächen, Tiefen, Kunsthalle Vienna, Austria; Castello di Rivoli, Rivoli Torino, Italy (2009); *A retrospective at* Mücsarnok – Kunsthalle Budapest, Hunagry (2009); *Die Düsseldorfer Schule. Photographien 1970-2008* at aus der Sammlung Lothar Schirmer, Bayerische Akademie der Schönen Künste, Munich, Germany (2009); *Art of Two Germanys / Cold War Cultures*, Los Angeles County Museum of Art, Los Angeles (2009).

ED RUSCHA

Ed Ruscha was born in 1937 in Omaha, Nebraska. In the mid-1950s he traveled to Los Angeles to study at the Chouinard Art Institute. He still lives and works in this city, which has had a notorious influence on his work. Ruscha is considered to be one of the precursors of Pop and Conceptual Art, and he has developed his practice in the fields of painting, drawing, photography and artists books. His artworks often involve meaningless words and phrases, such as road signs or sentence fragments found in city streets.

Ruscha has also developed an important body of work as a photographer. Initially published as a book, *Twenty Six Gasoline Stations* (1962) shows the number of gas stations on Route 66, between L.A. and Oklahoma. The images are unexpressive and monotonous, and they lack traditional technical and compositional consideration. As a mere register, this series of images helped to advance the anti-aesthetics that would be embraced by conceptual artists in the years to come.

Ruscha has shown extensively around the world. In 2005 he represented the United States in the 51st Venice Biennial with an installation called *Course of Empire*, named after the well-known series of nineteenth-century paintings by American artist Thomas Cole. While Cole depicted the rise and fall of civilization in the face of nature, the installation by Ruscha portrayed changes in city landscapes that reflect those undergone by people and ideologies. Also in 2005, the Whitney Museum of American Art held the exhibitions *The Drawings of Ed Ruscha* and *Ed Ruscha and Photography* and the National Gallery of Art in Washington held the exhibition *Cotton Puffs, Q-tips®, Smoke and Mirrors*. Ruscha's work has been exhibited internationally for three decades and is represented in major museum collections.

MARUCH SANTIZ GÓMEZ

Santiz Gómez was born in 1975 in Cruzton, within the municipality of Chamula, Chiapas. She started taking photographs when she was 17 years old. Tzotzil is her mother tongue, and as it often happens within this ethnic group, she proudly uses it. The town of San Juan Chamula is located in the highlands of Chiapas and its church is a perfect example of the syncretism between Pre-Columbian and Spanish cultures. Native customs predominate in this town.

The work by this artist alludes to the preservation of Chamula traditions. Santiz Gómez gathers the traditions of her people—which co-exist in Mexico with those of a modern Western nation—so their identity will not be lost. But she also tries to make their customs known and appreciated by others, especially by certain sectors of the Mexican population who, immersed in their quest for the "first world," often forget the ethnic plurality of the country where they live.

The photographs included in this exhibition are a good example of her work. They depict simple objects and situations, such as a cat on a bench, a basket with *chayotes*, or some wigs bound together to be used as a broom. These images represent native beliefs written in Tzotzil and, when translated, they bring us closer to the artist's world. In the picture with the broom we read: "Sweeping in the afternoon is bad, because luck might run out and money may vanish too."

Her work is part of the *Archivo Fotográfico Indígena* (Indigenous Photographic Archive), a project that started in 1995 by gathering photographers belonging to the native peoples of Chiapas. Santiz Gómez has been part of several important group shows such as La Mirada. Looking at Photography in Latin America Today at the Daros Collection, Switzerland (2003), at the Shanghai Biennial (2004), the Taipei Biennial (2005), and the traveling exhibition The Hours which was shown in Sydney, Australia and at the Irish Museum of Modern Art (2005). Her work was also part of La era de la discrepancia, organized at the MUAC, Mexico (2007).

STEPHEN SHORE

Stephen Shore was born in New York in 1947 and has been the director of the Photography Department of Bard Collage since 1982. Shore began shooting very early and without formal schooling. At 14 years of age he showed his work to Edward Steichen, then the photography curator of the Museum of Modern Art in New York. The relevance of his work was acknowledged by a solo show at the Metropolitan Museum of Art in 1971 when he only was 24 years old.

Shore's work documents everyday life in the United States—the American dream represented without glamour such as the birth of the suburbs, presented by a simple wall, streets and a lonely passerby. Along with William Eggelston, Shore was one of the pioneers of color photography. Walker Evans, one of the best-known American photographers of the 1920s and 1930s famously stated that "color photography is vulgar," making color photography as artistic expression an abomination. Despite their documentary appearance and simplicity, Shore's photographs reveal an impeccable technique and capture everyday beauty.

In 1972 Shore traveled to the Southwest from New York on a long road-trip to Amarillo, Texas. In his 1982 book *Uncommon Places*, published by the Aperture Foundation, the artist describes this trip, explaining, "my first view of America was framed by the passenger's window." *Presidio, Texas, February 21, 1975*, the photograph included in this exhibition was shot during that trip and is also presented in that book.

Stephen Shore has been represented in multiple exhibitions, among which the following solo exhibitions stand out: *The Biographical Landscape* at the International Center of Photography, New York, Worcester Art Museum, Worcester, MA, Henry Art Gallery, University of Washington, Seattle (2006); *Stephen Shore: American Surfaces* at P.S. 1 Contemporary Art Center, Long Island City, New York (2005-2006) and Sprueth Magers, Munich.

MELANIE SMITH

Melanie Smith was born in 1965 in Poole, England. When she finished studying art she moved to Mexico City, and was invited to the first exhibition of installation art ever made in the country: A *propósito (On Purpose)*, curated by Guillermo Santamarina in 1998. She soon found places to exhibit her strongly conceptual installation, video and photo pieces. Slowly the life and dynamics of Mexico City appeared in her work, always with references to minimalism and video art.

Her work as an abstract painter has strongly influenced her installations and videos. For example, *Orange Lush* (1997), a work in which Smith collected orange objects from the streets to make a series of mixed media paintings in orange tones—a reference to the bright colors found in Mexico City.

In 2007 Smith presented a series of installations, videos, ensembles, paintings and photographs titled *Spiral City Off Balance* at The Laboratory of Art and Ideas in Beldar, Colorado. *Photo for Spiral City II, III* and *IV* are photographic stills of her *Spiral City* multi-media project—aerial views of Mexico City taken from a helicopter that follows a spiral flight pattern over the metropolis. This piece is a direct reference to Robert Smithson's *Spiral Jetty*, the 1970 Earthwork made in the Great Salt Lake in Utah, which consists of a wide spiral made of basalt rocks at the lake's edge. Smith's photographs show Mexico City from above, as a seemingly endless network of houses and streets. The spiraling movement allows us to perceive the visual, cultural and political impact that the city has had in the works by this artist, and her reference to Smithson puts her piece in the context of an exploration of the relation between culture and nature.

Melanie Smith has had solo exhibitions throughout the world, including *Spiral City* and other *Vicarious Pleasures*, MIT List Visual

Arts Center, Cambridge, the Museo de Arte de Lima, Lima (2009); *Parres Trilogy* in collaboration with Rafael Ortega, Miami Art Museum (2008); *Spiral City / Ciudad Espiral* The Laboratory of Art and Ideas at Belmar, Lakewood (2007).

THOMAS STRUTH

Photographer Thomas Struth was born in 1954 in Geldern, Germany, near Düsseldorf, where he studied at the Kunstakademie. He studied with painter Gerard Richter, and later with photographers Bernd and Hilla Becher. The influence of these important artists is apparent in his early photography, where the main subject is the architecture of cities like Düsseldorf and New York, where he traveled in 1978 after receiving a study grant. His photography is also influenced by the photographs of August Sandler and Walker Evans. Later, and as a consequence of his collaboration with psychologist Ingo Hartmann, he developed an interest in photography as a tool for exploring the human subconscious. Struth's images portray the loneliness and isolation of individuals in large cities, while they also point to the city as a source of social identity. After his *City* series, Struth worked on a series of family portraits where he explored—along with Hartmann—how human beings see and how they see themselves. This premise led to make the *Museum Photographs* series, which is the best-known group of works by this artist. In these photos we see groups of visitors in well-known museums like the Louvre in Paris, the Pergamonn in Berlin, the National Gallery in London or the Prado in Madrid. These images show groups of people looking at artworks, while the characters in the works seem to be looking back at them.

In *Paradise 2,* one of his most recent series, the images of the trees and lush vegetation in the jungle evoke the stillness of a distant paradise. The calm and grandeur of nature makes us think of our individuality and of how it has become increasingly opaque in a globalized world.

Struth's work has been shown in Europe, the United States, Canada and Latin America. Some of his most important solo exhibitions include *The State Hermitage*, Saint Petersburg, Russia (2008); *Thomas Struth*, MADRE, Museo d'Arte Contemporanea Donna Regina, Naples, Italy (2008); *Making Time,* Museo Nacional del Prado, Madrid, Spain (2007) and *Thomas Struth: Images of Peru*, Museo de Arte de Lima, Lima, Peru (2005).

SIMON STARLING

Simon Starling was born in 1967 in Epson, England. He is currently living and working in Copenhagen. Starling studied at the Maidstone College of Art (1986-1987), at the Photography Nottingham Polytechnic (1987-1990) and holds an MA in Fine Arts from the Glasgow School of Art (1990-1992).

Simon Starling is interested in the production process of objects. In many of his artworks Starling uses well-known modern icons—originally meant for mass-production—and remakes them as crafts through long and complicated processes that often involve traveling. Through these processes, Starling explores the conditions of production in a global context where objects are often made up with parts coming from different areas of the globe. In his 2002 piece *Flaga* (1972-2000) Starling drove a 1974 Fiat from Turin—where it was no longer made—to Poland, where he replaced some parts of the car with others made in the plant that Fiat had opened in that country, and then drove back to Italy. His work in this exhibition, *Four Thousand Seven Hundred and Twenty Five (Motion Control / Mollino)* made in 2007 for an exhibition on the Alps that took place in Sondrio, Italy (*Imagini, Forme e Natura delle Alpi*, 2007), is a 35mm film that shows a wooden chair in detail. The work is an example of Starling's narrative and juxtapositions. The chair is a design developed by the multi-talented architect Carlo Mollino (Turin, 1905-1973) who was inspired by the furniture of the rural communities in Northern Italy. The chair has been filmed with the aid of a high-tech device based on a computer that controls the movement of the camera. In this piece, the modern folk-inspired design is mixed with state-of-the-art technology used by the film industry. The view of the piece may be seen as a reference to the landscape of the Alps, but also to Mollino's interest in skiing.

Starling showed his work in the Scottish Pavillion of the 50th Venice Biennial (2003). He has shown his work in solo exhibitions in institutions such as the Casey Kaplan Gallery in New York (2007), the Städtischen Kunstmuseum zum Museum Folkwang, Essen, Germany (2007), the Galleria Franco Noero, in Turin, Italy (2006) and Cove Park, Cove, Scotland (2006) and the Kunstmuseum Basel, Museum für Gegenwartskunst, Basel, (2005-2006). In 2005 he was awarded the prestigious Turner Prize and in 2004 he was shortlisted for the Hugo Boss Prize.

TERCERUNQUINTO

The Tercerunquinto collective, was formed in Monterrey, Mexico in 1996 by Julio Castro (Monterrey, Mexico, b. 1976), Gabriel Cazares (Monterrey, Mexico, b. 1978) and Rolando Flores (Monterrey, Mexico, b. 1975). The collective works with definitions of space and its usage. Their pieces often take the form of interventions that question the division between public and private, as well as notions of architecture and urbanism and habitation.

Questioning the borders that limit space has lead Tercerunquinto to make pieces such as the intervention in the Mexican Consulate General in Miami, an institution that is next to the Mexican Cultural Institute, during Art Basel Miami, 2002. Some of the characteristics that stand out in the practice of this collective are including the reactions of the audience as part of their pieces and establishing a dialogue with the architecture by transforming it. For this project, Tercerunquinto removed some of the walls separating the Consulate from the Cultural Institute, so that any person who went there for official business became part of the exhibition at the Cultural Institute. The visitors of the exhibition at the Cultural Institute could also be seen by the people in the Consulate.

The piece *Escultura publica en la periferia urbana de Monterrey (Public Sculpture in Monterrey's Urban Periphery)* was developed for a slum on the outskirts of Monterrey, Mexico, an informal community where most of the houses are built by squatters who take over land. The houses are constructed out of recycled materials such as cardboard, wood and other found objects. This work was staged as a series of interventions, of which only the first one was directly generated by Tercerunquinto. The intervention consisted of building a cement slab on an empty field, an architectural foundation which was left open for any number of future uses. The community took over this "formalized" built space for many public and private events and it became a kind of public square and market, a hair salon and even the site of political rallies that promoted voting. This site was eventually "privatized" when the neighbor next door took it over and fenced everything around the open spaces. The work, a system more than a sculptural object, existed as a real-time representation of existing communal processes of construction in that informal settlement.

Tercerunquinto has participated in numerous group and solo exhibitions, of which the following are the most important: *I Am What I Am,* at the Ikon Gallery in Birmingham, England (2008) and *Investiduras Institucionales* at the Centro de las Artes de Nuevo León in Monterrey, Mexico (2007). Included among their group shows are: *Habitat/Variations,* at the Centre d'Art Contemporain Geneva, Switzerland (2007) and *Urban Spaces* at Dina 4 Projekte in Munich, Germany. (2006). They were awarded the *Blue Orange* prize in 2004.

TATIANA TROUVÉ

Tatiana Trouvé was born in Conzenza, Italy in 1968 and lives in Paris. Trouvé works with time and memory as her subject matter. Her work creates dimensions where memories, ideas, imagination and the constant flux of time live side by side. She builds spaces with different materials such as metallic structures, leather strips, water containers and structures with rough surfaces that relate in a variety of formal structures, creating landscapes that bring sculptures together in autonomous dimensions.

Trouvé's installations are self-sustainable universes that generate spaces which recover the sequences of delay and memory. The different dimensions that she manipulates in her pieces—spatial, conceptual, and material—allow for various elements to live side by side and to give rise to new experiences and ideas on perception.

Trouvé has created a site-specific work for this exhibition in response to the interior courtyard at the Maison Rouge, a work that mutates as the exhibition travels. The installation utilizes some of the principles latent in her drawings, where the borders separating interior from exterior live, coexist and give rise to a new spatial dimension. In this sculptural installation, the metal trees, bed, water containers, and other elements often used by the artist in her work, transform gradually through proximity, creating alternative narratives.

Tatiana Trouvé's work has been shown in museums around the world. Some of her most important exhibitions include *Tatiana Trouvé* at the Centre Georges Pompidou (2008), *Medio día- media noche* at the Centro Cultural Recoleta (2007), Museum of Modern Art of Paris (2006), *SingulierS- Art Contemporain en France.* Musee des Beaux Arts de Guandong (2005). Her work has also been shown at the 50ª and 52ª Venice Biennials and in 2003 she was part of the Prague Biennial. In 2007 she was awarded the Marcel Duchamp Prize.

PABLO VARGAS LUGO

Born in 1968, Vargas Lugo has a BA in Visual Arts from the National University of Mexico (1988-1993) in Mexico City. He currently lives in Lima, Peru. In his paintings, collages and installations, Vargas Lugo shows an interest for textures and bright colors. His works deal with issues such as natural catastrophes, flying machines, city life, the passing of time and the unavoidable transformation of matter.

Although at a formal level his works might seem cheerful and engaging, because he often uses bright colors against white backgrounds and stresses the intricate handiwork involved in their making, many of them deal with obscure or tragic matters. In his 2005 *Grand Hotel* series, Vargas Lugo depicts a group of overlapping flags—like those found on the façades of some hotels—to show the contrast between the luxury that may be afforded by certain social groups, and the decay caused by environmental damage. In this context, the emblems of powerful and not-so powerful countries appear at the same level. The presence of a pirate flag gives a touch of humor to the piece.

Vargas Lugo was awarded the Jóvenes Creadores grant of Mexico's National Council for the Arts (FONCA) in 1997 and he was part of the AIR House artist in residency program in Vienna in 1998. His work has been shown at the Los Angeles County Museum of Art (2005), the UCLA Hammer Museum (2003), the Museo Del Barrio in New York (2003) and the Schloss Molsberg Pavilion in Germany (2002).

PAE WHITE

Pae White was born in Pasadena, California in 1963. While her pieces relate to the architecture that surrounds them—as space and as structure—the main feature of her work is the way in which she uses color. The crossover of cultures in the city of Los Angeles, where White lives and works, has been an important influence on her work.

Her mobiles, shaped as unusual cascades and chandeliers, are made by sewing together hundreds of geometric, brightly colored paper figures. They are delicate, suspended compositions that move with the most subtle breeze. Each cutting works as a brushstroke that seems abstract when seen up close, but at a distance they look like natural landscapes, schools of fish or `flocks frozen in time.

In some of her works, sculpture adopts the shape of functional objects, where strange animals look as furnaces and clocks are made of paper. On the other hand, White modifies existing architecture by adding unexpected colors and textures that emphasize its use, but also transform its everyday presence into an extraordinary fact.

In the 2007 Munster Skulptur Project, she presented a series of bells that played modern love songs, such as *Girl, You'll be a Woman Soon* by Neil Diamond - reminiscent of the ones placed along the *Camino Real* (King's Road) in California. She also made miniature marzipan models of the traditional vehicles used to sell tacos in L.A., a favorite dish of Mexican immigrants. White has shown her work in solo exhibitions in places like the Hammer Museum (2004), the Hirschhorn Museum and Sculpture Garden (2007), and Scottsdale Museum of Contemporary Art (2008). She has recently participated in the 53rd Venice Biennale (2009) and the Whitney Biennial (2010).

MARIANA YAMPOLSKY

Mariana Yampolsky was born in Chicago in 1925. She studied Social Sciences at the Chicago University from 1941 to 1944. In 1945, after the death of her father, she traveled to Mexico City where she became part of the *Taller de Gráfica Popular* (TGP) (Popular Print Workshop) directed by Leopoldo Méndez and Pablo O'Higgins. The work of the TGP was focused on making art available for everyone—making it an important part of society's development—a goal she kept until the end of her life. In 1948 Yampolsky became interested in photography as something that could be both a document and an artwork. At first, she took pictures to record her life, but little by little, that interest became a vocation—a work she developed until she died in 2002.

More than 15 books have been published and several solo exhibitions have focused on Yampolsky's work. Her photos have also been part of approximately 150 group shows in Mexico, South America, Europe and Asia. She worked as an editor of elementary and middle school books and she curated several photography exhibitions. Her work is an accurate reflection of her interest in Mexican culture, especially its native people. Her images often depict women and children—one of her main subjects—looking proud, serene and deeply honorable. These works were carefully composed and they show her interest in exploring the contrasts between textures, light, shadow and color.

Her work *Adornos, Tzintzunzan, Michoacán (Ornaments, Tzintzunzan, Michoacán)* is an example of the originality of her prints, where forms stand out through strong contrasts, one of the main features of her work. The image represents typical crafts of the Michoacán region in Mexico. They seem like simple objects which are abstract shapes placed against a dark background; nevertheless, the table under the objects and the log that may be seen in the lower left corner remind us of the earth and the countryside, a place Yampolsky always captured with a peculiar and clear beauty.

Yampolsky's work has been exhibited in important institutions such as The Museum of Photographic Art in San Diego (2004), Centro de la Imagen in Mexico City (2002), Antiguo Colegio de San Ildefonso in Mexico City (2005) and El Paso Museum of Art (1993). In 2007 she was part of the Munster Skulptur Project. Her work is in the permanent collection at LACMA, Los Angeles and SFMOMA in San Francisco.

PREFACIO

El Museum of Contemporary Art San Diego y el Museum of Latin American Art están complacidos de mostrar conjuntamente las presentaciones, que combinadas, componen la exposición *Mexico: Expected / Unexpected*, perteneciente a la colección de Isabel y Agustín Coppel. La colaboración entre MCASD, MOLAA, CIAC (Colección Isabel y Agustín Coppel) y la Secretaría de Relaciones Exteriores de México es una colaboración afortunada que trae esta reconocida colección a los Estados Unidos por primera vez, tras una extensa itinerancia europea, y la comparte entre estas dos instituciones del sur de California para presentarla a una mayor audiencia.

Esta exposición no sólo incluye extraordinarios ejemplos de artistas mexicanos de hoy en día, Gabriel Orozco, Francis Alÿs y Damián Ortega vienen a nuestra mente, sino otros artistas latinoamericanos prominentes están representados también; desde maestros del pasado como Lygia Clark y Hélio Oiticica a artistas internacionales de la actualidad como Rivane Neuenschwander y Tatiana Trouvé. Es más, estos artistas se unen a sus coetáneos en Europa y los Estados Unidos como Ed Ruscha y Maurizio Cattelan, Doug Aitken y Terence Koh. La contextualización resultante es un logro significante de la exposición que trata de cuestionar y expandir qué es "lo mexicano" dentro del arte contemporáneo de México y cómo otros, desde dentro o fuera, lo perciben. Mientras MCASD ha demostrado por largo tiempo su compromiso con este tipo de propuestas, MOLAA está ahora complacido de unirse en tal esfuerzo.

Primero y principalmente agradecemos a Isabel y Agustín Coppel quienes han comprobado ser sagaces coleccionistas y generosos patrocinadores. Apreciamos profundamente los esfuerzos de Mireya Escalante, directora de CIAC y Ana Belén Lezana, manager curatorial de CIAC quienes han trabajado sin descanso para hacer posible esta exposición. La curadora del proyecto original de *Mexico: Expected / Unexpected,* Mónica Amor y el asesor del proyecto Carlos Basualdo deben ser felicitados por su brillante concepto. Desde entonces se ha realizado un trabajo curatorial adicional: la cuidadosa división de la exposición entre las dos instituciones y la inclusión de nuevas obras a la muestra. En ese aspecto, los directores de ambas instituciones, queremos agradecer a Lucía Sanromán, curadora asociada de MACSD, y en MOLAA a Cecilia Fajardo-Hill, curadora en jefe, e Idurre Alonso, curadora. Estamos agradecidos por los esfuerzos de recaudación de fondos realizados por Edwina Brandon, vice-presidenta de asuntos externos, y Wendy Celaya, vice-presidenta asociada de desarrollo, ambas de MOLAA. MCASD también desea reconocer el incansable trabajo de búsqueda de patrocinios de Jeanna Yoo, directora de fomento. El catálogo ha sido habilidosamente diseñado por el director de arte de MOLAA, Steve Vladimiroff.

Finalmente agradecemos a nuestros patrocinadores sin ellos no podríamos haber presentado al público esta provocadora y estimulante exposición. En MOLAA agradecemos nuestro patroanador presentante Wells Fargo y Thank Goodness It's Sofia, apoyo adicional de Robert Gumbiner Foundation, Arts Council for Long Beach, City of Long Beach y el fondo anual de exposiciones de MOLAA. MCASD agradece al

Consulado General de México en San Diego por su apoyo a la exposición, y a The James Irvine Foundation Arts Innovation Fund, the County of San Diego Community Enhancement Fund, y the Institute of Museum and Library Services. El apoyo institucional para MCASD es provisto en parte por the City of San Diego Commission for Arts and Culture, a quien estamos profundamente agradecimos por su apoyo continuo hacia esta exposición.

Nuestro deseo es que el público viaje la corta distancia entre San Diego y Long Beach para visitar ambos museos y vean las dos partes de la muestra. Estamos seguros que disfrutarán esta singular oportunidad de ver "una sóla" exposición en dos instituciones de arte contemporáneo en donde se analiza simultáneamente las dualidades de lo local y lo internacional, lo establecido y lo emergente, lo anticipado y lo inesperado.

Hugh M. Davies
The David C. Copley Director y CEO
Museum of Contemporary Art San Diego

Richard P. Townsend
Presidente y CEO
Museum of Latin American Art

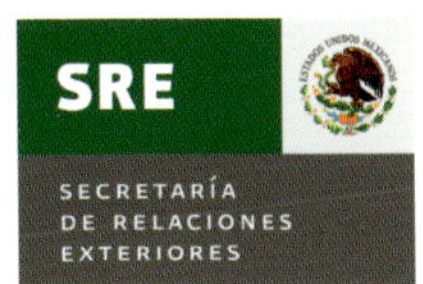

Presentación

Los Estados Unidos y México son dos naciones no sólo muy dinámicas, que cambian, crecen y se desarrollan a paso firme, sino también dos países orgullosos de sus múltiples raíces culturales y de la forma en que ello se ha traducido en la conformación de sociedades plurales, ricas en su diversidad.

Al encontrarse, como lo hacen en la larga y compleja frontera que comparten, se crean sinergias que, si en algún rubro son por demás ricas y evidentes, es en materia cultural. El significado y el peso de una nueva identidad artistica común a las muchas comunidades que conviven y se encuentran en esa frontera, por ejemplo, es sin duda algo digno de estudiarse a profundidad, como lo será igualmente la influencia de esa identidad en una mayor y mucho más estrecha relación de amistad y fraternidad entre ambos países.

La exposición *México: Expected / Unexpected*, de la colección Isabel y Agustín Coppel, Está conformada por obras de artistas en su mayoría mexicanos que no sólo subrayan los encuentros y desencuentros entre tradicíon e innovación en el arte contemporáneo mexicano sino también cómo esos encuentros y desencuentros pueden ir más allá de nuestras fronteras o deberse a la influencia de visiones que, al traspasarlas, han llegado al corazón de lo que actualmente hacen los artistas en México.

Estoy segura de que la exposición *México: Expected / Unexpected*, que se presenta de forma simultánea en el Museum of Contemporary Art de San Diego y en el Museum of Latin American Art en Long Beach, California, aportará un mayor entendimiento acerca del arte mexicano contemporáneo.

Agradezco a las instituciones que han hecho posible traer esta gran muestra de la riqueza cultural de la que los mexicanos nos sentimos tan orgullosos, al Museum of Contemporary Art de San Diego y al Museum of Latin American Art. Un agradecimiento muy especial, por supuesto, a la Colección Isabel y Agustín Coppel y a la visión y el empeño de quienes la han hecho posible.

Patricia Espinosa C.
Secretaría de Relaciones Exteriores, México

México: Expected / Unexpected

Ensayo del cátalogo original de Mónica Amor (curadora de la exposición) y Carlos Basualdo (Asesor de proyecto), para la exposición inaugural de Mexico: Expected / Unexpected *en La Maison Rouge, Paris, 2008*

La intención de esta exhibición es la de subrayar el papel de la colección como suerte de herramienta epistemológica, relacionada con el sitio cultural ocupado por los diferentes agentes, responsables de su formación: los coleccionistas mismos, principalmente, curadores, asesores, especialistas y galerías. Esta compleja red de instituciones y operadores no se prestan a un claro análisis, y lo mismo puede decirse sobre los objetos acumulados en la Colección Isabel y Agustín Coppel. Esto último, es el resultado del intercambio y la desigualdad entre las trayectorias que comprometen las incertidumbres de producción y las ambivalencias que le dan forma a cualquier operación cultural en nuestra actual economía global. Como consecuencia, la mexicaneidad, por utilizar un neologismo geográfico que Roland Barthes[1] asoció con las expectativas que se generan por el significador de identidad, de esta colección y de su exposición será resuelta a través de líneas de investigación, en cuyo intercambio, diálogo, influencia, impureza, disonancia y multiplicidad, se encuentran las estrategias fundacionales.

Otro acierto de la exhibición de la siempre cambiante y creciente Colección Coppel es el intento por explorar el arte contemporáneo (mexicano) mientras subraya las relaciones y conexiones con sus predecesores canónicos y sus productores contemporáneos. Mas allá, dos cuadros de referencia enmarcan el esfuerzo curatorial realizado aquí: por un lado, esta presentación intenta direccionar una colección que se encuentra abierta a las dinámicas globales que sirven de combustible al arte contemporáneo de nuestro período, y por otro, intenta mostrar que la Colección Coppel se encuentra, igualmente, comprometida con un grupo creciente de artistas contemporáneos mexicanos y con una audiencia local, cada vez más grande. El que ambos proyectos sean complementarios, es una de las premisas que dan forma a esta exposición y a la lógica propuesta para el espectador en los espacios físicos de la Maison Rouge. Como resultado, podemos esperar que la audiencia aprecie como la Colección Isabel y Agustín Coppel defiende el arte contemporáneo nacional e internacional, mientras interroga sobre las fundamentales diferencias entre aquellas dos categorías. Estas, por supuesto, son preocupaciones antiguas, llenas de riesgos y dificultades. Pero nuestra intención es generar controversia, a través de esta exposición, que ahora más que nunca, lo local y lo global, lo auténtico y lo extranjero, el original y la copia, son conceptos que permean entre cada uno y tienen muy poco que decir sobre la producción cultural cuando se piensan por separado.

La Colección Isabel y Agustín Coppel presenta figuras clave dentro de la escena del arte contemporáneo mexicano, como Francis Alÿs, Melanie Smith, Gabriel Orozco, Abraham Cruzvillegas y Damián Ortega, entre otros.

Partiendo del trabajo de estos artistas, la exposición intenta expandirse diacrónicamente en un esfuerzo por establecer las posibles influencias y antecedentes del trabajo de estos artistas. Asimismo, junto al trabajo de una generación joven de artistas, encontramos también el trabajo más histórico de artistas

---

[1] Roland Barthes, "Rhetoric of the Image," in *Image, Music, Text* translated by Stephen Heath, New York: The Noonday Press, 1977, 32-51.

como Gordon Matta-Clark, Lygia Clark, Ed Ruscha, Dan Graham y Hélio Oiticica. Pero la exhibición también desdobla de la misma manera sincrónica en que los incorpora, a artistas internacionales más jóvenes, cuyos trabajos muestran las preocupaciones conceptuales y las resoluciones estéticas de los mexicanos.

Ese es el caso de Tatiana Trouvé, Rivane Neuschwander, Pae White y Terence Koh, entre otros. *Mexico: Expected / Unexpected*, como el título lo indica, intenta desestabilizar las categorías que uno asocia con los conceptos del arte mexicano, la colección mexicana, lo local y lo internacional, lo auténtico y la copia. En un movimiento que resuena con lo que parece que está tomando lugar en otras áreas de la cultura mexicana, como el cine o la literatura, la Colección Isabel y Agustín Coppel, así como esta muestra, proyecta una imagen del arte contemporáneo mexicano que es inestable, rico y complejo, impredecible y en el que la tradición e innovación están constantemente en juego. Esperamos que el resultado comprometa a la audiencia, los sorprenda, sólo ahí donde el espectador hubiera esperado la sencillez del cliché.

La exposición está rudamente organizada en secciones o cuartos sin una trayectoria establecida y con un constante interjuego de trabajos y espacios facilitados por la planta asimétrica de la Maison Rouge. Aquí, haremos énfasis en algunos de esos intercambios para subrayar la naturaleza sugestiva de la exhibición que insiste en la posición relativa de las obras y artistas, así como en la calidad constructiva de la narrativa propuesta por la colección/exhibición. Sin embargo, en vez de una narrativa de evolución y de progreso reflejado en una idea monolítica sobre la gente y el lugar, proponemos historias cortas que se reflejen entre sí, sin aspirar a un clímax o conclusión.

En la galería de entrada, el trabajo en neón de Doug Aitken y Kendell Geers, y una cita programada por Jonathan Monk, presentan un marco predicativo en el que la oportunidad, más que la casualidad es la que determina su relación con México, o mejor aún, a la inestable mexicaneidad perseguida en la muestra. El primer trabajo, titulado *99 Cents Dreams*, 2007, por Aitken, relacionada con el sueño de plenitud y disponibilidad, y al accesible consumismo que las tiendas de todo por un dólar representan en los Estados Unidos de Norteamérica. En este contexto, y en relación con los trabajos siguientes, la pieza desplaza el modelo económico existente del otro lado de la frontera, un modelo que en cierto momento pareció estar al alcance de México bajo el auspicio de NAFTA. Una segunda pieza de Geers, introduce la noción de límites y fronteras por esto entendemos los límites físicos del espacio de exposición, asi como las fronteras geográficas de Estados Unidos y México, que han jugado un papel tan fundamental en la cultura moderna y contemporánea de México. En la pieza se lee *B/ORDER* (frontera) cuando la primera letra no parpadea. Cuando parpadea, se lee ORDER (orden). Un defecto técnico similar puede detectarse en un neón adyacente del mismo artista, en este se lee *D/ANGER*, 2003 (peligro-coraje), y mientras el juego de palabras, y la inestabilidad del significante escultórico, puede relacionarse directamente con las estresantes situaciones políticas del país de origen de Geers, Sudáfrica, el marco diferencial provisto por la exposición los convierte en un importante comentario sobre las fronteras políticas entre México y Estados Unidos. Un trabajo, titulado *Meeting 50* (2005-2007), y validado por el texto recortado en vinil, es parte de una serie de encuentros que el artista propone en el futuro distante, en una lugar, fecha y tiempo de la elección del artista. Este se llevará a cabo en la Ciudad de México, en 2017, entre el artista y el coleccionista. La *rendez-vous* propuesta por el artista, potencialmente existe al comprar la pieza y de alguna manera se altera por su papel de apertura en esta exposición. Tan dependientes como son estas reuniones de Monk, siempre dependiendo de otro, son también los encuentros entre trabajos, productores y prácticas estéticas propuestas por la colección y la exposición. La plataforma visual sugerida está basada, entonces, en un desplazamiento estético y en resonancias poéticas que entre pasan lecturas cerradas y definen estructuras. Una larga sección de la muestra liga formalmente, a través de una seri de resonancias tipológicas. Obras realizadas en diversos medios (pintura, escultura, video, instalación) al mismo tiempo que aluden, a medida que deshacen, nociones establecidas de mexicaneidad, tales como imágenes de muerte la relación entre ciudad y naturaleza, la poética de la mano de obra, y lo precario de la vida cotidiana. Aquí encontramos el silencio de los iconos de Carlos Amorales (*Panorama*): imágenes de figuras y formas delineadas en negro, rojo y blanco que acumulan, en un archivo sin sentido que aspira a un entendimiento imposible, y las sublimes vistas de parvadas de pájaros en las fotografías en blanco y negro de Graciela Iturbide. Esta relación lateral entre el aparente orden del archivo de Amorales (profundamente arbitrario al momento de considerar su lógica), y la caótica dimensión de la naturaleza, se elabora más allá en la yuxtaposición de la serial pero indistinta *Gasoline Stations*, 1962 de Ed Ruscha (señaladores de lugares entre espacios, el camino a ninguna parte, la tierra de nadie) y la localizable y vívida fotografía de México, de Helen Levitt (*Untitled, Mexico, D.F.*, 1941). En la intersección de estos paradigmas opuestos pero contradictorios, encontramos una obra abstracta de Pae White (*Freeze Festoon*), una cascada festiva de papel en una configuración móvil que repite el tema de la acumulación arbitraria mientras recuerda las decoraciones baratas que adornan las celebraciones populares en México y otros lugares de Sudamérica. Estas resonancias inesperadas se desdoblan adyacentemente hacia más asociaciones predecibles entre las fotografías de toreros de Rineke Dijkstra (*Montemor, Portugal, May 1 A, B y C*, todas de 1994) y del esqueleto preformativo de Terence Koh (*Untitled (Skeleton Pintings)*, 2006), ambos físicamente distantes (en el espacio de exhibición), pero conceptualmente cerca al *Niño Maya de Tulum*, de Manuel Álvarez Bravo, de 1942, donde el niño y el relieve del cráneo en la pared, son compañeros naturales.

Los otros tres cuartos, lateralmente conectados al espacio de exhibición principal, llevan más lejos el ensayo de esas operaciones de asociación. Empezando con *Untitled (Sitting Donkey*, Trento, 2004) obra que presenta un animal que constituye un icono humorístico relacionado con México, seguimos con Jack Pierson y la pieza *Si, Si, Si*, 1995, seis letras tridimensionales con los colores de la bandera mexicana, y finalmente el texto en vinil del mexicano Jorge Méndez-Blake, *Sin título (Sigue el llano en llamas)*, 2007, una alusión a la novela de 1953, *El llano en llamas*, de Juan Rulfo, sobre la vida rural de México durante el período de la Revolución. Un espacio conectado está organizado alrededor de la producción de la forma basada en (literal y estilísticamente) las operaciones de construcción. Aquí podemos encontrar trabajos de Gabriel Orozco, Gordon Matta-Clark, Lygia Clark y Hélio Oiticica, contrastando con trabajos de Simon Starling y Manuel Álvarez Bravo. Finalmente, temas centrales relacionados con el Surrealismo, la cultura popular y las contradicciones de la vida urbana se tejen en la obra de Francis Alÿs, Damián Ortega, Enrique Guzmán y Pablo Vargas Lugo.

Uno podría decir que la columna vertebral de la exposición es un trabajo de sitio específico que se encuentra ubicado en el centro del patio de la Maison Rouge, de la artista italo-francesa Tatiana Trouvé, que ancla las siguientes características: aquellos trabajos que hacen énfasis en las afinidades estructurales y constructivas y las varias resonancias iconográficas que exploran nociones de nacionalismo y pertenencia. Esta pieza, con su estética surrealista y seudomasoquista, sus aperturas y cierres, sus ramificaciones materiales y su naturaleza expansiva desgasta los reclamos de identidad que una exhibición y colección geográficamente obligada debería tener, y sugiere, por otro lado, que México es una imagen elusiva, tanto para extranjeros como para locales. El artista belga Francis Alÿs (uno de los artistas más prominentes de México) también direcciona esta falta de elusividad de lugar e identidad en su video *Zócalo*, 1999, realizado en colaboración con el artista mexicano Rafael Ortega. En este plano, 12 horas de documentación sobre el movimiento de la sombra del asta bandera, en uno de los sitios históricos más importantes de México, la plaza mayor de la ciudad y el lugar de las manifestaciones públicas y de los espectáculos de propaganda. El video de Alÿs retrata a la población protegiéndose del inclemente sol, parándose debajo de la sombra de la estructura. Hablando sobre la natural dependencia de los encuentros públicos, el espacio público, los monumentos y los espacios históricos (los que aquí se encuentran reunidos sólo buscan protejerse del sol), Alÿs, un extranjero que ha convertido a México en su lugar de residencia, desvela la frágil naturaleza de aquellas instituciones y la infraestructura que da visibilidad al concepto de nación (aquí la ondulante bandera pasa a segundo plano, es un fragmento que nadie ha venido a honrar). Su proceso de trabajo lo resume muy bien:

> "... paso mucho tiempo caminando por la ciudad... El concepto inicial del proyecto normalmente surge durante un paseo. Como artista, mi posición es parecida a la de quien pasa constantemente tratando de situarse en un ambiente en movimiento. Mi trabajo es una sucesión de notas y guías. La invención de un lenguaje va de a mano con la invención de la ciudad. Cada una de mis intervenciones es otro fragmento de historia que estoy inventando, de la ciudad cual estoy haciendo un mapa".[2]

Viajar y hacer mapas, la construcción del lugar a través de la imaginación; estas han sido poderosas metáforas para la producción artística de los últimos 25 años. Y su vigencia dentro del siglo veintiuno descubre nuestra exacerbada condición de viajeros permanentes abiertos a ideas migrantes, fronteras permeables y certezas desplazadas. Ignorar la vulnerabilidad de la construcción de una nación, cultura e identidad, es ignorar la liga fundamental entre el arte moderno y contemporáneo, centro y periferia, uno mismo y el otro. Es también ignorar el contexto fundacional de los objetos de arte: su relación con las instituciones, el mercado, y los problemas que competen su dirección. Corresponde a los artistas el inventar historias y reinventar la ciudad, corresponde a las exhibiciones y curadores el narrar esas trayectorias, y a las colecciones y coleccionistas el rendirse a la nostalgia y forjar nuevos, inconsistentes y siempre incompletos archivos de cultura contemporánea.

Mónica Amor (Curadora de la exposición)
Carlos Basualdo (Asesor de proyecto)

---

[2] http://www.postmedia.net/alys/zocalo.htm . Acceso septiembre 12, 2008.

Entrevista a Isabel y Agustín Coppel

por Mónica Amor y Carlos Basualdo, 15 de Febrero de 2008
Filadelfia, PA. Estados Unidos

IC: Isabel Coppel
AC: Agustín Coppel
MA: Mónica Amor
CB: Carlos Basualdo

MA: ¿Cómo comenzaste a coleccionar y cuál fue tu primera pieza?

AC: Visité algunas exposiciones en Culiacán y me hice amigo de un artista que ya murió. Con él empecé a conocer un poquito más de arte. Realmente la primera pieza que siento que compramos para la colección fue en Los Ángeles, en la galería de Tere Iturralde. Era una pintura de Cordelia Urueta de los años 40´s, de una mujer con vestido blanco bailando ante un espejo, que tiene un poco la estética de Diego Rivera. A Isabel y a mí nos encantó, y aún la tenemos colgada en el comedor de la casa.

MA: ¿Cómo se llamaba el artista que los introdujo al mundo del arte? ¿Te acuerdas?

AC: Se llamaba Miguel Esparza Blancas. Era un artista que conocía bien lo que estaba ocurriendo en Nueva York y de alguna manera trataba de interpretarlo en Culiacán. Era un gran seguidor de la obra de De Kooning de los años cincuenta. Aspiraba a desarrollar su propio lenguaje con un estilo mexicano, pero nunca tuvo mucho éxito.

MA: Y más tarde, al progresar su interés por coleccionar, ¿hay algunas influencias en particular, algún coleccionista o artista que haya sido o sea importante para ustedes?

AC: Hay una coleccionista en Culiacán, la señora Vita Podesta, que lleva mucho tiempo coleccionando. Compró hace como 25 años un cuerpo de obra de artistas muy importantes: Picasso, Diego Rivera, Juan Gris. Disfruta muchísimo su obra y además le resultó muy buena inversión; es algo que le significa mucho en su vida. Es una señora encantadora, nosotros somos sus amigos, nos invita a su casa y conversamos de muchísimos temas. Siempre ha tenido un espíritu muy joven y moderno.

CB: Me interesaría saber ¿por qué el arte? Y también si fue una decisión de los dos. ¿De dónde viene esa decisión?

AC: A los dos nos gustaba mucho el arte y disfrutábamos enormemente ir a conocer obras, buscar museos, entender el tema.

MA: ¿En el contexto artístico de Culiacán? ¿Algún museo en particular?

AC: En Culiacán hay un museo, MASIN, que tiene obra de los años cincuenta y sesenta en México, y también algunos artistas de principios de siglo. Pero más bien iniciamos esta búsqueda en los viajes. Siempre estuve muy metido en temas de comunicación, de filosofía y de organización. Me interesó tratar de entender cosas complejas, y fue como un reto entender por qué existía este mercado del arte y por qué se valoraba tanto determinado objeto. Me planteé como una incógnita intelectual la búsqueda de los significados de las cosas y el entender qué estaban viendo otras personas que yo no estaba viendo. En el camino empezamos a comprar obras de arte moderno mexicano, no de los grandes como Tamayo ni Rivera –salvo un Orozco que adquirimos hace muchos años–, sino de artistas periféricos al modernismo mexicano, artistas que son muy buenos, pero no tan conocidos internacionalmente.

MA: ¿Todavía tienen esas obras?

AC: Todavía tenemos y disfrutamos esas obras, todas. Pero en un momento dado frenamos ese proceso y empezamos a ver con más amplitud el tema del arte y lo que estaba sucediendo en el mundo. Pasamos en directo y con total convicción a coleccionar arte contemporáneo internacional. Recuerdo muy bien una tarde a principios de los 90´s en la Zona Rosa del DF, en la sala de la Galería Arvil con Armando Colina y Víctor Acuña. Armando fue muy contundente; me decía: "lo que tienes que buscar es Warhol, él es el artista más importante, él cambió la estética en el mundo, él es el verdadero creador del Pop Art, un artista con un cuerpo de obra inmenso". Nuestra primera adquisición de arte contemporáneo internacional fue una instalación muy grande de Gary Hill, *Learning Curve*.

CB: ¿Cuándo? ¿Puedes darnos alguna fecha?

AC: Como en1991 o 1992.

IC: También te surge mucho el interés por el arte cuando viviste en Nueva York, después de graduarte de la universidad.

AC: Sí, estuve viviendo en Nueva York 10 meses.

MA: ¿Cuándo?

AC: A mediados de los 80´s. Me tocó ir a algunas exposiciones increíbles, realmente a disfrutarlas como un observador más. Recorrí la ciudad, visité galerías y todos los museos.

MA: ¿Con algún guía o por tu cuenta?

AC: Solo, por mi cuenta. Tenía un amigo argentino que me acompañaba. Ahora lo tengo perdido.

CB: Pero ¿cómo se pasa de una situación en la que no hay tanto arte, en la que el arte es algo relativamente remoto, a una en la que es habitual el recorrer galerías? ¿Cómo se produjo esa transición? ¿Qué fue lo que inicialmente provocó tu curiosidad?

AC: Yo creo que la primera vez que fui a Europa con mi papá, un verano estando ya en la universidad, fue trascendental. El visitar el Museo del Prado, el Louvre en París con él de guía, me fascinó, fue una gran experiencia.

CB: ¿A tu papá le gustaba el arte?

AC: Le gustaba el arte muy clásico: Goya, Velásquez, Rubens, las guerras, la pintura histórica, heroica y en general los temas épicos.

CB: ¿Había pintura en tu casa?

AC: Había pintura, pero de la que se compra en las calles de París, paisajes parisinos, y un retrato interesante de mi mamá; es todo lo que había, no era un tema. Ese verano que fui con mi papá a Europa e invitamos un par de amigos míos, yo tenía 19 o 20 años, estuvimos tres semanas recorriendo las principales capitales. Visité por primera vez los grandes museos; entonces me nació la curiosidad de saber más sobre el expresionismo, los impresionistas y la historia del arte en general.

Recuerdo que en nuestra luna de miel, Isabel y yo fuimos a Tahití. En ese viaje llevaba conmigo una versión muy vieja de mi padre de la obra de Somerset Maugham, *La luna y seis peniques*, que trata sobre la vida de Gauguin. Todo el viaje fue una experiencia bellísima.

MA: Y volviendo a la obra de Gary Hill, ¿qué los motivó a comprarla?

AC: Yo estaba seguro que Gary Hill era el mejor videoasta en ese momento y creí que era importante comprar algo totalmente conceptual, muy histórico y significativo. Recuerdo que hice un análisis amplio de quiénes eran los videoastas y cuáles eran sus obras más interesantes. A Isabel le gustó la obra de Hill y decidimos comprarla.

MA: Pero tú no tenías nada de video hasta ese momento; estabas coleccionando pintura mexicana. Entonces, ¿cómo fue ese salto? ¿Viste la pieza en un viaje? ¿Quién te introdujo?

AC: Una obra similar, titulada *Learning Curve (still point)*, la vi por primera vez en el Museum of

Contemporary Art San Diego, instalada en un cuarto oscuro. La pieza consiste en un mesabanco con una silla colocada en uno de sus extremos. La mesa se amplía y termina en un pequeño monitor en el cual se proyecta una ola que rompe continuamente. En la versión que nosotros adquirimos, al final del mesabanco hay una
pantalla plana muy larga, con la misma imagen.

CB: Pareciera que desde el principio estabas pensando en términos de importancia histórica, de ubicación en un panorama más amplio, como si hubiese habido una intención programática en la colección. No parece haber sido una cuestión de vivir con cosas que a uno le gustan, sino más bien de componer una totalidad, ¿es así?

AC: Siempre. Sobre todo con la segunda parte de la colección, que fue algo mucho más pensado. Sí quería tener un cuerpo de obra que tuviera sentido y que me interesara a futuro, y no nada más en el momento en el que me gustó.

IC: Más estudiado, porque en el arte contemporáneo, si no estudias, no es tan fácil saber por dónde vas o qué quieres, qué te interesa. ¡Y Agustín vaya que estudia!

MA: En ese proceso de aprendizaje, de estudiar, ¿con quién te parece que mantienes un diálogo más sistemático? ¿Con instituciones, con coleccionistas, con artistas, curadores, críticos? ¿Hay algunas personas en concreto? ¿Algunas instituciones en específico?

AC: Constantemente aparecen ideas y puntos de vista muy diferentes, muy nuevos, inimaginables muchas veces, que sorprenden. Y entre los que opinan de arte, los que saben de arte, hay diferentes niveles.

Con el tiempo hemos venido platicando con muchas personas y hemos sostenido el diálogo con quienes creemos que nos aportan más. Hay mucha gente que habla constantemente de arte, pero no parece tener mucha idea. Claro que al principio cuesta trabajo entender toda esta dinámica. Posiblemente una de las cosas más importantes es aprender que uno no sabe de muchas cosas. Eso es muy valioso: saber que no sabes, y asumir que el tema del arte tiene varias capas y un sinnúmero de profundidades.

Conocer a Carlos y a ti Mónica, ha sido una etapa muy interesante para nosotros, porque tienen una perspectiva del arte que incluye corrientes artísticas con las que no estábamos familiarizados, como algunas que sucedieron en Italia y Brasil…, así como una visión más global, la importancia de cada pieza en un ambiente más internacional. Generalmente las galerías tienen un punto de vista sumamente limitado y no se dan cuenta de lo reducida que es su perspectiva. Algunos museos también se casan mucho con su época y con su momento, y terminan siendo obsoletos. El buen arte trata de provocar preguntas y de generar rupturas.

En México, por ejemplo, los artistas anteriores a Gabriel Orozco, que tuvieron mucho éxito, lo ven mal; les parece que su obra es una burla. A nosotros nos han dicho en muchas ocasiones que se va a caer a pedazos, que su obra no tiene futuro. En esa provocación te das cuenta del valor mismo de Orozco. Otros curadores, como Pedro Alonzo y su esposa Lane Coburn, tienen una visión muy joven del arte, abierta. Con él en particular hemos tenido muy buena relación.

También hemos tenido contacto por muchos años con los galeristas José Kuri, Mónica Manzutto, Enrique Guerrero, Jaime Riestra, Patricia Ortiz Monasterio, Marian Goodman, Andrea Rosen, Stephen Friedman y otros más muy importantes a los que nos gustaría conocer mejor, así como con los coleccionistas César y Mónica Cervantes, Patrick y Mariana Charpenel, Jose Noe y Marcela Suro, y con algunos curadores como Yvonne Force, Taiyana Pimentel y Ana Elena Mallet.

MA: ¿La relación con ellos es una visión internacional del arte?

AC: Sí, con Pedro Alonzo fue con quien compramos la obra de Gary Hill; él ha sido muy buen asesor. Con Yvonne Force hemos tenido una relación intermitente, pero de muchos años. Ella nos ha ayudado a entender otras propuestas y artistas.

Hemos tratado de seleccionar con quién tener cierta relación y con quién entablar relaciones más duraderas.

El desarrollo de la colección, las asesorías, las relaciones, los estudios y las diferentes adquisiciones las hemos hecho trabajando en equipo con Mireya Escalante, quien ha sido una parte muy importante en toda esta aventura.

MA: ¿Ustedes viven con el arte que compran? Obviamente, me imagino que no con todo, pero quizás hacen un esfuerzo por rotar las obras. ¿Cómo sistematizan este esfuerzo para experimentar los trabajos de alguna forma?

IC: Sí vivimos con el arte. En Culiacán tenemos el arte moderno latinoamericano que adquirimos primero, y en San Diego tenemos más del contemporáneo. La verdad, se siente mejor el contemporáneo, queremos estar rotando continuamente.

Es increíble cuando encuentras la pieza correcta, la que te gusta ver todos los días; cada vez que pasas por ahí, ves algo diferente, es lo que más disfrutamos.

AC: Realmente las casas, si lo analizamos, son galerías de arte. Queremos reestructurar la de Culiacán; es un proceso interesante. Cuando tienes una colección como la nuestra, se necesita una real curaduría para exhibir hasta en la propia casa. Ya no podemos colgar obras sólo porque nos parece bonito aquí o allá. Al hacer una curaduría de verdad, se encuentran conexiones que entonces dificultan el cambiar de lugar las piezas. Debe haber piezas suplentes, porque prestamos obra, pero las casas terminan siendo pequeñas galerías que exhiben exposiciones temporales.

MA: Claro, por eso les pregunto si lo han sistematizado de alguna forma. Es difícil reemplazar una por una.

IC: No es fácil; se requiere reconfigurar el sentido. Cambias tres o cuatro piezas, o no las puedes cambiar.

MA: ¿Qué tipo de interacción tienen con los artistas que han comprado? ¿Hay algún esfuerzo por parte de ustedes por conocer a esos artistas?

AC: Hemos conocido pocos, hemos platicado con algunos de ellos y nos hemos llevado buenas sorpresas en la gran mayoría de las ocasiones. Yo siento que en este momento los coleccionistas son muy bien vistos por los artistas, o sea, son muy abiertos, intentan explicar sus ideas y atendernos. Hemos tenido una buena relación con quienes hemos conocido. A mí en lo particular no me gusta mucho contaminarme de su personalidad, porque uno tiene una idea de una obra y ciertas referencias; así funciona mejor. Tiene uno que ver lo que hacen y tener esa tolerancia de sus propias vidas, porque no se están buscando role models, sino otras cosas.

MA: ¿Hay algún artista con el que mantengan alguna relación más personal?

AC: Con Sofía Taboas nos llevamos muy bien, al igual que con Pedro Reyes, Miguel Calderón y también con Gabriel Orozco; nos da mucho gusto verlos.

MA: ¿Cómo cambió su percepción del arte a través del coleccionismo?

AC: Pues es mucho más interesante el punto de vista que uno desarrolla como coleccionista. Son como dos cosas distintas: la apreciación del arte en sí mismo y la búsqueda natural de los coleccionistas, ya sean de discos antiguos, de zapatos o de lo que sea. El coleccionista es activo, es parte de la escena; hay un interés especial de estar buscando esa pieza única y poderla reconocer en el momento. Ahora que asistimos a la exposición de Frida aquí en Filadelfia, vimos piezas que en determinado momento estuvieron disponibles y era difícil entender que eran obras maestras; así nos puede estar pasando en muchas cosas, no sólo en el arte, sino en los negocios, en las relaciones, en las amistades. Hay situaciones y momentos que son claves y que no se ven a simple vista. Esto es como una formación para saber ver y apreciar; eso tiene un valor en la vida entera. Soy del mundo empresarial cien por ciento; el arte es de verdad un cambio de mentalidad, un descanso, un espacio de libertad, mi gran pasión que he podido aplicar y aprovechar en muchísimas cosas, en los grupos de trabajo, en equipos humanos, en las diferentes estrategias, en tener el ojo para saber qué sí vale y qué no vale.

MA: ¿Te ha pasado ver una obra que, como tú dices, la percibes inmediatamente como algo valioso, como algo que vale la pena, pero que dices no, no es para la colección?

AC: Sí, yo creo que nunca hemos comprado algo que no nos guste realmente, aunque estemos seguros de que es muy valioso. Además, las piezas se tienen que ver primero en su importancia y segundo en el contexto de la colección.

MA: O sea que hay una cuestión de gusto que es muy importante.

AC: Pues sí, sólo en una o dos ocasiones compramos algo que se nos hacía una buena inversión, pero terminamos por venderlo. Tener cosas que no nos gusten de fondo únicamente porque "hay que tenerlas", de alguna manera contamina la colección.

MA: ¿Cuál fue el enfoque inicial de la colección, cómo lo eligieron y por qué era importante para ustedes?

AC: Yo creo que no sabemos, realmente es una especie de enigma. Aunque yo le hubiera definido un enfoque con anterioridad, me parece que con la muestra que Mónica está curando ha encontrado un sentido muy interesante y diferente, que no habíamos alcanzado a ver. Considero que el querer definir la colección demasiado, querer explicarla, dedicarte a un medio o a una época, le quita fondo y placer al proceso. Y le quita coherencia, porque la coherencia está más bien en las obras. Nosotros creemos en el mensaje mismo del arte. Por ejemplo, esta muestra que se está haciendo en París, nos da una serie de relaciones nuevas muy interesantes que estamos descubriendo. Eso es lo inesperado de la colección, que tenga esa capacidad de tener varias lecturas.

MA: Se pudieron haber escogido otras obras, o a las mismas obras se les podría haber dado otra lectura distinta. Es quizá ese espíritu heterogéneo el que permite esa apertura. Ahora bien, ¿qué determina la incorporación de una nueva obra? ¿Cuáles son los elementos que determinan la incorporación de una obra a la colección?

AC: Es muy subjetivo; a veces estamos buscando algo de alguna época y terminamos comprando otra cosa. En cierto momento, una pieza o un artista hacen mucho sentido en la etapa en la que va la colección. Por ejemplo, teníamos mucho tiempo buscando un Nauman, y pues no se nos había dado el momento ni la pieza; por fin encontramos algo que se podría adecuar muy bien y lo compramos. También tiene que ver con una realidad de los recursos, no hay recursos ilimitados; pero si tuviéramos dinero sin límites, que no es el caso, también se podría perder el atractivo, porque entonces se trata de comprar lo top, lo más caro que hay en todos lados; entonces ya estaríamos comprando una pieza de Celebration de Koons. No creo que sería lo mejor para la colección, pero eso es otra historia; de todas formas ojalá lo hubiéramos hecho hace algunos años, por lo menos el perrito de globos.

MA: Esta experiencia con la curaduría, esta muestra, la experiencia de trabajar con las obras, de buscar relaciones... ¿Sienten que hay un reflejo o hay un paralelo entre la forma en que se establecen relaciones entre las obras a nivel curatorial y la forma en que uno incorpora una obra para la colección?

AC: Sí, por ejemplo, a las obras de Gordon Matta-Clark que se incluyeron se les dio mucha importancia. Yo no pensaba que Matta-Clark estaría tan bien con una pelota de fútbol de Gabriel Orozco, pero ves la pelota y lo de Matta-Clark, y tiene mucho sentido.

IC: Viendo nuestra colección desde otra perspectiva, hemos encontrado nuevas conexiones, hemos aprendido a relacionar cosas que no se nos habían ocurrido, lo que es muy interesante.

MA: ¿Qué tipo de diálogo te parece que están buscando entre las obras de los artistas mexicanos y los artistas internacionales, o los artistas de otros países, y cómo tratan de establecer ese diálogo?

AC: Creo que siempre ha habido un diálogo. En su momento, a mí me interesó mucho el diálogo de Rufino Tamayo y Siqueiros sobre el nacionalismo. Porque Rufino exhibía más por fuera y su obra nunca tuvo un mensaje político, y eso era muy mal visto en ese entonces; pero en realidad la obra de Tamayo se siente mexicana e internacional. Yo siempre fui más liberal, en pro de un mexicanismo como el que representaba Rufino Tamayo. Hoy más que nunca los artistas mexicanos están participando a nivel internacional con mucho éxito, traen una fibra mexicana, no con un obvio folclorismo, sino en una forma más profunda. Eso me parece muy valioso para México, que ya está participando en una competencia internacional en todos los ámbitos, al igual que otros países. Yo creo que hay un mensaje de globalización, por decirlo de alguna manera, en estos nuevos artistas. Lo mismo ocurre en la arquitectura, en el cine... Ya ves cómo los directores nuevos están teniendo tanto éxito al mostrar una visión particular que el mundo está apreciando; y eso es un gran orgullo para México.

MA: O sea que las resonancias locales están incorporadas de una manera más estructurada en formas de ver, formas de usar los materiales. También se ve un poco en la muestra que esas resonancias locales pueden reverberar en otros contextos.

CB: Me acuerdo de eso que decía Jorge Luis Borges en su ensayo de 1936, "El escritor argentino y la tradición:" "en el Corán no hay camellos".

MA: ¿Te parece que hay un sentido de misión en su actividad como coleccionistas?

AC: Yo creo que al tema del arte siempre se le quiere dar una misión, algún sentido de responsabilidad social; muchos están constantemente buscándolo. En el momento en que está uno en busca de esa misión, todo se afecta más, incluso la misma responsabilidad social, ya que el valor principal es la obra misma. Las obras de la colección las tenemos porque son muy buenos artistas y también excelentes piezas, o por lo menos así lo valoramos. Si hay alguna misión en la colección, es más bien la de destacar dónde hay talento y dónde hay creatividad de verdad, más que ayudar a que a un grupo le vaya bien. No quisiéramos engañar a nadie, lo que queremos y buscamos para la colección son obras que hacen vibrar, que valen la pena, que tienen talento.

MA: ¿Están interesados en compartir la colección con una audiencia? ¿Han pensado en las formas en que eso pueda tener lugar?

AC: Por supuesto que nos gustaría que las obras estuvieran expuestas al público. No se compraron para no exhibirse. Vamos a ir encontrando los lugares y los momentos adecuados. Ahora ya hay un proyecto.

MA: Habla un poquito de eso, me parece que sería importante.

AC: Hay un hermoso jardín en Culiacán; es un espacio del gobierno estatal, un espacio público. Y hay una asociación que yo presido llamada Sociedad Botánica y Zoológica de Sinaloa, AC. Tuve una relación muy buena con quien ideó el Jardín Botánico, el ingeniero Carlos Murillo, que ya murió. Con él trabajé durante 15 años aproximadamente, tratando de mejorar el espacio. Hicimos muy buen trabajo, se mejoró mucho el jardín y en determinado momento, por esto del arte, pensé que sería bueno empezar a incorporar algunas obras al lugar.

Comenzamos entonces a hablar con algunos curadores mexicanos, y tomamos la decisión de invitar a Patrick Charpenel a trabajar en el proyecto. Él hizo una propuesta muy interesante, muy de fondo, de cómo convertir este Jardín Botánico en un espacio de descubrimiento de arte contemporáneo, con obras integradas al jardín por artistas que trabajaron in-situ en Culiacán.

IC: Aquí tambien, como en la colección misma, ha venido trabajando con nosotros de manera muy profesional Mireya Escalante como coordinadora de los proyectos, adquisiciones y relaciones; ha formado un verdadero equipo de análisis, estudio y trabajo. Su participación en la colección y demás proyectos es muy valiosa, y a la vez es razón y causa de mucho de lo que sucede.

MA: ¿Y hay algún espacio interno, dentro del Jardín Botánico, que se pueda utilizar para las obras que requieren un espacio más convencional?

AC: Va a haber una especie de galería en unos edificios que está diseñando Tatiana Bilbao, pero son chicos, como para una muestra chica de arte. Todo lo demás está integrado al Jardín. La instalación es permanente y va a requerir mantenimiento. Hay obras de James Turrell, Gabriel Orozco, Dan Graham, Francis Alÿs, Julian Opie, Olafur Eliasson, Pablo Vargas Lugo, Simon Starling, Teresa Margolles, Rikrit

Tiravanija, Tino Seghal, Diana Thater, Richard Long, Mario García Torres, Sofía Taboas, Kyoto Ota, Fernando Orte, Pedro Reyes, etc.

MA: ¿Para cuándo creen que esté listo el proyecto?

AC: En unos dos años. Ya se están terminando algunas de las obras y el Jardín en sí mismo necesita muchas mejoras. Es un espacio interminable en cuanto a mantenimiento, donde hay que tomar decisiones estéticas todo el tiempo.

MA: ¿Les parece que puede haber otro tipo de actividades culturales alrededor de esa instalación?

AC: Sí, es un espacio ideal para ello; de hecho, ya hay muchísima actividad en el Jardín Botánico, como visitas de escuelas. Es un lugar muy especial y yo creo que va a ser muy interesante para Culiacán.

CB: Es interesante que vos, por un lado decís que lo que más te importa es la obra misma y que la obra sea fuerte, pero por otro lado hay como dos cosas que parecen percibirse. Por un lado, una intención de responsabilidad social que en Estados Unidos sería un "give back to the community" porque lo del Jardín Botánico es justamente lo más lejos a un vanity project que uno puede pensar, porque no se trata de hacer un palacio y mostrar master works totalmente fuera de contexto, sino de trabajar con un jardín que tiene una relación con la naturaleza.

MA: Y con la ciudad.

CB: Sí, con la ciudad que involucra una serie de connotaciones que tienen que ver con el uso y con la gente, y el integrar arte de manera que la gente pueda descubrirlo. Me parece un proyecto muy significativo a nivel de pensarlo como responsabilidad social y, por otro lado, percibo todo el tiempo en tu discurso y en el modo en el que vos trabajás una intención de apoyar a la gente de talento que vos encontrás, sean tanto artistas como arquitectos, escritores, etc. En este proyecto para La Maison Rouge hay dos escritores mexicanos escribiendo para el catálogo y te veo siempre muy curioso de conectarte a otros campos. Pareciese que la colección se insertase también en algún sentido dentro de un proyecto de apoyo, de mejora de las condiciones de vida del lugar en el que ustedes viven y en el que ustedes se formaron. No sé cuán consciente estás vos de eso.

AC: Sí estoy consciente de ello, aunque no lo reflexiono tanto, porque más bien estoy enfocado a que esto funcione, que es todo un reto. Yo creo que lo valioso, si lo logramos hacer bien, es que cada uno de los visitantes al Jardín Botánico entre a la experiencia del jardín mismo con sus encantos naturales, y tenga un inesperado contacto con el arte contemporáneo, el cual, en Culiacán, es casi inexistente. Esto les va a abrir la mente y les va a generar un interés. Va a ser una experiencia inolvidable para todos los jóvenes y en general para todos los visitantes. No hay duda de que ese es un interés real.

IC: Pero ese siempre ha sido tu interés, el de difundir el gusto por el arte para que haya un cambio en el pensamiento de la gente, para que tengan una oportunidad de ver otras cosas, de ver de qué manera se aplica a su vida ese cambio, esa flexibilidad que te da de alguna manera el ver arte.

CB: Y esto lo sienten tanto en relación a una persona anónima, como el posible visitante del Jardín Botánico, o también en relación a sus amigos, a los que ustedes incentivan y con los que suelen viajar a ver arte. Creo que existe un intento muy claro de parte de ustedes de promover el arte que les interesa y coleccionan.

IC: Son como redes que se van tejiendo, y de alguna manera van llegando a diferentes ámbitos que a lo mejor no imaginabas. Sobre todo la gente en Culiacán siente que está participando de alguna manera muy directa con este proyecto.

AC: Cuando iba a caminar en la mañana por el Jardín Botánico con el ingeniero Murillo para supervisar el trabajo, todo mundo nos felicitaba, como si estuviéramos en campaña política. Para mucha gente de Culiacán, el Jardín Botánico es sumamente importante; todos los días van a caminar ahí, meditan, reflexionan, y ver la transformación de ese espacio ha sido algo muy especial.

MA: ¿Cuál es el futuro de la colección?

AC: Seguir canalizando la colección como colección en sí misma; encontrar piezas y obras que ayuden a fortalecerla, a hacerla más y más interesante, más coherente en diferentes formas. Seguir adquiriendo piezas que tengan relevancia para la colección. En Guadalajara hemos tenido pláticas para hacer algo con la Universidad de Guadalajara, y si eso sigue adelante, probablemente la colección se muestre en unos años de manera más permanente en dicha ciudad. Por supuesto, una meta muy importante es terminar el Jardín Botánico. Es una labor complicada, muy complicada, que ha costado mucho trabajo y mucho tiempo porque no sólo es el tema del arte, sino el de la botánica, el de la construcción de los proyectos, el de las visitas de los artistas, etc. En fin, se trata de un esfuerzo colectivo muy grande. Ahora están trabajando en el landscape asesores de México y de diferentes lugares. En esta vida vale más hacer una cosa muy bien hecha que cien regulares.

MA: Y esa experiencia te va a determinar un poco que otros proyectos se embarquen o qué línea vas a tomar con respecto al futuro del público en la colección.

AC: Sí, por ahora hasta aquí estamos. Si logramos sacar bien esto del Jardin, ya pensaremos en otros proyectos.

IC: Así es.

17 MEXICANOS GLOBALES

Sabina Berman

EL EXILIO

SAM ZYMAN compone y estrena sus piezas musicales en Nueva York, pero es mexicano. Corrijo: y es mexicano.

Estudió medicina en México, aunque siempre, paralelamente, hacía música, como intérprete. Un día su esposa Nancy Carrasco le señaló la convocatoria de un concurso de composición. Samuel compuso música por primera vez, un octeto: no ganó el concurso pero sí la certeza de lo que quería hacer el resto de su vida. Muy pronto emigró a Nueva York para estudiar en el conservatorio Julliard. Y ahora, desde Juilliard, donde enseña y donde ensaya sus nuevas composiciones, su música se está difundiendo por el mundo.

De nuevo: y Samuel Zyman es mexicano.

No puede dejar de serlo ni quiere. Lo mexicano se siente en su música, pero de una forma inédita, singular. Si los críticos desconocen su biografía, no lo notan en ciertos ritmos, ciertas inflexiones. Si la conocen, no tardan en señalar su sabor "latino".

En el 2007, su Suite para dos chelos se presentó en el Palacio de las Bellas Artes de la Ciudad de México interpretada por dos de los mayores chelistas del mundo: Yo Yo Ma y Carlos Prieto. Cuando ambos se inclinaban en el proscenio para agradecer el aplauso del público, Yo Yo Ma lo llamó con un ademán. Sam caminó por el pasillo de la butaquería hasta el proscenio con la intención de alargarles desde ahí la mano a los dos chelistas y Yo yo Ma lo jaló diciéndole:

"Come up Sam, I´ll help you." ("Sube Sam, yo te ayudo.")

"Poco elegante", acota Samuel, así —de la mano de un japonés nacido en París y que vive en Norteamérica— subió a recibir el aplauso de un público que lo conocía poco, paradójicamente el del país de su nacimiento.

ALEJANDRO GONZÁLEZ IÑÁRRITU se formó como cineasta en México. Hizo radio como locutor y programador; hizo muchas horas de imagen para las cortinillas de Televisa y como comercialero; hizo su ópera prima, Amores perros: todo en México.

Entonces decidió cambiar de domicilio a Hollywood. Es decir, a la zona residencial de Santa Mónica en Los Ángeles, desde donde Hollywood no es una quimera, sino la industria de cine que se desperdiga por toda la ciudad.

Salir de México con esposa e hijos, cambiar de residencia, de pronto ser Nadie, cuando en México ya era reconocido por la gente en la calle. Don Nadie en una ciudad en la que Julia Roberts hace compras seguida de un cortejo de fotógrafos; donde Spielberg entra a una cafetería y 16 manos se alzan saludándolo; y donde una tarde, cuando El Negro, como llaman sus cuates a Iñárritu, entraba por el patio de atrás a su propia casa, un vecino llamó a la policía creyéndolo un ladrón.

Lo más difícil, narra Iñárritu, fue saber que ponía tres mil kilómetros de distancia entre sus dos hijos y sus abuelos. Sus abuelos, sus tíos, sus primos: la banda familiar.

¿No es eso la Patria? El lugar donde vive nuestra gente amada. ¿Y no es ese el exilio? No poder subirte a un transporte y llegar a casa de los abuelos.

"Ni modo", se responde a sí mismo Alejandro, con aire reflexivo. "Para bien y para mal les tocó ser mis hijos." Él y su esposa María Idalia los llevan seguido a México para que convivan con la familia. "Pero no es igual", dice Alejandro.

Iñárritu bregó tres largos años para preparar desde Los Ángeles su segunda película, 21 gramos, toda ella en inglés y con actores norteamericanos, aunque muchos de los creativos fueron mexicanos o latinoamericanos. El libro cinematográfico es de un mexicano, la música es de un argentino; la edición, la cámara, el diseño de arte, la hicieron mexicanos.

Como Zyman, Iñárritu se considera, sin asomo de duda, mexicano. Hay una intensidad emocional, una escala de valores y un permiso para imaginar, casi surrealista, en sus películas: todo ello muy mexicano. Además, Iñárritu es un activo de la comunidad mexicana angelina y da la cara por sus causas.

Famosamente, al recibir el Globo de Oro por Babel de manos del gobernador de California, El Negro le hizo una bromita: "Search me, I have my papers", le dijo a Arnold Schwarzenegger, "Búsqueme, traigo mis documentos". Así se igualaba a los millones de migrantes mexicanos ilegales. Por cierto que Arnold torció el gesto.

ALFONSO CUARÓN me llamó por teléfono una mañana. Con Cuarón, uno no puede saber nunca de dónde llama. Tiene una casa como de sueño en la campiña de Italia; renta un departamento en Londres, donde se encuentra el estudio en que ha filmado sus últimas dos películas; en Nueva York estuvo todo un año trabajando en otro departamento y hasta hace dos años ahí estaban las oficinas de su compañía de producción, Esperanto, aun si es en Los Ángeles donde suele reunirse con los productores de los estudios de cine. Además, viaja seguido a México, donde lo llaman otros asuntos de trabajo y donde vive la mayor parte de su familia.

Para mí que el hogar de Alfonso es su teléfono celular con roaming internacional.

"¿Dónde estás, Alfonso?", le pregunté.

"En un aeropuerto", me contestó, "voy rumbo a México, a presentar Children of men".

Alfonso quería rebotar conmigo algunas ideas que pensaba expresar a los reporteros cuando se topara con ellos en el aeropuerto de México. Por ejemplo, cuando le preguntaran cómo se concibe a sí mismo.

"Yo soy un pirata", dijo que les iba a decir, "voy y vengo".

Le dije: "Já, qué romántico, pero para mí que eres algo más contemporáneo: un bracero mexicano de lujo".

Lo dije y Alfonso se rió.

Al día siguiente leí en el periódico el encabezado de la sección de espectáculos: Cuarón, bracero de lujo. A los reporteros también les había gustado el mote.

Cuarón, como Iñárritu, como **GUILLERMO DEL TORO**, el director que completa la tercia de ases de nuestros cineastas emigrados, sienten una filiación con los otros millones de migrantes mexicanos. Quinientos mil mexicanos han salido de México cada año, desde hace diez; anteriormente el flujo era de unos doscientos mil anuales. 9 millones viven hoy ilegalmente en los Estados Unidos de Norteamérica. 20 millones viven legalmente ahí. Además hay comunidades mexicanas considerables en Canadá, Alaska y España, y aunque menores, en el resto de Europa.

Igual que esos migrantes, los tres ases del cine, como tantos otros artistas mexicanos nacidos en la década de los 50, deshicieron sus hogares en México para ir a buscar mejores oportunidades de trabajo. Igual que ellos, conocen el desasosiego de no pertenecer, la añoranza diaria por la Patria, el resentimiento por la incapacidad de los gobiernos mexicanos y mantienen una lealtad sentimental al país: igual que los braceros del hambre, los braceros de lujo han ayudado a cruzar por la frontera a amigos, dándoles trabajo.

E igual que ellos, son fieles al español y a la cultura mexicana. Cuarón está al tanto de la nueva novela de importancia, de la última película nacional, de la bronca interminable de nuestra política, lee Letras Libres y el Proceso, aunque esté filmando en Londres.

LO GLOBAL

GAEL GARCÍA BERNAL, el actor mexicano más activo en el cine mundial, se queda pensativo cuando le pregunto si se considera un bracero de lujo.

Me dice: "Cuarón, Del Toro, Iñárritu, sí tuvieron que emigrar para poder hacer películas grandes. En el México que a ellos les tocó (hacer sus pininos), (un México sin industria de cine), era imposible. Además, desde México no hubieran podido lograr una distribución mundial. Así que ellos sí fueron braceros de lujo. Yo en cambio, nunca sentí la necesidad de emigrar". Enfatiza la palabra necesidad.

Pero igual tus películas mexicanas no fueron distribuidas internacionalmente, le apunto. Hoy todavía es a través de Londres o Nueva York o Los Ángeles que una obra de arte se distribuye internacionalmente.

"Sí", asiente Gael y permanece meditabundo. La verdad no le resuena bien el término bracero de lujo. Lleva tácita una condición de necesidad, de escasez, que no se ajusta a su experiencia.

La suya es por el contrario una experiencia de abundancia de oportunidades y de extraordinaria movilidad. Gael no ha emigrado: entra y sale de México, vuelve y se va, eso varias veces cada año, según el lugar en que las películas que filma suceden. Y para sus proyectos mexicanos, que son varios, tiene acceso al capital de Hollywood, de México y de Europa.

"¿Artista global te conviene mejor?", le pregunto.

"Sí", contesta más convencido, le suena mejor. Pero me anota algo más. "No quiero estructurar demasiado con el pensamiento algo que en la realidad carece de estructura", me dice.

"¿La globalización de la cultura carece de estructura?", le pregunto.

"Así es. Está sucediendo, día a día; día a día está reinventándose."

Estructurarlo sería precipitarse en un error táctico, parece decir Gael. Demasiados vectores están moviendo el fenómeno, demasiados actores participan en él.

Esa forma no planeada de estar en medio del suceso de la globalización de la cultura, esa forma de estar abierto a lo que ocurra, de estar disponible a participar en formas todavía inéditas; esa forma de no interrumpir el flujo de creatividad común con una convicción demasiado personal: en ello reside parte del éxito de Gael.

Por lo menos en dos bandas internacionales de artistas participa Gael. La banda latinoamericana global y la banda de treintañeros global. Con la primera ha hecho películas memorables, Y tu mamá también, Babel, Ensayo sobre la ceguera, Diarios de motocicleta, entre otras; con la segunda ha hecho también

cine, digamos The Science of Sleep; teatro, Together, e incluso ha grabado una canción de rock, Cristóbal, que también es el tema musical de su ópera prima como director, Déficit.
"¿Cuántos idiomas hablas?", le pregunto a Gael.

"Español e inglés, perfectamente. Pero puedo charlar en portugués, en italiano y en francés."

Me confiesa algo más: ha oído decir que los niños aprenden idiomas con una facilidad incomparable, y sin embargo él mismo a los 30 años, viajando entre países, entre directores, entre películas, se sorprende de agarrar al vuelo los idiomas. "Acabo de hacer teatro en Islandia, y había mañanas en que me veía a mí mismo hablando islandés. Bueno no, hablando algunas palabras en islandés, así como si nada."

La penúltima vez que vi a **GABRIEL OROZCO**, el artista plástico, fue en un programa de la televisión norteamericana, de la PBS para mayor precisión, transmitido en Calgary, donde yo me encontraba haciendo teatro.

Se le miraba a Orozco fotografiando los melones en un supermercado. Luego fotografiaba las latas de atún apiladas en forma de pirámide. Podía haber estado en un super de cualquier ciudad de Occidente.

¿No es eso también la globalización?: la estandarización de eventos cotidianos como ir a comprar la comida en un supermercado idéntico a cualquier supermercado del mundo. También otra señal de la globalización: la foto de una pirámide de latas de atún: el equivalente para los pintores renacentistas de un óleo de un grupo de naranjas y manzanas.

De hecho Orozco estaba en París. Las siguientes imágenes lo mostraban fotografiando una bolsa de papel estraza movida por un vientecito en una calle color sepia, inequívocamente parisina.

Orozco se paró ante un contenedor de basura y fotografió una bola de papel desgarrado en tiras.

La última vez que lo vi, fue en un pueblo mexicano. ¿Malinalco, Chiconcuac, San Miguel de Allende?, no lo logro recordar. Un pueblo de esos bien cuidados que hay en México y que se llenan de luz ámbar en las tardes. Lo reconocí de lejos ahí al fondo de una calle: Orozco fotografiaba los alambres que coronaban una barda inconclusa de ladrillos.

En efecto, como Gael lo expresa, no hay un control central en la globalización de la cultura. No hay una Hormiga Reina ni un Hugo Chávez, ni un Banco Mundial que señalen el rumbo o pongan las reglas.

"¿Hay sin embargo algún acuerdo entre los cineastas mexicanos globales?", le pregunto.

“Nada.” “¿Un manifiesto?” “Nada.” “¿Un manifiesto ni siquiera informal?” “No, nada.”
Y sin embargo, entre la diversidad de factores que juegan en la globalización de los artistas mexicanos, hay factores principales.

1. Un mundo cada vez más redondo gracias a una intercomunicación que nuestros abuelos hubieran considerado imposible.

2. Una cultura globalmente difundida, en cuyo repertorio de valores estéticos se precian dos que suelen ejercer los artistas mexicanos globales con naturalidad:

    a. La captura justamente de lo global, que es la señal distintiva de la época.

    b. Y lo excéntrico –lo que está fuera del discurso central de la cultura en Occidente–.

3. La generación más grande de millonarios que la historia ha conocido: millonarios desperdigados por los cinco continentes que pueden comprar arte –y de hecho lo están comprando, formando así un mercado global, especialmente para las artes plásticas–.

4. La crisis de las artes en México, en la que conviven:

    a. La generación numéricamente más grande de artistas habida, artistas educados en las excelentes escuelas públicas de arte y que logran afinar sus dones gracias a una diversidad de becas y subsidios.

    b. Una política cultural que ha fallado en dos áreas. Una, promover el surgimiento de industrias culturales. Dos, enlazar la obra creada de los artistas mexicanos con la sociedad.

Así, los artistas contemporáneos mexicanos se descubren con sus instrumentos bien afinados y sin promotores ni público. Acicateados por un miedo, el miedo al autismo, y una ambición, la globalización, es que cientos de ellos han emprendido el viaje hacia el mundo.

SER EXCÉNTRICO O NO.

Octavio Paz advirtió que los mexicanos somos, culturalmente, occidentales excéntricos. Es decir, culturalmente pertenecemos a Occidente, pero no a su centro; la nuestra es una tradición cultural imantada desde la distancia de la tradición central occidental. Paz lo escribía por los años sesenta, en la ciudad que por entonces era considerada por los latinoamericanos el centro de la cultura occidental, París, y lo escribía como un estado inescapable para un mexicano. Las cosas se han movido.

Ahora mismo, no existe un centro principal de lo cultural. Aunque tampoco es verdad que vivamos ya en un mundo plano, como algunos observadores de la globalización presumen prematura y optimistamente. No, estrenar con éxito una obra de teatro en una ciudad latinoamericana, digamos Buenos Aires, no tendrá las repercusiones de estrenarla en Londres. Si en Londres fuera un éxito, se remontaría en 30 ciudades; si en Buenos Aires es un éxito, su fama permanecerá enclaustrada en Buenos Aires.

Así, el mercado de las artes sí se ha expandido por el planeta entero, pero las decisiones para la distribución global de las artes se toman todavía en unas cuantas ciudades: Nueva York, Los Ángeles y, en menor grado, Londres, París y otras capitales europeas.

En esta cultura global, la expresión de Paz, occidental excéntrico, se ha vuelto más bien una opción para cada artista mexicano. Cada uno debe elegir qué tan excéntrico quiere ser; y qué tan occidental.

Gabriel Orozco es nieto directo de Marcel Duchamp y sólo un fervor nacionalista le descubrirá filiaciones con Diego Rivera o Frida Kahlo. Mary-Anne Martin, la galerista de arte latinoamericano con base en Nueva York, dice que los compradores de piezas de Orozco a menudo desconocen que es mexicano y de saberlo les parece "un dato meramente incidental".

En cambio, Samuel Zyman reconoce en su propia música influencias claramente mexicanas. "No soy nacionalista", dice. "No me gustan los nacionalismos. Pero soy mexicano, hablo español, crecí en México, viví en la realidad mexicana y es parte de cómo veo el mundo, de cómo veo todo. Ser mexicano es parte esencial de quien soy."

Rememora una infancia donde la música mexicana le entraba por todas partes. "En los taxis, en la radio, en la televisión, vas a placitas donde tocan bandas. Además, estuve y estoy en contacto con la música clásica mexicana, la música de los grandes compositores. Y estudié con el compositor mexicano Humberto Hernández Medrano..." Ha escrito obras "deliberadamente mexicanas" en dos casos en que así se lo pidieron. "Encuentros, que compuse para representar a México en la Expo 92 en Sevilla. Y mi segunda sinfonía, que compuse para conmemorar el 50 aniversario del Instituto Nacional de Nutrición."

"Era el 96, México estaba en crisis, se vivía la devaluación. El doctor Segovia, entonces director de Nutrición, me dijo: 'Escríbeme una obra que nos retorne el orgullo de ser mexicanos, titúlala La Recuperación del Orgullo'. Me estaba pidiendo una obra nacionalista y eso fue lo que hice. Pero aún en obras que no llevan esa agenda, me sale lo mexicano, y lo judío."

Los críticos detectan de inmediato en Samuel Zyman la influencia de compositores del canon occidental. Bach, sobre todo, ritmos de jazz también. Suelen encontrarle lo judío a continuación, que en varias obras se anuncia desde el título, como en su Kol Nidrei. Lo mexicano se lo notan típicamente cuando el crítico conoce su biografía; entonces lo catalogan como músico mexicano o latino, eso dependiendo de la biografía cultural del crítico.

El caso del coreógrafo **LUIS SERRANO** es distinto. Serrano ha elegido "lo mexicano" como sello de identidad para globalizar a la compañía de Ballet de Monterrey.

Serrano nació en Cuba. Como bailarín clásico desarrolló una sólida trayectoria en compañías de primer nivel de Cuba, Venezuela y Estados Unidos. Al asumir la dirección artística del Ballet de Monterrey (BdM, según su logo), Serrano y la fundadora de la compañía, Yolanda Santos de Hoyos, se propusieron internacionalizarla. Para ello eligieron dos rutas: elevar el nivel técnico de los bailarines y propiciar nuevas obras con música mexicana.

"Más identidad clásica en lo formal y más identidad mexicana", escribe Fey Berman sobre el camino que trazaron para el BdM desde el año 2007 y que en el 2008 da sus frutos en la gira que realizan por varias capitales.

Cada noche el programa del BdM se cierra con Huapango, del músico nacionalista Moncayo, "tema mexicano hasta el tope y que requiere gran energía y obliga a los bailarines a movimientos minuciosamente complejos y espectaculares. Los hombres hacen audaces saltos y giros en el aire. Las mujeres se suspenden en la punta del pie pareciendo suspendidas. Los hombres levantan y giran a las mujeres llegando ambos a poses inesperadas y llamativas."

"Esta pieza", dice Serrano, "es el sello de la compañía. Con Huapango marcamos una personalidad propia bien identificable".

GUILLERMO GÓMEZ-PEÑA, el célebre performancero, elige en cambio declararse ni de aquí ni de allá, sino del cruce de fronteras. Su arte es ese: retratarse en el cruce de las fronteras entre identidades establecidas. Capturar el híbrido que ocurre en el momento de cruzar.

Guillermo nació en la Ciudad de México. Veinteañero, estaba dedicado a un poema épico sobre un viaje intergaláctico cuando lo conocí en la Capilla Alfonsina, donde también yo tallereaba mis versos libres, y era un tipo sumamente divertido y peligroso.

Una breve muestra. Una tarde tomábamos cervezas en un restaurancito argentino y hablábamos de todo y de nada, nada más que por matar el tiempo, y Guillermo se fijó en el señor que leía un periódico en una mesa contigua. El periódico le cubría el rostro y medio cuerpo y no vio al chavito bigotudo que era Guillermo acercarse y prenderle fuego con un encendedor y volver a sentarse para apreciar "el evento".

Veinteañero todavía, "sofocado por una cultura estática y jerárquica", Guillermo cruzó a vivir en California y ahí cruzó la frontera invisible entre los inmigrantes latinos y los chicanos, empezó a andar con los segundos a pesar del tabú que lo prohibía.

Ahora en San Francisco es líder del grupo de artistas autonombrado La Pocha Nostra y es uno de los actores más influyentes del performance como arte.

¿Mexicano, chicano, mexa-mericano, artista multi-cultural, occidental excéntrico, gringo espolvoreado con chilango?, ¿qué diablos es Gómez-Peña?

El Diablo que disuelve fronteras. Que muestra su artificio. Su crueldad política. Su tontería existencial.

Últimamente se autonombra "un mexicano post-nacional", es decir, un mexicano cuya identidad no depende del arraigo a un territorio o a la inclusión en una entidad política. Y también se autonombra uno de los próceres de una nación virtual llamada Latinoamérica del Norte.

Pero lo dicho, realmente Gómez-Peña se rebela a cualquier identidad estática. Sus eventos son cruces de fronteras –fronteras culturales, de género sexual, de lenguaje, fronteras entre la política y el arte, la práctica y la teoría, el artista y el espectador–.

Gómez-Peña se expresa, más famosamente, a través del performance, pero realiza igualmente video, instalaciones, fotografía y escribe ensayos y libros; y en algunos de sus eventos estéticos hace todo eso al mismo tiempo.

Si Zyman deja fluir por su música, fluir y entrelazarse, sus distintas herencias culturales y deja la definición al espectador crítico; si Gabriel Orozco está cómodo como artista occidental; si Luis Serrano elige como sello distintivo lo mexicano (a pesar de ser él mismo cubano); Gómez-Peña ha hecho de la autodefinición siempre en vías de convertirse en otro el terreno de su arte.

Es ciudadano del cambio y su Patria es el movimiento.

HERMAN@S MEXA-MERICAN@S

De cada tres familias en México, una tiene un familiar viviendo en Estados Unidos. En mi familia, esa es mi hermana, **FEY BERMAN.** Mi hermana mexa-mericana.

De lo que vengo escribiendo en este ensayo buena parte se lo debo a ella. A sus artículos y entrevistas y a las largas conversaciones diarias que sostenemos vía Skype. Lo que apunto y apuntaré de Samuel

Zyman, de Mary-Anne Martin y de Luis Rubio, lo tomo de lo que ella ha publicado sobre ellos. Igual sobre lo que apuntaré del cine mexa-mericano.

Fey observa fascinada la suerte de los artistas mexicanos que a través de Nueva York están globalizándose. También escribe de la naciente nueva cultura de los mexa-mericanos. También, de la vida cotidiana de los migrantes mexicanos.

Fey me hace notar que la vida de los mexa-mericanos y el arte de los artistas mexa-mericanos o mexicanos escasamente se tocan. Los artistas, en general, no se han considerado los voceros de los primeros. Aunque los momentos de excepción, donde sí lo han sido, ya forman un cuerpo significativo. En el cine, hay todo un género que informalmente se nombra "de tema de migrantes". Entre las películas y documentales de este género, Fey me señala dos. Una por poco convencional, otra por ser la que mejor ha capturado el sentimiento de la migración.

Una. Sleep dealer, de **ALEX RIVERA**, él mismo neoyorquino de padres ecuatorianos, imagina una "cibermaquila" en un futuro cercano. "El sueño de la derecha norteamericana vuelta película de ciencia ficción: disponer de la abundante mano de obra de los braceros mexicanos y no tener con ellos ninguna obligación social: en Sleep dealer los obreros permanecen del lado mexicano con el sistema nervioso enchufado a un sistema cibernético, de manera que su energía realiza a larga distancia el trabajo rudo y barato en las metrópolis de Estados Unidos e incluso lucha sus guerras en otros continentes."

La segunda película que me señala Fey es La misma luna, la película en español que más taquilla ha tenido en el mundo.

La misma luna nació de la colaboración de dos mujeres, una de un lado de la frontera y la otra del otro lado. **LIGIA VILLALOBOS**, norteamericana de padres mexicanos, quien escribió el guión (por cierto que en inglés) empleando sus memorias infantiles. La otra, mexicana, **PATRICIA RIGGEN**, que dirigió la cinta.

La misma luna captura el sentimiento que a Ligia Villalobos le parece el que atraviesa los hechos de la migración. El abandono. Al cruzar una frontera uno abandona un país. Al establecer del otro lado nuevas amistades uno abandona las pasadas. Al lograr estar bien en la nueva Patria uno renuncia a la Patria original.

Sobre el éxito arrollador de La misma luna, Patricia Riggen ha dicho que "todo cuanto ha sucedido es un milagro". Ligia Villalobos, más sajona, con los pies más asentados en la tierra, ha dicho que "esta pequeña película abrirá la puerta a los siguientes directores y guionistas de las siguientes películas latinas".

Fey también ha escrito sobre **MAX LIFCHITZ,** pianista, compositor, director de orquesta y del grupo musical Consonancia Norte/Sur.

Virtuoso como intérprete, Lifchitz como compositor exige el virtuosismo de sus intérpretes. Su música es brillante, arrebatada, pasional, post-moderna. A menudo política. Y su influencia en la música contemporánea, importante.

Yellow ribbon, una serie de obras cortas a la que sigue agregando, consta hasta ahora de 46 obras cortas escritas en el transcurso de 26 años y celebra la libertad política y artística de Occidente. Cada obra está dedicada a uno de los 54 estadounidenses secuestrados en Teherán, en 1979, y además refiere a la prohibición de la música que el Ayatola Homeini impuso en la radio.

Tlatelolco de villancicos rebeldes rememora la masacre de universitarios mexicanos del año 1968, con todo su estruendo y su tristeza inconsolable.

Elegía recuerda la guerra de Vietnam. *Still Life*, para doce voces femeninas, fue compuesta en memoria de las víctimas del ataque terrorista a las Torres Gemelas de Nueva York en septiembre 11 del año 2001.

El penúltimo CD de Lifchitz, dedicado a la música mexicana de piano, fue considerado por la revista Fanfare "...fácilmente el CD de piano más interesante grabado en 1996". Su último CD salio apenas en otoño de 2008.

"¿Cómo es posible que no se hable de Lifchitz en México?", me pregunta, casi me reclama, mi hermana mexa-mericana, escandalizada.

Su azoro es justo, es como si una familia no reconociera a uno de sus miembros más conspicuos. Todavía más porque Lifchitz siente y ejerce su membresía en la cultura en español: amén de que la refleja en su propia obra, se ha auto-designado como su difusor. El grupo que fundó, Consonancia Norte/Sur, ha estrenado en Estados Unidos cerca de 800 composiciones de autor latinoamericano y ha grabado con una porción de esa música más de dos decenas de CDs .

Le pregunto a Fey si es algo inédito lo que está sucediendo en la cultura mexa-mericana. Me lo confirma, es algo nuevo. Para empezar, sólo incómodamente se le puede llamar cultura mexa-mericana a este intenso cruce de artistas de uno y otro lado de la frontera, que además tampoco marca una separación con los artistas latinoamericanos. Para continuar, la efervescencia creativa no tiene precedentes ni tampoco su visibilidad en Norteamérica.

El 8 de abril del 2008 asisto con mi hermana a una cena de gala en el Lincoln Center de Nueva York. En el escenario, cien niños neoyorquinos—italianos, afro-americanos, orientales, judíos, irlandeses, vaya:

esa mezcla que se llama lo neoyorquino—bailan el jarabe tapatío, quebraditas, aires veracruzanos, y de cuando en cuando estallan en una porra. ¡Me –xi-có, Me –xi-có, Ra ra rá!

Con esta ceremonia se cierra un año en que dos millones y medio de niños dedicaron sus clases de artes a indagar sobre México y donde aprendieron sus bailes.

La iniciativa, del National Dance Institute y de la institución civil mexicana CONARTE, se complementó con la instalación de un programa gemelo en la Ciudad de México. Maestros neoyorquinos avezados en ello, educaron a maestros mexicanos para instalar la enseñanza de danza en las escuelas primarias del primer cuadro de la capital del país.

EL PORVENIR DE LOS GLOBALES

Gael García Bernal opina que no es sabio estructurar lo que fluye mejor sin estructura, la cada vez mayor participación de artistas mexicanos individuales en el juego del arte global.

Guillermo Gómez-Peña en cambio ve en esa ausencia de proyecto común más bien un abandono del estado mexicano. Lo ha dicho en innumerables ocasiones: el estado mexicano sencillamente no ha logrado articular una reacción al "inmenso fenómeno de la migración mexicana".

Cabe agregar: tampoco ha logrado reaccionar al inmenso fenómeno de la globalización cultural.

En 1990, el escritor Carlos Fuentes escribió desde Londres, donde reside la mayor parte de cada año, un artículo invitando al gobierno mexicano a capturar la oportunidad que abría un mundo repentinamente interesado en el español. Advertía que debían existir Casas México por doquier, para enseñar el español y como puertas abiertas a nuestra cultura.

"México debe hacer valer su liderazgo cultural en el mundo de habla hispana", declaró en el año 2000 Lourdes Arizpe, quien en ese momento terminaba su gestión como directora de cultura de la **UNESCO**.

Quien al cabo capturó la oportunidad que Fuentes vislumbró y Arizpe reiteró, fue España. Creado en 1990 por el Ministerio de Relaciones Exteriores español, el Instituto Cervantes ahora cuenta con 58 centros en el mundo.

En ese contexto, que cada artista global mexicano siga volando por el amplio cielo del orbe como un ave solitaria, no es una elección: es lo único posible. Si acaso por momentos encontrará otras cuantas aves para formar una parvada momentáneamente mexicana.

Y por eso iniciativas aisladas, emprendidas desde lo muy personal, pero que trascienden a un artista individual mexicano, como la alianza del National Dance Institute de Nueva York y **CONARTE** o como la exposición de la **COLECCIÓN COPPEL** en París, cobran la importancia de lo excepcional.

La colección Coppel es el mapa del gusto por el arte de una pareja, **ISABEL** y **AGUSTÍN COPPEL**. Los Coppel han ido adentrándose en el arte guiados por el placer y el interés, las mejores guías posibles tratándose de arte. Las primeras piezas que compraron fueron obras mexicanas y modernas. Luego, han ido adquiriendo obras latinoamericanas e internacionales contemporáneas.

El acierto de esta exposición es conservar los trazos de ese mapa excéntrico –con lo mexicano como semilla del interés por lo global–.

Un mapa excéntrico e inesperado para el espectador extranjero, donde podrá sorprenderse ante lo mexicano visto como una forma peculiar de lo occidental.

Un mapa excéntrico exhibido justamente en Europa, inicialmente en uno de los centros de Occidente, París.

Una idea feliz.

LA MÚSICA DE DOS CHELOS SOLITARIOS

Una tarde Carlos Prieto y Yo Yo Ma bajaron sus arcos, habían estado tocando dúos, y dejaron sus dos chelos lado a lado, en sendos sostenes de acero, en el centro de una estancia, y salieron a platicar con el compositor Samuel Zyman.

Carlos Prieto bromeó: "A ver qué hacen los chelos solitos. A ver si tienen chelitos, o algo".

Siguieron platicando y entonces, ya serio, Prieto le propuso a Zyman que hiciera "algo" para los dos chelos.

De ahí surgió *Dúo para dos chelos*, que Prieto interpretó con otros chelistas en distintas ciudades de América. No fue sino nueve años después que Yo Yo Ma y Carlos Prieto finalmente tocaron el dúo compuesto para ellos; sucedió en la Ciudad de México y fue en ese concierto que Yo Yo Ma le alargó la mano a Zyman para que trepara desde la butaquería al escenario más famoso de su Patria de origen, el Palacio de las Bellas Artes, donde recibió el aplauso del público mexicano.

Así de móvil se ha vuelto el escenario de las artes.

CARLOS REYGADAS planeó la historia para una película, Luz silenciosa, en su casa y luego salió al mundo para encontrarle el paisaje. Se decidió por el desierto del norte de México, donde habita la comunidad menonita, porque era un espacio casi vacío, con apenas construcciones y con pocos habitantes. Ahí su historia adquiere el sabor de un drama esencial.

Guillermo del Toro por su parte escribió el guión de El laberinto del fauno para filmarlo en México. Dificultades de financiamiento lo decidieron a filmarla en España, con leves cambios al libreto.

Sin duda el signo de la cultura global es la movilidad.

Un disparo en el desierto del Sahara afecta la vida de una adolescente japonesa, luego de repercutir en California y México. Tal es el mito que construyeron Alejandro González Iñárritu y el escritor **GUILLERMO ARRIAGA** en Babel, hablada en cuatro idiomas, y que se ha erigido como una metáfora de la época.

Guillermo Gómez-Peña escribe en su reciente libro El nuevo border mundial de una "nueva cultura híbrida emergente en todo el mundo". "Una cultura de fusión", "de multisincretismos", "de sampling", "de pastiches", "de yuxtaposiciones", "de interconexiones culturales".

Emergente: es decir, que surge sin comando central ni plan maestro y que adquirirá un nuevo nivel de organización por sí sola.

¿Cómo será ese "otro nuevo nivel de organización" que adquirirá la cultura global?

Ah, el suspenso que abre la pregunta se llama el presente.

Unexpected

Elmer Mendoza

Fueron un Hombre y su sombra los que pensaron que una ciudad no era un conjunto de edificios construidos en múltiples lomeríos, sino un espacio humano donde no se ponía el sol; sin embargo, la sombra se fue sin despedirse. Unos dicen que montó una fábrica de mapas en El Cairo, otros que compró una isla en Suecia y que de allí no la mueve nadie.

El Hombre sin sombra no creía en fantasmas, ni en la escala de valores del uno al diez, ni en la pureza de las formas. Después, no fue otra cosa que un viajerosedentario.

El Hombre tardó en salir de su desconcierto, en recuperar su equilibrio y en convencerse de que cada cosa tiene su razón y de que no siempre importa comprenderla. Pronto dejó de llamar la atención por su carencia. Años después, todos querían conocerlo, ¿por qué? Sospechaban que poseía una valiosa colección.

Encendió su puro. Se encontraba en su jardín acompañado de tres personas que ansiaban saber de su famosa colección. Hay varias cosas que me impactan de Gabriel Orozco, expresó: la forma en que ironiza los materiales, la vida y los recuerdos que uno es, los que se han acumulado a lo largo de los años. Veo una obra de él y me quedo meditando en mí como si fuera el Ave Fénix naciendo de esas entretelas del mundo en que nada parece tener una explicación coherente. Fumó. El humo que expulsó se llenó de pequeñas brujas volando en sus escobas. Es una sensación intensa que no me abandona por días. Incluso una vez soñé con un desfile de espantapájaros encabezado por Alfred Hitchcock; recuerdo que llevaba un enorme cuervo en la cabeza y otro en el hombro. Volvió a encender el puro. Varias de las pequeñas hechiceras se retiraron con solemnidad.

Me preocupa la ciudad, confesaba, y desarrollaba interesantes discusiones sobre el trazo de calles, avenidas, plazas y los diez mil seiscientos cuarenta y dos colores que habitan el planeta. Su colección, le requerían los tres tipos, Cuéntenos de su colección, ¿es verdad que es de arte etrusco? Y él añadía que un grupo de arquitectos dibujó planos diversos que nunca terminó de estudiar: ¿Qué hacen ustedes con una temperatura de 40 grados? El Paraíso tenía fuentes, frondosos jardines, arroyos y se acabó. Tenemos demasiadas colinas, pero no puede ser de otra manera, ¿acaso el mundo no es redondo? Uno de los invitados, prestigioso jeque, que pretendía adquirir la colección porque creía que era de películas de Marlene Dietrich, abandonó el lugar ofuscado. Ese Hombre habla de pintores y proyectos como si fuera lo único en la vida, exclamó, antes de subir a su helicóptero y desaparecer. Él no lo tomaba a mal y extrañaba a su sombra: una acompañante que tenía explicaciones para todo, aunque no entendía cómo podía vivir en una isla pequeña y sin él. Bueno, concluía, si yo puedo vivir sin ella, ¿por qué ella no va a vivir sin mí?

Toledo es una espina, es muchas espinas. De pescado, de maguey, de cactus. Comentaba entusiasmado. Su arte figurativo no tiene un asidero posible: flota y es tradición, esoterismo, manierismo; modificas el punto de vista y entras en la parte oscura del universo y saltas del delirio a la tranquilidad como si estuvieras en un columpio y la noche fuera simplemente una sopa. Su obra es una sombra espesa. La naturaleza que salta sobre el lienzo cae mezclada en su misterio y en los dedos de un hombre de pocas palabras. Desde luego, vestido de blanco. Beben vino. Las brujas en el humo del puro se empeñan en cabriolas imposibles que él contempla divertido.

Les cuenta: Esta plaza es para que circulen las muchachas en flor, me explicó un arquitecto que me mostraba un proyecto. El piso es de mármol e instalaremos ventiladores para que todas se consideren Marilyn Monroe. Observé, calculé y advertí que nadie hablaría jamás de la ciudad por eso. No, le señalé, es otra cosa la que necesitamos: una ciudad humana, donde la gente se quiera a sí misma porque ama el sitio donde vive. Quiero una ciudad irrepetible. Esperada/Inesperada. Donde cada árbol y cada habitación sean voces seguras de sí mismas. Que nuestros visitantes se pregunten dónde están y que jamás se respondan a la primera

Me gusta el Arte porque veo lo oculto, escucho lo no dicho, siento la vida en mi cuerpo, es lo que me interesa del arte; ese sentimiento fuerte que hace posible una vida anticipada porque sabes que nada será igual que ayer. Todo será nuevo. El color, las formas y el espacio regulan el universo. Cada percepción se convierte en un vehículo que opera en sentido contrario: es decir, se convierte en una forma de ver el mundo. Este puro está muy seco, no es para fumar a nivel del mar, o a 41 metros como estamos aquí. A ver, ¿gustan uno? Tengo una caja de otros, más suaves. Los invitados declinaron y él encendió el suyo. De su barbilla saltaron las brujas a la fumarola que salía de su boca.

Cuando fundaron la ciudad es probable que solamente lo hicieran por los ríos y la cuenca agrícola. Creció alrededor de ellos. En este plano hay ciento tres puentes. Me expuso un arquitecto. De todos tipos: de madera, hierro, cubiertos, de concreto, una réplica del Golden Gate, otra del Saint Michel. No, lo interrumpí. Bueno, dejemos algunos, los que no copien algo, pero quiero dos imaginarios, que la gente llegue allí e infiera que hay un puente, que si intenta cruzar se mojará en el río, que sepa que allí hay un puente que la ciudad venera. Tal vez sólo admirable por la gente de buen corazón. El arquitecto hizo rollo los planos y se retiró. Pensé que tal vez no había leído El traje nuevo del emperador.

Los visitantes lo escuchaban nerviosos y el respondía sus preguntas. Coleccionar es una forma de vida, explicó el Hombre que no le gustaba salir en la tele ni hablar con periodistas. Es una fuerza que siempre te induce a pensar en el día siguiente, en lo que debes hacer para merecer los momentos de gloria que dan las obras de arte. Un hombre hace su historia llueva, truene o relampaguee y al final son contados los momentos trascendentes, los días que se equiparan a las grandes obras y que son los que te hacen pensar que merece la pena vivir. Como el poeta que es inmortal por un poema de los miles que escribió. Todos deberíamos crear esos momentos. Por favor señor, hemos venido de muy lejos, por ahí dicen que usted tiene una colección que se niega a negociar. Nadie sabe de qué es pero es lo de menos; pensamos que viniendo de usted debe ser algo entrañable. El Hombre observó el humo y bebió.

No se explicaba por qué pero extrañaba profundamente a su sombra. No quería rechazar a sus invitados a pesar de que se hallaba en el límite de la prudencia. Uno de ellos, lo animó a seguir. He perdido interés en su colección pero no en sus palabras, me encantaría que continuara. Le dio las gracias: Sé que usted patrocina un museo muy importante, lo felicito, para mí un museo es el ejemplo más vivo del humanismo cotidiano, ese que expresa las maneras en que transcurre la vida. Lo que se respira y por más pequeño que sea ningún visitante es limitado por sus paredes. Hay un aire revolvente que nos ubica en el tiempo y el espacio. El otro de los presentes insistió: Su colección, ¿tiene que ver sólo con obra del siglo veinte o... Movió la cabeza negando.

Respondió a su interlocutor más atento. El Arte, como los sentimientos, no tiene nacionalidad. No siempre soy capaz de explicar la atracción, leve o desmesurada, de un cuadro. Se puso de pie para abrir una botella.

Las pequeñas se alegraron y reanudaron sus juegos. Volaron y volaron. Entonces tocaron el timbre con suavidad. Guardó silencio. Sin duda, alguien más en busca de mi colección, pensó. Tal vez ese señor chino que no he querido recibir. Las brujas fueron a ver quién lo buscaba y quedaron magnetizadas con la visitante y la acompañaron. Era su sombra que se deslizó suavemente hasta la estancia con las brujas revoloteando alrededor. El Hombre estupefacto se puso de pie. ¿Saben cómo abrazar una sombra? Pues él tampoco. Varias preguntas vinieron a su mente pero decidió no hacerlas. La recién llegada observó el espacio y lo aprobó con un movimiento de cabeza. Los visitantes experimentaron una aguda extrañeza pero no se movieron.

Aceptó la presencia de la sombra que se entretenía con las brujas, escanció vino y continúo con absoluta propiedad: "Las obras de arte se convierten en obras de arte sólo cuando niegan su origen", planteó Teodoro Adorno, en un ligero instante en que dejó de ser el gato de Julio Cortázar. Es una expresión que me encanta porque rehuye todo racionalismo. ¿Cuál es el origen de una obra de arte? Sonrió, se llevó una galleta de marinero a la boca y bebió de su copa. ¿Qué es lo que niega? Se sacudió una miga. Se podía tocar su regocijo. Hasta las brujas sonreían instaladas en la cara de la sombra que había ocupado el asiento dejado por el jeque.

Una colección es un camino infinito. Y él era un peregrino que escapaba a cualquier explicación, incluyendo la de el principito, que era un viajero frecuente en un planeta habitado por una persona. ¿Cómo se vende eso?

A veces no puedes ver toda la obra que forma tu colección, pero te sientes bien sabiendo que la tienes, que está por ahí bien resguardada. Opinaban que era ecléctico, que su pasión no tenía límites, que arriesgaba demasiado. Fumó. Las brujas volando en sus escobas buscaron el humo. Sabes que nada le pasará y que ese lugar que cada pieza tiene en tu corazón está bien ocupado. La sombra aprobó con un gesto.

Después de una larga fumada: Señores, mi colección no está en venta, casi soy yo mismo, ¿cómo podría venderla? Pero, insistió un noble de un país en ruinas, Por más valiosa que sea, debe tener un precio, ¿aceptaría usted una sombra como pago? Se hizo el silencio. Señores, fue un placer. Piénselo, añadió el noble con gesto de pocos amigos. No necesito su sombra, señor, ¿qué no entiende? No la necesito porque tengo la mía. La sombra reaccionó rápidamente y se colocó de tal manera que se viera; la verdad es que no ajustaba perfectamente pero fue suficiente para que el noble ofreciera disculpas y se retirara desconcertado.

En cuanto estuvieron solos le sonrió, se hallaba de nuevo en su silla. Las brujas se quedaron quietas. ¿Tenías ganas de verme? Afirmó. Espero que no te haya decepcionado la ciudad, no es la que soñamos. La sombra hizo un gesto de neutralidad. ¿Dónde has estado viviendo? Sintió que recibía la respuesta en su mente: En Rapa Nui. ¿En esa isla, por qué? Me gusta el horizonte. La sombra lucía relajada y las brujas volaban de uno a otro sin descansar. ¿Qué es todo ese escándalo de tu colección misteriosa? No sé, estoy por exponerla, es de arte contemporáneo y espero que realmente sea algo Inesperado. Te sigue deleitando el factor sorpresa. Conversaron animadamente mientras concluía el puro. Debo volver. ¿Cómo, no te quedarás? Hay Hombres que no necesitan su sombra: eres uno de ellos. ¿Sólo has venido a decirme eso? No lo sé, las sombras no tenemos memoria. Se despidieron. A los minutos reaccionó: se hallaba realmente animoso, relajado, completamente dueño de sí mismo.

¿Y las brujas, dónde quedaron las brujas?

MCASD BOARD OF TRUSTEES

MOLAA BOARD OF TRUSTEES

FOUNDER

Robert Gumbiner, M.D. (1923 - 2009)

MOLAA ANNUAL EXHIBITION FUND

William Escalera and Francisco George
Joan Friedman and Robert Braun
June and Ewel Grossberg
Hilary Poochigian
Susan Ware and Burke Gumbiner
Jorge Virgili

Museum of Contemporary Art San Diego Staff

DIRECTOR'S OFFICE
Hugh M. Davies, Ph.D., The David C. Copley Director and CEO
Lilli-Mari Andresen, Executive Assistant
Megan Whitaker Nesbit, Administrative Assistant

BUSINESS OFFICE
Charles E. Castle, Deputy Director and CFO
Trulette M. Clayes, CPA, Controller
Catherine Lee, Human Resources Manager
Jen Riley, Accountant
Tiffani Mai, Accounting Clerk

CURATORIAL
Kathryn Kanjo, Chief Curator
Robin Clark, Ph.D., Curator
Lucía Sanromán, Associate Curator
Neil Kendricks, Film Curator*
Jenna Siman, Curatorial Manager
Cameron Yahr, Assistant Registrar
Jeremy Woodall, Preparator
Thom Demello, Preparator
Ali Hennessey, Research Assistant*
Margaret Fischer Lees, Education Assistant
Nicole Oder, School Programs Assistant*
Wes Bruce, Teen Programs Assistant*

ADVANCEMENT
Jeanna Yoo, Chief Advancement Officer
Robert Sherer, Senior Annual Giving Manager
Cynthia Tuomi, Stewardship Manager
Heather Cook, Advancement Associate
Julia Altieri, Membership Coordinator
Lesley Emery, Events Coordinator
Diana Mason, Advancement Coordinator
Angela Bartholomew, Grants Coordinator
Megan Skidmore, Advancement Assistant

COMMUNICATIONS
Rebecca Handelsman, Senior Communications and Marketing Manager
Mara Daniels, Visitor Services Supervisor
Cindy Kinnard, Lead Visitor Services Representative
Leah Masterson, Communications Associate

GRAPHIC DESIGN
Ursula Rothfuss, Manager of Graphic Design
Kasey Reis, Graphic Design/Production Coordinator*

HOSPITALITY AND EVENTS
Edie Nehls, Hospitality and Events Manager
Eric Reichman, Hospitality and Events Coordinator
Mike Scheer, Senior Technical Coordinator

RETAIL SERVICES
Monique Fuentes, Manager of Retail Operations

FACILITIES
James Patocka, Facilities Manager
Tauno Hannula, Facilities Technician
Christian Akers, Facilities Technician

SECURITY SERVICES
Justin Giampaoli, Chief of Security
Javier Martinez, Security Specialist
David Mesa, Security Specialist
George Garcia, Senior Security Services Rep.
Luis Chavez, Senior Security Services Rep.*

**Part-time*

Museum of Latin American Art Staff

PRESIDENT'S OFFICE
Richard Townsend, President and CEO
Irma Arvizu, Executive Assistant

CURATORIAL AFFAIRS
Cecilia Fajardo-Hill, VP of Curatorial Affairs / Chief Curator
Idurre Alonso, Curator
Selene Preciado, Assistant Curator
Gabriela Corchado, Associate Registrar
Emily Calvert, Collections Management Assistant
Gabriela Martinez, AVP of Education
Rebecca Horta, Education Coordinator
Susan Beckley, Volunteer Manager

EXTERNAL AFFAIRS
Edwina Brandon, VP of External Affairs
Lisa Nashua, AVP of Foundation and Government Relations
Wendy Celaya, AVP of Corporate Relations and Major Gifts
Marcy Rodriguez, Membership Manager
Leonardo Bueno, Development Assistant
Susan Golden, VP of Communications
Martha Guzmán, AVP of Communications
Steven Vladimiroff, Graphics Art Director
Adrian Covarrubias, Graphic Design Assistant
Eva Melgarejo, AVP of Events
Christina Cruz, Event Sales Coordinator
Denisse Galvan, Museum Events Assistant

FINANCE AND RETAIL
Christopher Gordon, VP of Projects and Finance
Tim Buckingham, AP/AR Manager
Melinda Lim, Accountant
Kara Stephenson, Assistant Store Manager

HUMAN RESOURCES
Mirella Romero, AVP of Human Resources

OPERATIONS
Lee Gumbiner, VP of Operations
Octavio Olmos, Operations Assistant
Jason Stabile, Visitor Services Manager
Mario Calzada, Visitor Services Associate
Helen Charles, Visitor Services Associate
Jennifer Sales, Visitor Services Associate
Randy Collins, Facilities Manager
Chukwunyere Ebegbulem, Maitenance
Andrew E. Brown, Maintenance
Paul Luna, Facilities
Maria Jimenez, Housekeeping
Anthony Hampton, Security Manager
Jose Rizo, Security Supervisor
Jonathan Guzman, Security Guard
James Seleznoff, Security Guard
Mitchell Rodrigues, Security Guard
Brian Thornton, Security Guard

PHOTOGRAPHIC CREDITS

Marc Domage, Francisco Kochen, Enrique Macias, Pablo Mason, Fredrik Nielson, Michel Zabé

COURTESY

303 Gallery, New York / Colette Urbajtel / Galerie Peter Kilchmann, Zurich / David Zwirner Gallery, New York / galeria kurimanzutto, Mexico City / Marian Goodman Gallery, New York and Paris / Cultural Association "The World of Lygia Clark" / Eggleston Artistic Trust / Rose Gallery, Santa Monica / Peres Projects, Berlin and Los Angeles / Laurence Miller Gallery, New York / Galería Luisa Strina, Sao Paulo / The Estate of Gordon Matta-Clark/ Galería OMR, Mexico City/ The Estate of Ana Mendieta Collection/ Galerie Lelong, New York/ Casey Kaplan, New York/ Tanya Bonakdar Gallery, New York/ Galeria Fortes Vilaça, Sao Paulo/ Projeto Hélio Oiticica, Rio de Janeiro / Phillips de Pury & Company, New York / Galleria Franco Noero, Torino / 1301PE, Los Angeles / Jaime Bravo, TEA / Roberto de Armas, TEA / Mark Bradford and Sikkema Jenkins & Co., New York / Yishai Jusidman / Galería KBK, Mexico City

CIAC ACKNOWLEDGEMENTS

CIAC would like to thank those at La Masion Rouge, TEA, Stedelijk Schiedam and BPS22 who made the presentation of this exhibition possible. It has been a pleasure collaborating with them.

We would like to specially acknowledge Leonel Morgan, Pablo Aguado and Nancy Casielles.

FRONT COVER
CARLOS AMORALES (b. 1970, Mexico)
Panorama, 2007
set of 30 collage paper drawings

BACK COVER
CARLOS AMORALES (b. 1970, Mexico)
The Horny Ghost 07 / El fantasma calenturiento 07, 2007
oil on canvas